Rent Two Films AND Let's Talk in the. Morning

Using Popular Movies in Psychotherapy

**John W. Hesley
& Jan G. Hesley**

John Wiley & Sons, Inc.

New York • Chichester • Weinheim • Brisbane •
Singapore • Toronto

Library of Congress Cataloging-in-Publication Data:

Hesley, John W., 1943–
    Rent two films and let's talk in the morning : using popular movies in psychotherapy / by John W. Hesley, Jan G. Hesley.
       p.   cm.
    ISBN 0–471–17043–7 (paper : alk. paper).
    1. Motion pictures in psychotherapy.   I. Hesley, Jan G., 1951–
    II. Title.
    [DNLM: 1. Psychotherapy—methods.   2. Motion Pictures. WM 420
  H585r   1998]
  RC489, M654H47 1998
  616.89'14—dc21
  DNLM/DLC
  for Library of Congress   97–36627

Printed in the United States of America.

10 9 8 7 6 5 4

To a wonderful mother,
Maribelle Barnes Hesley Griffin

Credits

We owe thanks to many people, but none more than to our clients. Without their willingness to try a new approach in searching for solutions to their problems, we would not have become aware of the value that films can have in that process. We appreciate deeply their fundamental contributions to this book.

Jim Levine, our agent, was the first to suggest that this idea might interest other therapists. We appreciate his labors in honing vague concepts into a book proposal and his counsel during the long passage toward fruition. At times, had he not offered sage advice and reassurance, we no doubt would have abandoned the idea altogether. Richard Simon of *Family Therapy Networker* introduced us to Jim. We are deeply indebted to Rich, who, on the basis of an article we wrote for FTN, encouraged us to pursue other writing projects.

The generous contributions of Foster Cline, M.D., cannot be repaid sufficiently. We thank Foster for his enthusiasm, insights, and belief in the feasibility of using films in therapy. He helped us understand the connections with traditional psychotherapy and convinced us that films could be used effectively with a broader range of clinical issues than we had first envisioned.

At John Wiley & Sons, Jo Ann Miller saw value in our work and took the time to help us better understand a process we had used uncritically for a long time. Tracey Thornblade worked closely with us to refine, streamline, and tame sometimes unruly language. Jo Ann and Tracey alternately prodded and nurtured, providing the creative support we needed to sustain the project from start to finish. We appreciate their patience and expertise.

We thank our terrific family. Chris Hesley explained patiently to his elders what "20-somethings" see in contemporary film. Kate and Kip Hesley allowed us to view movies nightly for a year and did not file complaints of child abandonment with the state. Finally, to our dear friends who no doubt wondered how a project could obsess two people for so long, we say thanks for wondering in silence.

Prologue: Lights, Camera, Action!

Therapists often try new techniques when a client's problem cannot be resolved using a familiar approach. Our work is no exception. We trace our use of films in therapy to one client in 1989, a mathematician whose wife told him she would leave him if he didn't get help for his depression. He had no interest in therapy and disliked therapists, whom he regarded as scientific lightweights. But her ultimatum convinced him to attend sessions long enough to satisfy her that he was trying. Then he planned to drop out.

With some concern, I (John) accepted him into my practice, trusting that we would make connections eventually. But after several weeks I began to have doubts. He had little to say, and nothing I said seemed to make an impact. The only subject that engaged him was baseball; he could quote statistics from 1903 (the first World Series, he explained). Dutifully, I searched for how statistics might become a metaphor for change. But all my suggestions were met with a blank look that said I was indeed the scientific lightweight he suspected I was: "I don't understand why you're asking what those numbers *mean*. They don't *mean* anything. They just are."

One weekend, Jan and I saw *Field of Dreams*. The film moved us deeply because it is about a man (Ray) who is captured by an insight and risks everything to follow its path. The path leads to a conversation with his deceased father that ultimately heals old wounds. But the film is also about baseball. And when I saw my client a few days later, I asked if he had seen the film. He hadn't, but was intrigued. On an impulse, I asked if he would go see it and tell me what he thought.

When he came in the following week, he was troubled. He had watched the movie twice and thought it was "interesting," but he couldn't figure out why I'd asked him to see it. He *knew* that therapists had ulterior motives for their suggestions, but what was mine? By the end of the session, he still hadn't found a satisfactory answer, so he said he was going to watch it a third time. "I'll figure out what you had up your sleeve—sooner or later."

The next week was a watershed. The client had suddenly noticed the film's ending, which he had missed the first two times. (For those who haven't seen it, at the end of the film Ray's deceased father appears as a young ball player and they play a game of catch. The conversation between them settles important issues that had been unresolved at the time of the father's death.) The third time around, the scene had struck with particular force.

He talked about his father who was dying from lung cancer. The client had not seen him in 10 years, although they talked by phone on holidays. His childhood memories, he explained for the first time, were filled with conflict. His father had largely ignored him, and as soon as the client could leave home, he had, never to return. I asked what the film had in common with the relationship with his dad.

CLIENT: It was that last scene, where the ghost of Ray's father comes back as a kid. I got to thinking—When you're a kid, your parents are bigger, smarter, and in control. You never think they might be walking around in a fog. So when they treat you bad, you believe they're doing it for good reasons. . . .

JOHN: Even if you don't understand those reasons.

CLIENT: Yeah. You just figure they know what they're doing. But in that scene, Ray knows his dad was just a normal kid—he'd done his best, but life just wore him down. He didn't hate his son. Ray might feel bad about that, but he couldn't blame his father for being normal.

JOHN: Is something familiar about that?

CLIENT: Sure. When Dad pulled away from me I thought it was because I wasn't good enough. But when I thought of him in my shoes (or me in his), I wondered if he felt like I do now. Sometimes I'm so damned discouraged I can't even talk to my kids—it hurts to try. I don't like being that way, but that doesn't help me do it better. Now, I wonder if he was going through the same thing I am.

JOHN: He's still around. You could ask.

Two weeks later he left for Arizona to visit the family from which he had cut himself off years before. When he returned, he came to therapy because he wanted to be there, not as a favor to someone else. The conversation with his father had healed old wounds and opened new areas for exploration. And the film had been the catalyst of this change.

The point is not that the movie was an exact analogue of the client's family history. His interpretation of the film in essence rewrote the script. But the film touched him emotionally and helped him make a connection to his father on an affective level. It offered possibilities about their relationship's history that piqued this mathematician's curiosity. And it reframed the father-son relationship so that he could put himself in his father's place. The film—and my suggestion that it had some connection to him—was a puzzle. He had to check out his impressions while he still had time. Ultimately it helped him reconcile with his father.

In the months after that experience, I used films more often with clients. And as I became enthusiastic about the approach, Jan tried films with her clients too. We found that working with movies in therapy offered advantages from the beginning. Clients brightened up when we talked about movies. They seemed to appreciate taking the spotlight off their own problems and talking about a related topic that was cheerier. Moreover, they made connections that urged therapy along in new and productive directions. In time, our clients taught us what was most important in selecting films for use in therapy, setting the scene for an assignment, and talking about the film in therapy.

In discussing our use of films with other therapists, we learned that many counselors suggest films to clients but are reluctant to do so on a regular basis. Therapists encounter two main difficulties in using films more often. First, they usually recommend movies they have seen recently rather than films that are thematically related to the problem of a client. Therapists simply cannot keep in mind the many films that are appropriate for specific problems. Second, therapists are not comfortable discussing films with clients in a therapeutic setting.

This book will satisfy those concerns. Using movies in therapy is no more complicated than other approaches. After all, film is a predominant part of our culture and most of our clients' lives.

In the first section of this book, we discuss how therapeutic work with popular films fits within the tradition of psychotherapy. We suggest ways to select films, make assignments, and process homework. In the second section, we offer an anthology of films to address a number of clinical issues, discussing helpful films for each problem area. These films and many more are then briefly summarized in the third section of this book which contains a category index to films and a title index. These indices make up the therapists' quick reference guide, offering films appropriate for a number of problems encountered in counseling settings.

We'd like to add a word about our classification of films. Obviously, each film speaks to a number of different clinical issues. *Field of Dreams,* for instance, concerns a father and son relationship, but also addresses issues such as grief and loss, intimate relationships, transition to adulthood, and marriage. Because we have used this film most often for its moving and inspirational qualities, suitable for many people who have given up on life, we have listed *Field of Dreams* under the category of "Inspiration." We hope that by providing two indices—a list of films by major category and a title index that includes all relevant categories—the clinician will be able to find an appropriate film quickly and easily.

We know that therapists who incorporate films into therapy will be surprised and delighted with the creative interpretations their clients draw. We are continually amazed at the nuances clients see that we have not, the connections they make that speak almost magically to their problems. Of course, it is not *really* magic. Films don't hold any magic not already in the mind of the client. As Dorothy and her friends found in talking with the Wizard of Oz the secret is always inside. But if a movie can help a client unlock that truth, it has done its job.

Contents

PART I

VideoWork:
Theory and Application

Chapter 1

Introduction to Video Work

Susan was 32 years old, a college graduate, twice engaged but never married, working as a clerk in a grocery store. She was in a stalemated relationship with Steve, a confused young man. At times he'd say he loved her and wanted more commitment. At other times he claimed he wanted to be on his own. Susan knew the relationship was making her unhappy, but she didn't know what to do. "I really love him," she explained. "I think he'll eventually get it together." Susan's parents and friends advised her to leave. She said they didn't understand.

As her therapist, I (Jan) wanted to help Susan view the relationship from a different perspective. She saw her choice as staying or leaving, but I wanted to encourage her to look beyond the obvious. She had tried to please Steve by changing her hairstyle, abandoning friends, and giving up hobbies. She hoped he would like her better and fall more deeply in love with her, but at the same time she was ignoring whether she liked the person she had become. I asked her to put aside the issue of what to do with Steve and watch a movie. I told her it would be useful to view from a different angle a problem very similar to her own.

The film was *Singles,* a movie about a group of friends in their twenties in Seattle. I suspected Susan would identify with it because the characters resembled her friends, and I believed she would relate to the

3

protagonist, Janet, a young woman in love with a rock musician. I asked Susan to be aware of her feelings as she watched the film and to note any insights that might occur. She agreed to rent the film during the next week so we could discuss it when she returned. And the following week in the therapy session, she was eager to talk about her experience.

"It was easy to see why you wanted me to watch that movie. I'm a little like Kyra—she played games with her boyfriend. But mostly I'm like Janet, and her boyfriend was a *lot* like Steve. I got mad when I realized you wanted me to see that I'm in the same trap she was in. I wanted to turn it off, but I told you I'd watch it so I did. That scene with the plastic surgeon really got to me."

In the scene to which Susan was referring, Janet discusses breast implants with a physician. She had noticed pictures of movie stars at her boyfriend's apartment, all of whom had larger breasts than she. So she debates with the surgeon how much to increase her breast size: he argues for less, she for more. Finally he tells her to consider what she is doing. If it is necessary to change her appearance so dramatically to attract her boyfriend, the surgeon asks, what does that say about his ability to love? And what does it say about her willingness to sacrifice her identity? Susan readily saw the connection, and she was angry.

"All this time I've been trying to make him believe I was enough. He could make a commitment to me and stop looking around. But after I saw that movie I thought about my mother, who had breast cancer a few years ago. My dad helped her through it, and it didn't change a bit what they felt for each other. I started thinking about Steve. If I have to work so hard to make him want me now, what if something like that happens to me? I've been making a big mistake. If he chooses me now, it's not the real me. I've got to get back to who I am and let him decide if that's enough. Also, as I watched that rock musician—you know he wasn't a very good musician—I started wondering what I see in Steve. I've got a lot more thinking to do."

FILMS IN THERAPY

VideoWork is a therapeutic process in which clients and therapists discuss themes and characters in popular films that relate to core issues of ongoing therapy. In VideoWork, we use films to facilitate self-understanding, to introduce options for action plans, and to seed future therapeutic interventions. We select films for both positive and negative associations. Some films dramatize possible solutions. Others show predictable outcomes if dysfunctional patterns remain unaltered.

As in Susan's case, the subject matter of the film usually corresponds to a client's main therapeutic issues, and one or more characters may be similar to the client. We explain thoroughly why a certain film is assigned, and we give specific instructions for the viewing. If a film includes language or a scene that may be offensive, we discuss that before making the assignment. As a rule, our clients view films during the week following the assignment. At the next session, we discuss their impressions.

We are not suggesting that merely watching a film is sufficient to bring about desired change. The ability of an inspirational film to effect change is short-lived, much like a New Year's resolution. Though some counselors (Horenstein, Rigby, Flory, and Gershwin, 1994; Solomon, 1995) have suggested that films are useful as self-help, our approach emphasizes the partnership of conventional therapy and film homework. VideoWork is one more strategy in attaining therapeutic objectives. It presupposes that competent therapists will make use of the insights their clients garner from films.

As with any intervention, there are risks. Films can influence behavior positively and negatively (Eisenberg, 1986; Harry, 1983). But by choosing from an anthology of therapeutically useful films, assigning them strategically, and establishing boundaries for the viewing, therapists can minimize the risks. Our goal in this book is to provide the information that clinicians need to use films safely and successfully.

THE ROOTS OF VIDEOWORK

Practitioners have long recommended books, plays, poetry, and the visual and performance arts as a means of teaching concepts of mental health and providing corrective emotional experiences (Pardeck, 1993). As early as 1840, Sir Walter Galt cataloged fictional and nonfictional literature recommended by psychiatrists for religious and moralistic education to hospitalized psychiatric patients. But it was not until the 1930s that the casual practice of prescribing therapeutic readings to patients was formalized into a practice known as bibliotherapy (Rubin, 1978).

In the *Bulletin of the Menninger Clinic,* William C. Menninger (1937) first described how selected literature might serve educational, recreational, and social purposes in psychiatric hospitals. According to Menninger, literature provides immediate gratification for patients and serves as a source of information. It encourages patients to invest in an interest outside themselves and thereby maintain contact with external reality. It leads to insight into their problems. And through discussing books with others, literature helps patients to identify with a social group.

Menninger also suggests guidelines for literary assignments. Clinicians should prescribe books to patients according to their needs, backgrounds, and symptomatic pictures. He recommends older as well as newer works; the salient issue is how clearly artistic works serve as appropriate channels of expression for the ideas and emotions of patients. He cautions clinicians to exercise sound judgment in utilizing the rich source of ideas found in fiction and requires that therapeutic readings be ordered only by the attending physician.

Bibliotherapists who followed Menninger echoed his concern for undesired effects. Hazel Sample (1940), in the first paper to treat bibliotherapy as a discrete field, cautions that fiction often contains unstated counterproductive values. Sample recommends that bibliotherapists carefully weigh a story's conflicts and its resolution. She warns that authors express their own ideas and opinions through characters in a story and that those ideas and opinions should enlighten rather than confuse a patient. Her conclusion is that readings can be an effective aid to therapy but that clinicians should exercise good judgment in the works they choose and how they are used in treatment.

BIBLIOTHERAPY IN THE ERA OF SELF-HELP

Initially both fiction and nonfiction readings were assigned. But in the past 20 years, as clinicians themselves produced self-help literature for the general public, nonfiction has become the dominant genre in bibliotherapy. Clinicians who recommend books to their clients cite evidence that such readings are effective adjuncts to therapy in many areas. Self-help books enhance self-perception, help clients cope with the traumas of divorce and abuse, effect attitude change, and reduce depression (Berg-Cross, Jennings, and Baruch, 1990). By the time many clients enter therapy, they have already read a number of self-help books.

Therapists report that readings give clients tasks that focus their thinking as well as a sense that they are participating more fully in therapy. According to Rubin (1978), readings help clients understand themselves better, verbalize their concerns, discover their problems in the stories of others, dispel isolation, develop a better sense of context. Readings also show how others have solved similar problems and clarify values. Readings also lead to honest self-evaluation.

Although some professionals periodically question whether self-help books are as helpful as claimed, therapists use them as teaching materials with clients who are eager for additional help. And therapeutic teaching materials have expanded far beyond the printed word. Audiotapes teach relaxation techniques, self-hypnosis, and anger management and provide affirmations that clients use in enhancing self-esteem. Professionally prepared videotapes present dramatizations that teach how to handle common problems in parenting and couple communication. Self-paced skills training on personal computer software is becoming available for home computers. These applications are effective new tools that therapists can use to reinforce and generalize therapeutic effects.

THE RELATION OF VIDEOWORK TO BIBLIOTHERAPY

VideoWork is an extension of bibliotherapy, sharing aims, advantages, and limitations. But it differs from current practices of bibliotherapy, most prominently in using fiction rather than nonfiction. Whereas nonfiction self-help materials offer guidelines for behavior illustrated by examples from ordinary life, films show ordinary life and let clients (in conversation with therapists) find guidelines that work for them. A film offers a wide range of interpretations determined by the specific needs of a client, by the directions a clinician gives for viewing, and by the connections that a therapist helps a client draw.

VideoWork also differs from bibliotherapy in terms of strategy. Films are occasionally assigned to reinforce an idea introduced in therapy sessions, but they are more often intended to encourage internal search and insight by the client. As clients watch films by themselves or with partners or family, they identify corresponding resources or limitations in their own repertoires that may not have emerged in therapeutic conversations.

For example, *The Bridges of Madison County,* which deals with conflicting needs for passion and stability, was assigned to a couple who complained that intimacy was missing from their marriage. When they returned, the wife admitted that the film caused her to realize that she had never forgiven her husband for an extramarital affair he had years before. Although watching the film was difficult for her (because it centers on an extramarital affair), she confessed that she had withheld intimacy as payback for her husband's infidelity—a fact that had not been obvious to her before the film assignment. Subsequent work involved helping her identify residual feelings about the affair and discussing how she and her husband might rebuild trust.

VideoWork does not require a therapeutic discussion of every assigned film. Although discussions usually follow film assignments, some clients experience strong emotional reactions but do not wish to talk about the film. The story line may have hit too close to home or the connections with a character may be too revealing. Often those clients immediately suggest a new way to resolve a problem without verbalizing or even knowing what led to the new idea. We treat their insight as if it were unmediated. Further discussion of the movie would be counterproductive.

One overprotective parent who was assigned the film *Ferris Bueller's Day Off,* a tale about a normal but rebellious teen, appeared unenthusiastic when she was asked what she thought about the film. "It was okay," she said, "but I didn't see much connection with our family. However, I've got something more important on my mind. It's Tim. Do you think he's too old for a curfew? I'm thinking of letting him decide when to come home. After all, he'll be in college in six months. Maybe I should give him time to practice being on his own." The mother had earlier rejected the same suggestion. The film made the difference, but she took the credit.

Finally, in comparing Video Work to traditional bibliotherapy, it is our impression that clients do film homework more readily than book assignments. Films are fun to watch, require only a small investment of time, and are already part of many clients' usual routines. Some clients do not like to read, but they watch films regularly and have excellent recall of plots and characters. Additionally, clients who might read only a single book during treatment are willing to watch a series of films that address a number of clinical issues.

FILMS AS THERAPEUTIC METAPHORS

A close relationship exists between Video Work and a clinical use of therapeutically constructed metaphors. Both involve surprise that disrupts habitual responses, both use rich images that require a client to supply personal content in order to construct meanings that are relevant, and both involve implied directives for change. Clinicians use metaphors to broach sensitive areas and to go beyond the conscious material that clients have identified in therapeutic conversations.

Films also introduce clients to ideas that might be too threatening if suggested directly. In Susan's case, the movie scene in which Janet talks with the plastic surgeon about breast implants served as a metaphor for what Susan was doing to attract her boyfriend. Although Susan had no intention of undergoing surgery, she was radically altering her personality to fit what she thought Steve wanted. The extreme measures to which Janet was willing to go struck Susan as ludicrous until she realized that in her own way, she was doing the same. The film provided Susan with a role model who finally decides that a love with so many conditions is not a love worth pursuing. Likewise, Susan decided to be herself and let the chips fall where they might with Steve.

Stephen S. Pearce, in *Flash of Insight*, describes how metaphors deepen the substance of therapy.

> Narrative and metaphor afford individuals the opportunity to distance themselves from events in their own experiences and become the protagonist in their own lives' narratives. Metaphor and narrative en-

able them to rehearse potential solutions until they achieve insight and new direction. Once material previously deemed intolerable is thought and rethought, it can gently knock on the door of consciousness and say, "Here I am." A metaphor is a story that allows people to bridge the gap between what is and what should be. (Pearce, 1996).

To bridge that gap, a therapist might use a movie such as *Cold Comfort Farm* to show a client how to make fundamental changes for the better. After the death of her parents, the heroine in this film, a young woman named Flora, moves in with relatives on a dilapidated farm where everybody is miserable. Metaphorically, Flora might be a therapist approaching a severely dysfunctional family or a client trying to make changes at home. Facing such a bleak setting, the temptation is to begin giving advice. But Flora is wiser. She discovers what each person wants, then shows each of them how to reach those goals. By the end of the movie, extraordinary changes have been made and everybody is happy. Films such as this *show* rather than *tell* clients how to work with people who are resistive to change. Clients learn valuable lessons about behavior change and envision how their own problems might be solved.

Thus films are metaphors that can be utilized in therapy in a manner similar to stories, myths, jokes, fables, and therapeutically constructed narratives. Films address the affective realm and add to the impact of cognitive insights. Because films galvanize feelings, they increase the probability that clients will carry out new and desired behaviors. Cognitive insights tell clients what they ought to do but affective insights give them the motivation to follow through.

IDEAL HOMEWORK FOR TIME-EFFECTIVE THERAPY

In an era of managed care, therapists are challenged to make therapy more cost-conscious without sacrificing effectiveness. This challenge necessitates a departure from the traditional 50-minute once-weekly session. Sessions are often scheduled farther apart, and there is no guarantee that clinicians will have more than a few opportunities to influence positive change. The problem, therefore, is how to get the most out of the time that is available.

In maximizing their effectiveness, therapists increasingly rely on therapeutic homework—structured assignments introduced by a therapist during sessions and completed at home by clients. According to Bandura (1969), the underlying assumption in assigning homework is that desired behaviors introduced in therapy sessions are practiced and mastered in a client's natural environment, leading to the development of effective self-regulatory functions. Therapists introduce concepts, assign homework that will reinforce key therapeutic points, and process the exercise in a follow-up session.

Several specific benefits of homework have been described by clinicians. First, therapeutic material may be more readily mastered. What is initially encountered in the therapy session is practiced and reinforced outside (Budman and Gurman, 1988). Therapists can also achieve a better continuity of care. By using daily and weekly report forms, they can monitor the details of a client's daily life, marking progress and change and modifying treatment approaches where needed (Beitman, 1987). Homework helps therapy be more relevant to daily life. Through practice outside sessions, the effects of therapy can be generalized throughout the client's environment (Bandura, 1969). Finally, homework can act as a hurdle or challenge that once mastered by the client, advances therapeutic progress and leads to greater self-reliance (Haley, 1973). Hence, using homework assignments in which clients practice new skills or reintegrate old ones is a technique by which connections may be made between the special setting of therapy and the client's life.

Benefits of Homework

- Enables clients to practice what they learn in therapy (Budman and Gurman, 1988).
- Helps clinicians track progress and modify treatment plans to achieve better continuity of care. (Beitman, 1987).
- Maximizes the effects of therapy in the client's own environment (Bandura, 1969).
- Advances therapeutic progress and leads to greater self-reliance (Haley, 1973).
- Serves as a bridge between therapy and life.

In making that connection, therapists assign imaginative as well as realistic tasks. Bereaved clients visit cemeteries where deceased relatives have been buried. They conduct imaginary conversations and write letters to their loved ones, bringing closure not completed at the time of death (Staudacher, 1987). Shy clients rank threatening social situations, then master the list item by item (Zimbardo, 1977). In all homework, therapists give rationales for assignments and thoroughly process exercises in subsequent sessions. Homework builds from one successful experience to another, as lessons from one assignment suggest new objectives for the next. Likewise, a film assignment that proves helpful to a client can be followed by another film that will facilitate additional insights.

VideoWork combines realism and imagination. We select a film because it resembles the situation of a client, but through associations, the client derives a wealth of material beyond the content of the film. As clients watch films, they have internal conversations with the characters of a film; they reflect on the relationships they are viewing and think of actions they might take (similar to or different from the characters on the screen) to solve their own problems. Films are dynamic experiences that compress information into a relatively small package.

A client named Delia, for instance, was doubtful at first that watching films would help solve conflicts with her son. She had brought 11-year-old Tony for help because, according to her, he was irresponsible. But it soon became clear that she was too demanding and that she held Tony to developmentally inappropriate standards. I (John) asked her to watch the film *Regarding Henry,* a story about a man who loses his memory after he is shot during a robbery, and to note carefully what transpires in one scene. Henry, who had lost his obsessive-compulsive behavior as well as his identity, deliberately tipped over his orange juice to make his daughter feel better about a glass of juice she had just spilled. It was a scene, I hoped, that would deliver the message, don't sweat the small stuff. My intention was to follow up *Regarding Henry* (metaphorically similar to Delia's mechanistic relationship with her son) with other films that modeled warm, supportive, and balanced parents. Delia returned from the assignment filled with questions and strong feelings.

DELIA: When he pushed that glass over, it made me cringe. I'd never do that. That's crazy. It's the opposite of what I want Tony to learn.

JOHN: You mean, you want him to be responsible?

DELIA: Yeah. And if I did irresponsible things, he would too.

JOHN: Maybe. But I thought Henry was trying to show his daughter that we all make mistakes and that it's not the end of the world when we do.

DELIA: You have to show a kid that? I try to be as perfect as I can be around Tony. So he'll know he could too if he'd just try hard enough. I don't want him to see me making mistakes.

JOHN: I understand. But remember how Henry's relationship with his daughter improved after he lost his memory? When he stopped pushing so hard? Why do you suppose that happened?

DELIA: Well, he started spending more time with her for one thing. He talked to her about what went on in her life every day. And she talked to him more.

JOHN: What do you think changed—to make her more willing to talk with her father.

DELIA: I don't know. He didn't bite her head off, like he did in the beginning. In the first part, she'd try to talk with him but then she'd just look down at the floor. She knew he didn't care what she was saying, he just wanted her to do what he said. But after he was shot, he started listening to her. More than that—he really got a kick being around her.

We then discussed how the child behaved even more "responsibly" after she and her father had established a warmer relationship. Delia applied the analogy to her son. She saw that she did not have to give up her desire for Tony to be responsible, but that, as Henry had discovered, she was holding her son to impossible standards. And the conflict was robbing them both of a loving relationship. Delia saw the problem, but she admitted she didn't know how else to parent. "I wouldn't know any other way to act with Tony." So a second movie assignment *(Parenthood)* provided a role model of parents who enjoy as well as train their children. Whereas the first film awakened Delia to the idea that she herself might

13

be contributing to her son's problem, the subsequent film modeled how she could interact more positively with her child.

Advantages of Films as Homework

- Compliance.
- Accessibility.
- Availability.
- Curiosity.
- Familiarity.
- Rapport.

COMPLIANCE

Although not every client will watch each film assigned, most clients will give this new approach a chance. It takes them by surprise. They are accustomed to having their therapists suggest a self-help book, but they have rarely looked to films for help with their problems. If the first experience with a film yields positive results, clients will likely be enthusiastic about similar homework assignments in the future. Once they're convinced that the approach works for them, they will be on the lookout for relevant films, sharing therapeutic films with friends and families. Overall, clients report that they enjoy discussing films, even when the material is emotionally charged and personally challenging.

ACCESSIBILITY

Emotionally distraught clients may do better with film assignments than with books; whereas reading assignments require an ability to focus that depressed or anxious clients find difficult, films require less concentrated attention. Clients with limited language skills can also benefit from films. Clients who are reluctant to venture out to a movie theater can watch films in their own homes. For couples in which one partner likes to read and the other doesn't, watching a movie is a task they both can agree on.

And we have found that adolescents in particular are almost always willing to watch a film.

AVAILABILITY

Movie watching can be shared by families even when other family members have not participated in therapy. This sharing facilitates productive conversations within the family. Clients borrow useful concepts from films to explain therapeutic issues to other family members or to share some of their concerns. One client whose husband had been unwilling to talk with her about their problems agreed to watch an assigned film. Afterward, she was able to tell him much of what was bothering her by talking about the characters and their interactions; he did not know that her feelings ran as deeply as was portrayed in the film. Once he understood what she felt, he was more willing to talk about the things that mattered to her.

Because therapists may also be sending messages to a client's family via the films they assign, they should think carefully about how a film will impact other family members as well as the client. We instruct our clients to explain to others in the family that the films they watch are part of therapy. When appropriate, we encourage them to invite others to watch. (It is not usually appropriate, for instance, in homes in which abuse is occurring.) And we issue an invitation for family members who have viewed films to attend a follow-up session, if they wish. We always assume that others in the family might see assigned films, so we make our selections with that in mind. If family members react negatively to a film we assign, we ask that they attend a therapy session so that we can address their concerns appropriately.

CURIOSITY

Because we carefully explain our rationale for using films, VideoWork assignments seem logical to our clients. But the films we pick are sufficiently removed from the problem at hand to potentiate clients' curiosity. Clients know that we have reasons for recommending a particular film, but they are not sure what those reasons are. They ask themselves which characters we see as similar to them and how the plot compares to their own situation. This questioning facilitates creative thought from the moment we mention a title. We have had many instances in which clients watched a film several times to make sure they "got" what they thought we intended for them to take from the film. This aspect adds intensity to a VideoWork assignment; films are puzzles to be solved. And when clients return from watching a film with only part of the message we hoped they would hear, we frequently ask them to view it a second time.

Tom, for instance, watched the film *Strangers in Good Company,* a movie about a group of elderly women who are stranded when their tour bus breaks down. The film had seemed an apt assignment because Tom's ailing 75-year-old mother was beginning to make more demands, and Tom and his brother were arguing about their responsibilities. Missing from Tom's description of the problem was a sense of empathy with what his mother was experiencing. "I don't understand why she doesn't see that it's important for her to go into a nursing home. She's just not facing facts."

Tom agreed to watch the film, but after viewing it, he said it had only reinforced his opinion that "old people are crotchety." He admitted that his interpretation was "probably not what you were after" and offered to watch it again. During the second viewing, one feisty character, independent but losing the ability to manage on her own, struck him with particular force. It was the first time, he said, he had ever been able to imagine himself growing older. "I could see it from her point of view; I wouldn't want to have people making my decisions for me. I guess Mother doesn't want that either." This observation offered more possibilities for discussion, but it took a second viewing to bring it to light.

FAMILIARITY

Films are familiar, part of the vernacular of the client, hence they require no leap to a specialized language sometimes encountered in structured homework. The subject of films often comes up in daily conversation. People use them as metaphors for life, and phrases from movies are commonplace. One of our clients said, after a particularly difficult weekend with her husband, "I may pull a Thelma and Louise on him," and we knew what she meant. Films can even epitomize entire generations. Movies such as *The Man in the Gray Flannel Suit, The Graduate, Easy Rider, The Big Chill,* and *Slackers* summarize what many people were experiencing during those eras. Clients are accustomed to measuring themselves and their life events against the images they encounter in films

RAPPORT

Much of a client's life is outside the direct experience of the therapist. Films shared by clients and therapists deepen therapeutic alliance by providing an experience they have in common and by putting therapists and clients on more nearly level ground. Undesirable authoritarian aspects of the therapeutic relationship are attenuated somewhat by film homework. A therapist's training and experience, ironically, may convince a client that they have little in common and hence may limit the positive influence that a therapist can have. Talking about films, a more neutral subject, often brings therapists and clients closer together. Clients assume that a therapist is an expert at doing therapy, but they perceive equality when talking about films.

As is true in all homework, practice allows clients to become more comfortable using VideoWork. They will get that practice if they take film assignments seriously. But for that to happen, therapists should view film homework as important to therapy and should provide clear rationales. The key factor in obtaining useful results in VideoWork is the con-

---

Seven Ways Films Aid Treatment Planning

1. Offering hope and encouragement.
2. Reframing problems.
3. Providing role models.
4. Identifying and reinforcing internal strengths.
5. Potentiating emotion.
6. Improving communication.
7. Prioritizing values.

---

fidence with which therapists introduce films into therapy—a confidence that begins by understanding the benefits of VideoWork.

OFFERING HOPE AND ENCOURAGEMENT

No film can by itself reverse a negative worldview. But therapists can select films that begin in despair and end in triumph, thereby giving rise to hope. Clients who can identify with characters trapped by their circumstances and who can share the characters' disappointments as well as unsteady steps toward liberation may find reason for optimism in their own situations.

For example, the film *The Shawshank Redemption* begins in bitter defeat and concludes in personal triumph—serving as a useful therapeutic metaphor for clients who have suffered significant setbacks. Few clients feel the hopelessness of the film's protagonist, Andy Dufresne, who is sentenced to life imprisonment for a crime he did not commit. But despite the odds against him, he refuses to give up. Other prisoners lose their individuality in the harsh prison environment and adjust their expectations to a routine that with time becomes addictive. But Andy endures his imprisonment and in the meantime takes steps to ensure a better future. In the end, he is triumphant.

Clinicians can draw parallels between Andy's predicament and clients' belief that they are trapped. Andy did not ask to be imprisoned; likewise, clients do not always choose their circumstances. Life has not been fair to Andy, nor is life always fair to clients. Freedom will result from what Andy does to help himself. And clients too must take action in order for their lives to improve. A film such as *Shawshank* meets clients on a level of hopelessness, then challenges them to devise ways to liberate themselves. The film illustrates the therapeutic adage that hope is not passive but grounded in action.

REFRAMING PROBLEMS

"The meaning that any event has depends upon the 'frame' in which we perceive it. . . . When the meaning changes, the person's responses and behaviors also change" (Bandler and Grinder, 1982). In practice, reframing occurs when a therapist draws different conclusions about an event than what clients had concluded. Reframes startle clients and cause them to reconsider earlier judgments. When therapists introduce respectful new perspectives, reframes serve to weaken the dominance of an unchallenged meaning. The reformulations do not have to be profound. Modest reframes can lead to large therapeutic advances. Reframing a child's "argumentativeness" as "spunk and creativity" helps a parent maintain a more positive outlook. An obsessive-compulsive can be congratulated for paying attention to detail. And the socially phobic client, while being encouraged to spend more time with other people, can be praised for deeper-than-usual sensitivity. Reframes don't make change less necessary, but they help change occur in a friendlier atmosphere.

Films, because they often reframe fictional crises, are ideal vehicles for reframing the problems of clients and for causing clients to entertain productive doubts about their own crises. What seems to be true at the beginning of a film is soon cast into doubt and by the end is reframed into an entirely different context. For example, a comedy such as *Starting Over*, a movie about life after divorce, presents divorce as a bleak event, almost hopeless. Then the film twists that point of view through surprising turns until a new understanding emerges—one involving renewed life. After watching *Starting Over*, clients may say, "Well I still believe that divorce is very sad, but not necessarily wrong in every case—certainly not hopeless." A very important reframe has taken place.

Some clients describe their families as irreparably flawed and believe that their situation is hopeless. But a film such as *What's Eating Gilbert Grape?* illustrates an exception to that attitude. Members of the Grape family have serious emotional and physical problems: mental retardation, major depression, codependency, and a severe eating disorder. But this troubled family sticks together and thrives. Therapists can use the film to demonstrate that even in the most trying circumstances, people still act forcibly to improve their lives. The film shows how one family refuses to accept stereotyped definitions of itself and can therefore find novel solutions. By extension, a client's troubled family can be reframed into a setting in which personal growth can take place.

PROVIDING ROLE MODELS

Some clients, reared in emotionally impoverished circumstances, have few mentors or guides. They want a better life but have not met people who demonstrate qualities or behavior from which they can learn. Clinicians help such clients find mentors or may even serve that function themselves. But role models for the specific issues clients are facing may not be at hand. In those cases, film characters are useful substitutes.

In a true-life film titled *Rudy,* a boy with modest athletic talent wants to play football at Notre Dame. His friends and family are unsupportive. They advise him to get a job and settle down as they have. But for Rudy, playing football at Notre Dame is a way to make a better life for himself. He is willing to pay any price to reach that goal. Eventually he succeeds, but not without many starts and stops. Just as Rudy suffers disappointments but holds on to his objective, clients can be encouraged to persist in their own endeavors despite setbacks they encounter.

Other films offer role models to clients with different needs. *Ruby in Paradise* depicts a woman who is unwilling to accept a stereotypical and dissatisfying gender role. She finds a job that brings her fulfillment. In *The Water Dance,* a paraplegic endures the challenges of physical and emotional recovery. The protagonist is a role model for clients with physical disease or traumatic injury. And in *Mask,* a heroic if eccentric single mother encourages her disabled son to live as normally as possible. These film characters and input from a therapist can offset the absence of actual role models. Just as earlier generations took their role models from written biographies and novels, today's clients can use film characters. Role models do not have to be real people. More important, they should embody viable ideas for how clients would like their own lives to evolve. Film role models are examples from whom clients can learn and be inspired.

IDENTIFYING AND REINFORCING INTERNAL STRENGTHS

Many contemporary therapists focus more on identifying and utilizing internal resources than on exploring clients' psychopathology, building on strength rather than weakness. Viewed from this perspective, clients are not dysfunctional so much as they are unaware of their assets and the means by which they can access them. Therapy helps clients recall forgotten or discounted resources, then facilitates opportunities for those resources to be applied. Films assist in reaching that objective by portraying fictional characters who resolve difficult problems, often with no more personal skills than those possessed by the clients themselves.

In the film *Parenthood,* a character named Gil is a father who doubts himself and whose doubts are intensified by a school psychologist who diagnoses Gil's son as emotionally disturbed. Gil has trouble balancing the demands of work and home, but he has one vital strength: He honestly cares for his children. He attends their ball games and dance recitals, gives good advice, and bandages wounds, both emotional and physical. By the end of the film, Gil learns that although he's no expert, he is a good father. Clients will feel better about themselves after watching the film. They will see that the skills Gil uses are mostly common sense. And like him, clients have more common sense than they give themselves credit for having. A film such as *Parenthood* convinces clients to use the skills they have.

Because films deal with stories of individuals rather than with abstract principles of human behavior, clients identify with the characters they encounter in films—people who also have their ups and downs. Film characters find resolutions to their problems through familiar and readily accessible skills. Clients recognize and appropriate resources from their own repertoires.

How does the leap from "reel life" to "real life" take place? Usually through conversation in therapy. Clients may watch a film such as *Parenthood* and fail to see the connections that would be helpful, partly because they discount the strengths they have in common with the movie characters. The therapist can call attention to these strengths and remind clients of attributes they have revealed that are similar to those of a film character.

I (John) had a client who felt that he was failing his teenage son because he "did not know how to talk with him, how to tell him what he needs to know to be a man." The same client, however, was an excellent sailor who had taught his son much under the context of showing the son how to sail skillfully. I asked my client to watch the film *A River Runs Through It,* about two boys growing up in Montana, to see a model of metaphorical instruction. Afterward, we talked about how the father in the film teaches his sons about life by showing them how to be competent at fly-fishing. With some prompting, the client made the connection between the movie father's fly-fishing instruction and his own sailing experiences with his son. "You're right," he said with surprise, "I've been doing that with my boy all along." The main value of the exercise was the client's new sense of competence as a father, acquired by identifying with a film character he viewed as wise.

POTENTIATING EMOTION

Films trigger emotions and open doors that might otherwise be closed. It is one thing to talk about a problem, quite another to feel it. Particularly for clients who intellectualize, viewing a film that elicits emotion and connecting the film to personal situations enhances therapeutic conversations.

Jim was 44 years old when he described for the first time the physical abuse he had suffered as a child. He told his story with little or no feeling: "All that happened a long time ago. My dad's dead now and there's nothing anybody can do. It doesn't even bother me anymore. I've gotten over it." But there were signs that the past was still very much alive for Jim. He was periodically despondent, and he didn't enjoy his three young children. He treated them gingerly, afraid that he would harm them the way his father had hurt him. After weeks of listening to Jim intellectualize his problems, I (Jan) wanted to encourage him to express his feelings. So I asked him to watch a film called *This Boy's Life,* novelist Tobias Wolff's account of his abuse by a stepfather.

The film contains many classic elements of child abuse: a single mother looking for a strong male image for her difficult son, the arrival of a too-good-to-be-true Prince Charming who changes into a tyrant after the wedding is over, a child's cries for help that go unanswered by a mother wanting to make the marriage work. The film documents Toby's strategies for survival, the escape from his abusive stepfather, and the reconciliation between mother and son. When Jim returned the following week after watching the film, he was somber. "That was the first time I've cried about anything since I was a kid," he said, "and I'm not sure that represents therapeutic progress. I swore that SOB would never get to me again. Now look what's happened."

But in the weeks to come, therapy became more intense and more productive. Viewing the film was, for Jim, a key that opened the lock on his unfortunate past. Many of the same feelings he had experienced as a child came back, and he saw that the problem had not gone away. His emotional reaction to the film, breaking through decades of denial, convinced him that he had not "gotten over" the abuse and that his background was contributing to problems in his marriage and family. The real problems were not his current family but that he was filtering his family life through screens of his past. As he talked more in therapy about his youth and the pain he'd suffered from his father, Jim slowly began handling present difficulties more successfully, separating fact from fantasy. He began dealing better with his emotional isolation not only from his family but also from friends. And it was important to Jim that the film had been based on real life. "If he did it, I can too," he said.

IMPROVING COMMUNICATIONS

Clinicians attempt to help clients communicate unfamiliar concepts to their partners, but a film can introduce understanding through readily grasped images. One client was puzzled about what his wife meant when she called him "cold and indifferent." But after watching *The Accidental Tourist,* a film about a repressed and inflexible man, he said to her: "Oh, *that.* I never knew *that* bothered you." We ask clients in relationships with strained communications to select a film with a message they want to convey to a partner. By watching the film together and explaining to the partner why they picked that particular film, they are able to enter into more productive conversations. Films thus serve as metaphors that more accurately represent the feelings clients cannot always put in words.

A client named Jean, a professional woman in her early 40s complained of having "lost her voice" years before. She valued her marriage of three years to Thomas, but she was afraid that she was reaching the same impasse with him that she had reached in an earlier marriage. She was unable to define what she needed from the relationship, and she could not confront him when he acted in ways she believed were unfair.

He was willing to make changes, but admitted he did not really understand what she wanted from him. He asked her to be more specific. And their relationship seemed to be founded on an assumption that he was the more capable of the two: Although she was frequently at a loss for words, he never was. I (John) encouraged Jean to explain her feelings to him, but she continued to fall back on a formula, "I've lost my voice." Thomas continued to say, "Be specific."

Jean was assigned *Matilda,* about a neglected child in a grotesquely dysfunctional family. The assumption was that because of her abusive childhood, Jean would appreciate Matilda, a precocious youngster who thrives despite self-absorbed and immature parents. I anticipated that she would understand the film better than Thomas and that she would explain it to him—a reversal of their usual conversational pattern.

Two weeks after the assignment, Jean said the movie had indeed helped her explain to Thomas how years of living with her "crazy" parents had silenced her. Although she loved him, she had not been able to break this habit of self-protectiveness with him. He said he found it hard to believe her family was as bizarre as Matilda's. But she replied that her family was every bit as dysfunctional, "just not as funny." In the weeks that followed, he seemed to better understand her avoidance of conflict and was careful not to attack her when she tried to talk. Though they continued to struggle with communication difficulties, Jean finally said, "I am beginning to regain my voice."

PRIORITIZING VALUES

According to Parry (in Friedman, 1993), "if the 'grand narratives' have lost their traditional capacity to inspire . . . all we have now are our own stories and such stories as we invent to encompass the clash between chaos and control that seems central to life in these days." We are not comparing Hollywood films to the great philosophies or religions, but social critics agree that popular films constitute one of the primary sources for the dissemination of cultural values in our time (Gergen, 1991).

Films do transmit values. They suggest norms, define the good life, and offer opinions about which goals are worthy and which are not.

There is, of course, a danger in the influence of a film. When clients accept underlying messages unexamined, they are vulnerable to the filmmaker's point of view. But when clients analyze films in the context of ongoing therapy, they find that films help them prioritize their values and aid in resolving ethical dilemmas.

The film *Short Cuts* features several stories from the pen of Raymond Carver that have no connection other than agreement that society is off course and that something must be done. The film has no heroes or villains, and one action doesn't necessarily cause another. The viewer is never certain if things are getting better or worse. While one character complains "People don't give a damn," another seems more optimistic: "We've got to start caring more for each other."

The film presents episodes that can encourage clients to contemplate how they would act in similar circumstances. In one episode, a man and his fishing buddies find a dead body in a river. Not knowing what to do, they reason that because they cannot help the dead woman, they might as well wait until returning home to call the police. But at home, the man's wife is horrified. She asks how they could continue fishing after they found the body. He doesn't understand why she is upset. His buddies pressured him to stay, but how would leaving have changed anything? What was wrong about what they did? The episode could be used in therapy to discuss personal responsibility, requirements for living in a community, and the necessity of sometimes opposing one's peers.

Although therapists are not ethicists, they deal with questions of right and wrong as choices impact their clients. By discussing films, therapists can avoid an implied directive to give advice. They can place the emphasis where it should be: on the client's development of useful ethical guidelines. Films open up therapeutic conversations so that clients can find their own ways.

Chapter 2

Integrating Films into Therapy

At a time when traditional philosophies and religions have lost much of their authority, films represent a source of cultural identity through the adoption of attitudes, beliefs, behavior, and even the language of film characters. The distinction between the fictional worlds that characters inhabit and the real world has become increasingly blurred as film characters and the celebrities who portray them assume lives of their own. Psychologist Kenneth Gergen notes in *The Saturated Self* (1991):

> When *Batman* opened, a crowd of 20,000 stood for hours to glimpse celebrities for a few seconds in person. How many of one's neighbors elicit such devotion? It may also be ventured that with the advances in film technology, the movies have become one of the most powerful rhetorical devices in the world. Unlike most of our acquaintances, films can catapult us rapidly and effectively into states of fear, anger, sadness, romance, lust, and aesthetic ecstasy—often within the same two-hour period. It is undoubtedly true that for many people film relationships provide the most emotionally wrenching experiences of the average week. (pp. 56–57)

Some social critics view this development as alarming. Neal Gabler, in a column in the *Los Angeles Times,* points to the darker side of the coin. According to Gabler, films provide raw material for heinous crimes; television newscasts turn ordinary people into performers enacting a movie script. Gabler relates a foiled holdup attempt at a southern California bank to a film titled *Heat:*

> The truth, of course, is that we had seen it before—just not on the news. We had seen it in the movies. . . . Whether through the perpetrators' lack of imagination or the inherent momentum of these sorts of things, the heist and the shootout followed all the old movie conventions, which is no doubt why the press felt so comfortable treating the event as if it were a movie and why viewers were so absorbed by it.
>
> It may be appropriate that a crime committed not far from the movie studios should become another testament to how thoroughly the movies dominate our consciousness. Although their heyday when more than 70 million Americans went to the movies each week is long gone, *film remains the primary way we refract reality and attempt to understand it.* (March 16, 1997. Reprinted in the Ft. Worth Star-Telegram. Italics added.)

This observation is completely accurate except that Gabler limits the "heyday" of films to attendance at movie theaters. People today watch many films through cable television and video rentals, and the demand for film continues to rise, as evidenced by a stream of made-for-TV movies that dramatize daily news events.

A recent controversy in the Dallas–Ft. Worth area concerned a network's airing of a television drama that depicted the murder of a local teenager, allegedly by two of her classmates. Attorneys for the defendants sought to ban the film locally, arguing that potential jurors would decide guilt or innocence based on the content of the film rather than the facts. The court, however, disagreed and ruled that stations could carry the film. (The regional stations voluntarily declined.) We think the attorneys made a valid point. A dramatic reenactment of a crime is entertainment, but viewers tend to confuse fictional accounts with the truth.

Life also imitates art in the therapeutic consulting room. Therapists sometimes refer to the soap operas they hear at work each day. Clients' lives can resemble recent films or television shows. Clients also compare themselves to characters in films they have recently seen. When they are having trouble explaining a point, they will say, "You know, it's a lot like what so-and-so did when she was going through a divorce," and they name a television or movie character rather than a friend.

Films are neither good nor bad in themselves, but they become so when viewers internalize the messages films contain. Our approach to films in therapy is to encourage clients to examine films for what is life affirming and reject what is not. We know that they will continue to watch films on a regular basis with or without our encouragement. We want films to become part of their lifelong emotional journey of greater authenticity and healing. If film relationships provide significant emotional experiences for clients—and we believe that they do—how can therapists enlist films for therapeutic purposes? The first step is to consider the relationship that therapists have to films and to delineate the specific skills therapists need to link film viewing to therapy.

WHAT THERAPISTS NEED FOR VIDEOWORK

As therapists, clinicians attend to the nuances of their clients' narratives, they encourage self-disclosure by accepting nonjudgmentally what clients offer, and they ask open-ended questions to gain a better understanding of viable goals. These same skills are required to discuss films with clients. Clinicians should listen to what clients are actually saying about films instead of just hearing the interpretations that they want or are looking to hear. Clinicians should work with the films that clients prefer without imposing their own aesthetic preferences. And their questions about films should be modeled on the news reporter who asks "who, what, when, where, and how," rather than be formulated to validate pet psychotherapeutic theories.

But further skills are required. First, therapists should learn to watch films therapeutically so they can describe the process effectively to their clients. Next, they should assemble a list of therapeutic films. And finally, they should think of films as cotherapists in the process of encouraging and utilizing insights.

HOW IS THERAPEUTIC VIEWING DIFFERENT?

VideoWork is not the same as entertainment. Viewers typically pay more attention to a film's plot and less to character development. VideoWork, however, concentrates on characters and their relationships. What is most critical is the process of change in and between characters. We ask clients to pay attention to how characters appear at the beginning, how they react to the conflicts they face, and how they are different by the end of the film. We ask that clients note how relationships improve or deteriorate as the story unfolds, what each character does to make things better or worse, and how the character appears to feel in response to changes.

Another difference between viewing for entertainment and viewing for therapeutic benefit is the emphasis on conscious identification. Anyone who watches a movie identifies with a character to some extent. But in VideoWork, we encourage clients to articulate their identifications. Which characters elicit the most personal identity? Which elicit the least? What behaviors would clients like to adopt? What attitudes seem useful in relating to others? How are the issues that the characters are struggling with similar to clients' own issues? Is a character's approach to problem solving similar or dissimilar to their own? What feelings does a client associate with a character? Are those feelings familiar? If unfamiliar but positive, can the client access untapped feelings and utilize them?

Viewing for Entertainment	Therapeutic Viewing
Plot	Characters
Action	Relationships
Outcome	Process
Excitement	Insight
Suspense	Analysis
"Movie stars"	Focus on oneself

A third difference between casual and therapeutic viewing has to do with articulating ideas for change derived from the film. We ask clients to consider the film's unique voice. How does that voice differ from the clients' families or friends, and what new perspectives do they hear? If the film were an encoded communication showing a new way of looking at their problems, what is the message? What new ideas for action emerge during the process of watching the film? How viable are the ideas it contains? If these ideas are potentially useful, how can a client put them into practice? If the ideas are impractical as they stand, can they be modified so they will work better?

We presented the VideoWork model to a group of management consultants during a weekend workshop, inviting them to participate in viewing a film therapeutically. With tongue in cheek, we introduced the process by explaining that they were about to watch "a film made by mystics, containing secrets of the universe." We asked them to focus on personal or business problems that concerned them and to imagine that the film contained a potential solution, which might emerge from a bit of conversation, a particular character, a theme, or a visual image. Then we announced that the film was *Groundhog Day,* starring Bill Murray in the role of a narcissistic television weatherman named Phil.

The follow-up discussion, scheduled for an hour, ran three-and-a-half hours. The group was surprised that a comedy could elicit so many potential answers to the questions they had posed. We began the discussion by asking them to talk about how the movie spoke to their concerns. Some participants had trouble seeing how the film related to their questions but were helped by others to find connections from information they had previously revealed. But the major breakthroughs came days later as participants discovered new insights. One participant, who had believed himself equally committed to work and home life, said that Phil's unbridled ambitions caused him to realize that he had been neglecting his wife and children. He vowed to create a better balance between his profession and his family. Another participant said that, like Phil, she had stopped doing the little things that had molded her employees into a cohesive organization—not because she was not a talented leader but because with success had come lethargy.

When we asked the group to describe what made the exercise work for them, they said that the film distanced them from their problems so they could see those problems in a new light. In talking about the film—which they easily saw as a relevant metaphor to the questions they had asked—they experienced creative insights. They also agreed that our introduction to the film had been critical in watching the film with an open mind. One man said, "I knew you had a purpose for that silly film, but I doubted I'd get it. I'm still not sure I got what you wanted me to, but I got enough. It's amazing to me that it worked."

CONSTRUCTING A LIST OF FILMS

Therapists should assemble a working list of therapeutically useful films that are available on videotape and should be aware of the films playing in theaters. It is important to identify several films that address each clinical issue because no film suffices for all clients and because clinicians work better with some films than with others. Part II of this book is an anthology of films that we have found helpful in our practice. But this anthology is just a starting point. Once clinicians begin to employ films frequently, they will find favorites that fit their therapeutic approaches and their clients' needs.

Therapists can legitimately disagree on which films are ideal for clients, and it is important that they are comfortable when assigning a film. A therapist who reacts negatively to a certain film should not be concerned that other therapists are using the same film successfully with their clients. Nevertheless, we believe that successful practitioners of VideoWork will be those clinicians who can be most flexible in their choice of films—guided primarily by the preferences of their clients. Almost any film that a client likes can be used productively in therapy, but only if the therapist treats a client's preferences with respect and enters into the exercise with a sense of curiosity about why the client picked that film.

Sometimes clients prefer films that therapists do not. For example, I (Jan) asked a 16-year-old girl with family problems to name the films she enjoyed the most. At the top of her list were "Freddy Krueger movies." I admitted that I hadn't seen them but asked her to describe which characters she liked the most and why.

CLIENT: I like Freddy Krueger because he can get into people's heads, know what they are thinking. I wish I could do that—it'd be better if I could. I get into trouble because I think people want one thing and it turns out they want something else. Or I get jumped on because I don't know that what I'm saying is going to upset them.

JAN: Which people, in particular?

CLIENT: Mom, mostly. I just fall into this deep pit when she's around. I start talking about something I don't know is going to upset her and then she goes off on me. If I could read her mind like Freddy Krueger does. . .

By taking this client's movie preferences seriously, I gained helpful insight into her problems and values. Moreover, rapport was enhanced significantly through finding a subject about which she was an authority. We would not assign slasher movies to any client, but mining for metaphorical value even horror films that clients have seen can be worthwhile.

A wealth of resources exists to help therapists select films that meet their clients' needs. The first resource is, as in our example, one's own clients, who will readily suggest films they have seen. Another resource is other therapists who use movies in therapy. Many of the films we use in our practice were recommendations from other therapists. Shannon B. Dermer and Jennifer Hutchings (1997), in a survey of marriage and family therapists, identified 100 films that therapists regularly use or deem useful for therapy in addressing marriage and family problems. *Family Therapy Networker* contains monthly reviews of new films from a clinical viewpoint. For therapists with access to the Internet, numerous film sites list both current and older films. On our Web site at www.hesley.com, we review new video releases that are useful for therapy. We also link to other Internet movie databases. But therapists themselves are the best resource for useful films. When therapists watch films with an eye for how those films apply to a client's problems, their database grows rapidly. A whole world opens for inspection and evaluation.

MOVIE CHARACTERS AS COTHERAPISTS

Therapists should think of films and characters as material that will be internalized by clients and available for future reference. Clients remember characters from films and can repeat key phrases and sequences long into the future. Although clients also recall remarks made by therapists, films are particularly useful as cues for insights, decisions, and productive emotions that had emerged at the time of viewing or in follow-up discussions with the therapist. These cues remind the client of insights and connections that are made in therapy.

For example, one couple in our practice watched *The Accidental Tourist* and agreed that they suffered from the same conflict avoidance that Macon and Sarah Leary do in the film. The Learys believe that the fewer arguments they have the better their relationship will be, even after they separate. Then Macon encounters an eccentric dog trainer named Muriel who teaches him that straightforward communication is a prerequisite for mature relationships.

After watching the film and discussing it in therapy, the couple agreed that they "needed more Muriel and less Leary" in their marriage and that they would contract with each other to expect and provide emotional honesty. In weeks to come, they chided each other good naturedly when they fell into old habits. "Bring in the dog trainer," they would say—a gentle reminder to honor their agreements for confronting interpersonal differences and to get back on track with their goals. Muriel, odd and therefore memorable, would always be ready to speak up if the Learys threatened to reappear in their marriage.

For this couple, the film served as an internalized cotherapist who would be with them long after therapy had come to an end. We find this function to be the rule with VideoWork rather than the exception. Former clients tell us that they recall "that movie you asked me to see, the one with the guy like me." Frankly, we have often forgotten the film we had assigned, but they have not. The image has continued to do its magic.

Internalized cotherapists can even be consulted for problems that arise after therapy is finished. One young client had been fascinated by the character of Curly, a hell–bent–for–leather trail boss who imparts sage advice in the film *City Slickers*. Several years later, when the client came back to discuss a new job, he said that Curly had been a constant companion since he had watched the movie as part of his therapy. "I'd picture Curly smoking his cigarette and leaning down from his horse. Then I'd ask him how I should handle something that was going on and wait for an answer. You know what? He'd usually come through with an idea I hadn't thought of." Once a client internalizes a fictional character, the imagination can apply the character's wisdom to new concerns. The process is simply a way to facilitate creativity.

CINEMA EXPERTISE NOT REQUIRED

Therapists who are not film buffs can relax. It is not necessary to be a film critic to use VideoWork. The purpose in using films is to augment therapy, not analyze movies. Clinicians should never become so enamored by a film that they lose sight of therapeutic objectives. Discussions often turn quickly from a film to a client's own situation. Therapists should not feel obligated to return to discussion of a film merely because it was assigned or because they are curious about a client's interpretation. In practice, some of the more successful instances of VideoWork have involved clients who barely mentioned the films assigned during follow-up visits but who described new therapeutic insights.

Some therapists are better than others at remembering plots and characters from films. Therapists who tend to forget a film's details should use the indices of this book to remind themselves of films that are suitable for clinical issues. Clinicians will also find that they can recall appropriate movies more easily by making up cheat sheets of favorite films and keeping them close at hand during sessions. Although several films can speak to a clinical problem, therapists will find a greater comfort zone in working with certain films rather than others.

All this advice notwithstanding, there is one basic and absolute requirement for using VideoWork with clients: *Therapists should genuinely enjoy movies.* If they do not, they are unlikely to show much enthusiasm for their assignments, and their clients might not take the assignments seriously. This intrinsic interest in films is probably the only quality about using VideoWork that cannot be learned.

TRY IT BEFORE YOU BUY IT

Before doing VideoWork with clients, therapists should experience the process for themselves. The box below shows how we suggest you go about the experiment.

WHO BENEFITS FROM VIDEOWORK?

Clients who are functioning moderately well in their home and work or school environments and whose problems involve interpersonal components are ideal candidates for VideoWork. We use films with individuals, couples, and families, with adults, adolescents, and some preadolescents.

A Test Drive with VideoWork

1. Pick a problem from your present or past.
2. From the anthology or the indices of this book, find the category that most closely matches your problem.
3. Choose a film—it is not important whether you have seen it before.
4. If you wish, invite a partner or friend to watch with you.
5. As you watch the film, note the characters with whom you feel identification, the emotions you feel, the similarities and dissimilarities to your situation, and your insights.
6. After the viewing, discuss the film with your partner or reflect on it by yourself. If the film had a unique message for you, what was it? What new ideas for new behavior did you have?
7. Pretend that a particular client had seen the film. What questions would you ask, and how would you use the film? What other films can you identify that might take the discussion a step further?

As a matter of practice, the working criteria are whether film assignments fit into the usual routine of clients and whether, in using films, we can facilitate new discoveries and perspectives or connections that will enhance therapy.

In our private practice, we have used films to address these areas:

- Parenting (including stepparenting, blended families, and adoption).
- Marriages and other intimate relations.
- Communication problems, conflict resolution.
- Chronic illness and traumatic injury.
- Loss and grief, depression.
- Shyness, irrational fears, anxiety.
- Family-of-origin issues.
- Substance abuse.
- Histories of emotional, physical, and sexual abuse.
- Divorce, custody.
- Eating disorders.
- Caretaking, dependency.
- Women's issues.
- Men's issues.
- Identity.
- Vocation.
- Religious concerns.
- Developmental stages.
- Death and dying.
- Understanding relatives and friends with severe emotional illness.

As consultants with organizations, we have employed films in facilitating discussions on sex discrimination, teamwork, ethics, and leadership. In continuing education workshops for mental health professionals, we have used films to address ethical concerns. And in churches, we have used films as focal points for workshops on death and dying, marriage, and values.

WHO IS NOT A CANDIDATE FOR VIDEOWORK?

We do not use films with small children except in family therapy as a means of encouraging the family to do something positive together. Given

36

a child's developmental limitations and our practice of discussing films a week after they are assigned, using videowork with young children is usually not effective. Other therapists, however, might find helpful ways to talk with children about films—particularly by showing film clips to parents and children in session and then discussing them immediately.

Clients with serious psychiatric disorders are not candidates for VideoWork. Because clients usually watch films in their own homes rather than in our office, it is difficult to deal with issues that come up during or immediately after a viewing. Obviously this risk is too great for clients who have trouble distinguishing reality from fantasy. But this risk is true as well for nonpsychotic clients with severe symptomatology. Therapists should not assign films that they believe, in their clinical judgment, might cause a client distress. It is helpful with all clients to briefly discuss a film and then assess the client's reaction to the idea of watching it. If the client is unsure whether the film will help, that is manageable. But if the client believes that watching the film would be too difficult emotionally, it is better to substitute a different type of homework.

We have found that we can trust our clients in this decision. In our experience, although clients may not know when a film will be helpful, they almost always know when it will be too hard to take. We describe scenes that are highly emotional if we think a film might cause difficulties to vulnerable clients (such as the funeral scene in the movie *Steel Magnolias,* in which a mother grieves for her daughter). If the film seems too threatening to them, clients are quick to say they do not want to watch it. Here is a rule of thumb: with clients who are more vulnerable, we describe films in far more depth than with clients who are more resilient and less emotionally distraught.

VideoWork assignments are very successful with couples. However, if there is violence in the home, we do not use film assignments. Films often introduce subjects that clients may have avoided in therapy, and that introduction is productive under normal circumstances. But when a couple has a background of violence, the risk of an unmonitored film assignment and an unpredictable reaction is too great.

We also do not assign films to clients who have recently had traumatic experiences similar to the characters in the film. Couples who have just narrowly avoided losing a child to illness are obviously not candidates for films such as *Lorenzo's Oil,* in which the protagonists agonize over a gravely ill child. But a couple that cannot manage a film immediately after a child's illness might well benefit from it five years later as they attempt to put the event behind them. We describe the film to such parents and ask them if they think they are ready for such an assignment—usually they have little doubt about whether they are. Clinicians should make decisions about a client's readiness for a film by using the same criteria they use with any high-impact homework. If they have doubts that a client's emotional strength is sufficient to deal with the feelings that a film may elicit, they should choose a less threatening film or not use VideoWork at all.

Another contraindication for a film assignment is when clients might assume from a film selection that a therapist identifies them with a particularly unattractive character. A repressed and angry mother of a troubled teenager could not help but see herself mirrored in the embittered and emotionally distant mother in the film *Ordinary People.* Recommending that film would likely result in an enraged client. In chapter 4, we discuss in more detail how to minimize the possibility that clients will read the wrong motives into film assignments. But if a therapist thinks that a certain character in a film fits the client in ways that will be offensive, the therapist should not assign that film.

Finally, if clients express a dislike of films in the intake interview, we do not use VideoWork. Plenty of people already enjoy films; there's no need to convince those who do not that they should. Clients who don't already watch movies will interpret film assignments as busywork and will not comply with the assignment. In our experience, this group represents no more than about five percent of the clients to whom we have introduced VideoWork. People in general, love movies.

WHAT ARE THE RISKS?

Because we avoid film assignments to clients such as those described in the previous section, we have never had a client experience significant problems with a film assignment nor have we heard of problems from other clinicians who use VideoWork. The worst-case scenario appears to be when clients indicate that a film seems off target and irrelevant to their needs. Usually a second film assignment proves more successful, particularly if we ask the client to choose the film. But if the second film is no more successful than the first, we abandon VideoWork in subsequent sessions.

Despite the relative safety of film assignments, therapists should take reasonable precautions. Films contain a rich matrix of images. Clients will most likely get more from a film than was intended, and clinicians must be able to manage whatever emerges. Clients should be psychologically strong enough to handle dramatic material, and that determination can only be made by a therapist based on a specific client's strengths and vulnerabilities. As we discuss in the next section, during the intake interview therapists can get a reading on how movies in general affect clients and on the prospects for assigning films in therapy. But ultimately the therapist alone, using clinical criteria, can decide whether film assignments pose unique risks for a client.

WHEN TO INITIATE VIDEOWORK

We introduce the concept of film assignments in the initial meeting with a new client. In addition to questions regarding family history, presenting problems, lifestyle, social support systems, and overall goals and objectives, we ask clients to name a few films they have found to be personally meaningful. We ask what kinds of films they prefer (action, drama, comedy, romance) and which film characters have had a personal impact. We question how their own attitudes and behavior are mirrored by the characters in the films they describe: Who are "the good guys, the bad guys, the angels, and the monsters" and how are they similar and dissimilar to the client? We also ask which films their families enjoy.

Including questions about films in the assessment helps diagnosis and enhances a common therapist/client language leading to greater rapport. It helps determine if using movies in therapy will be productive and, if so, which types will work best. We can avoid films that might create misunderstandings. And in clients' choice of movies, we find clues to their working role models, ideal self-images, internal resources, potential goals, perceived obstacles, degrees of imagination and creativity, and overall philosophy of life. Furthermore, by talking about films early in the therapeu-

39

tic relationship, we allow clients to express feelings that may be too threatening to express directly.

An illustration of this process is the case of a diminutive and soft-spoken young woman named Mary, referred by her family doctor after an incident of date rape.

Mary said she had attended a street dance, did not want to go home alone late at night, and had spent the night at a friend's home. During the night, her friend raped her. Surprisingly, she accepted the blame for the whole episode. She said that she had been drinking that night, "probably too much," and that she was naive in expecting her friend to honor her request "just to get some sleep." She was angry, but she expressed her anger in soft, unemotional tones. Although others urged her to report the incident to the police, she declined: "It would be my word against his." She wanted to forget the situation and return to a normal life. She went on to describe herself as a loser and cited the incident as more evidence: "It was the latest in a long list of mistakes I've made."

I (Jan) wanted to give her anger more direction and take the focus off her generalized negative self-attributions. I asked if she could think of a film that represented what she felt. Mary looked down sheepishly and then smiled bitterly. "*Extremities,*" she said, "It's a movie about rape. Not exactly what I went through, but that's the one that came up when you asked." As Mary described *Extremities,* she became angrier and her quiet voice intensified.

MARY: The woman's raped in the movie, violently raped. It was scary. He tied her up and held a knife to her. I thought he was going to kill her when he was finished. But somehow she slips out of the rope and turns the table on the guy. She traps him, shuts him up him in a fireplace, and sprays chemicals in his eyes so that he's blinded. I think she tortures him—*but he tortured her before, you know?* She's going to kill him, she *really wants to,* but her friends walk in and talk her out of it. [*Then she paused and her voice became firmer.*] Of course I'd never do anything like that—I can't imagine doing anything like that. But I can understand why she wanted to. You get so mad you want to kill a person who does something like that.

We began comparing the film to Mary's situation. In contrast to the movie, Mary had refused to take action. She suppressed her feelings of anger. But in describing the film, Mary expressed a full range of feelings, which was a new experience for her. In the context of a therapy setting, she identified more assertive options. Subsequently she decided that for her own self-respect she needed to report the incident. Her depression lifted as she took actions that she deemed appropriate.

VIDEOWORK IN AN ASSESSMENT

Burt was referred to me (John) by a physician who was treating him for ulcers and for moderate depression resulting from stress at work and at home. An accountant by profession, he had recently separated from his second wife, Judy, and complained that he "just didn't understand women." He said he undoubtedly worked too much but that he and his wife had agreed that he should do so to help buy a new home. He added that the extra work did not bring in more income because he was on salary but that he believed it showed his boss he was ambitious. Nevertheless his wife had left him, saying that their relationship was "not as much fun as before." Her words baffled him, and he concluded that she "didn't know what she really wanted." This situation, said Burt, was almost identical to his first divorce. His previous wife had told him that he did not know how to be in a committed relationship. "You don't have a clue how to be a husband," she had said.

Burt appeared surprised when I asked him about the movies he had recently seen and whether any might describe his conflicts with his wife. After a moment's thought, he laughed and said he knew one, a comedy called *Multiplicity*. He seemed self-conscious about the choice and added that he was not sure this film was what I had in mind.

BURT: It's really just a funny movie, you know. It's not serious at all.

JOHN: Your choice is fine. Tell me as much as you can remember about it. I haven't seen it yet.

Parenthetically, my not having seen the film was of little consequence. No therapist can be expected to be familiar with or remember

41

the details of every film that clients mention. Sometimes being unfamiliar with a film can be an advantage. New clients may assume that therapy is like visiting a family doctor who "fixes the problem." Hence a strategy by which clients are placed in a position of power—like Burt being the expert on the film *Multiplicity*—increases the likelihood that therapy will be a true partnership instead of a dependent relationship. My posing a question about a subject outside my "expertise," accepting the film Burt offered without judgment, and asking him to describe it were tangible ways of encouraging him to participate fully in therapy and of opening a conversational space for dialogue.

Burt warmed quickly to describing *Multiplicity*. The story, he said, was about a man named Doug who felt incapable of meeting the demands of his busy life. After working 12-hour days as a building contractor, he would return home to a wife who criticized him for not doing more around the house and for not taking a more active role with their children. He tried to improve but he could not satisfy the demands of home and job, and he felt a continual sense of failure. "Just like I do," Burt added. At the end of a day, Doug had nothing left over for himself. Time on the golf course, which he relished, was out of the question. He wondered how he could stretch the hours of the day, or maybe even himself. If he could split himself, he could please everybody else and still have something left over.

And that is exactly what happens in the film. A scientist clones Doug into two, then three, then four persons. Now he can give more time to his family as well as to his job and have extra time for golf. All goes well until the expectations rise. Because Doug has done so well at work, his boss expects him to do even more. And because he's become a superdad and an ideal husband, his wife holds him to higher standards. Eventually the clones are literally running into each other trying to satisfy everybody and creating chaos by making deals without telling each other. What begins as an ideal solution creates problems that are even worse.

Clients who are under stress frequently complain of time pressures: "I wish I could be two people." In *Multiplicity*, the metaphor is extended to its logical outcome, both good and bad. Doug's cloning helps satisfy the needs of more people, gets more work done, and frees up time for recreation. But the cloning also creates new problems that eclipse the original ones. In talking about the film, Burt began to reflect on his own strategy and its failure in his marriage. The harder he tried at work and at home, the more fragmented he felt. Eventually, he satisfied neither his wife nor himself.

I asked Burt to identify the clone most similar to himself. He picked the one dedicated to work. In that area, he felt comfortable that he was doing a good job despite increasing demands made by his boss.

JOHN: Which clone was least like you?

BURT: The one that stayed at home—the father and husband. I grew up in a family where my dad had a good job, paid the bills, and that was about it. He didn't do anything with me, no playing ball or anything like that. And I don't remember him and my mom doing much together. Mostly he watched TV, went to bed early, and was the typical couch potato. But don't get me wrong, he was a darned good provider.

Burt knew that Judy wanted more from him than what his father had given to his mother. Judy wanted companionship and intimacy, which Burt knew meant more than sex. As he described his marriage further, Burt began to realize that he responded to Judy's requests for greater intimacy by convincing them both that he was too tired and undervalued at work, making it possible for him to pull away and claim to be "too stressed out to have anything left." In retrospect, Burt realized that the overwork was mostly his own choice and a way to avoid facing his real problems. Before Judy began asking for more time with him, he did his work satisfactorily within a 40-hour work week. The truth was, he admitted, he really *was* clueless about how to be in a loving relationship. His problem, as he finally defined it, was not so much stress as an absence of skills in maintaining intimate relationships over a sustained period of time. Work stress was merely a convenient excuse.

Thus, at an early stage of therapy, a presenting problem was redefined. Discussing the film *Multiplicity* helped Burt transform a generalized complaint about which he could do little ("How can I satisfy everybody?") into a more concrete problem about which he could do something ("How can I learn to express intimacy in my relationships?").

The film discussion also moved therapy away from unproductive self-attributions ("I'm not the husband type and probably need a 'clone' to do that for me") toward self-efficacy ("I need to learn intimacy skills").

Michael White (1990) has termed this process "externalizing the problem," a process in which situational explanations replace personal attributions. In showing a client that a problem lies outside oneself and that it can and should be attacked with all one's resources, the course of therapy is shortened and clients experience more hopefulness about the future. For Burt, this change in perspective, occasioned by talking about a film comedy, narrowed his therapeutic agenda. In redefining his problem toward skills acquisition and away from personality reconstruction, Burt cut more directly to the heart of his unhappiness. He also saw therapy as less aversive than he had imagined it would be, and thus he committed himself more enthusiastically to it.

Chapter 3

Selecting Films for Therapy

New films or old? Movie theater or video store? Most of our film assignments involve videotape rentals because therapeutic viewing requires clients to concentrate on the material they are watching in a way that movie theaters make difficult. At home, clients can stop the tape to study a particularly insightful piece of dialogue. They can write notes or discuss a turn of the plot with a partner. And rentals are relatively inexpensive, a significant factor because we typically recommend several films to clients throughout therapy.

Six Tips for Successful Movie Matches

1. Select effective role models from films.
2. Match the content of a film to therapeutic issues.
3. Pick films that clients enjoy.
4. Show characters solving problems.
5. Take advantage of powerful indirect effects.
6. Choose films that evoke inspirational moods.

We like clients to identify with certain characters in the films they view, to find the themes compatible with their own situations (concretely or analogically), to find value in the ways characters solve problems, and to develop ideas for appropriating insights from the films in their own lives. In choosing films that will accomplish these objectives, we consider a number of attributes (see box on page 45).

EFFECTIVE ROLE MODELS

Sometimes the role models that clients need are unavailable in real life but can be found in films. This approach is not new. Appropriating role models from the movies is merely an updated version of something that has been done since the invention of the printing press. From the fictionalized or real worlds of business, sports, entertainment, history, politics, and religion, people have always shaped themselves by reference to larger-than-life characters.

Role models may indeed be larger-than-life, but to be believable, they must be similar to us in some respects—family background, life experience, vocation, lifestyle, or in the conflicts they face. They may be the same age, younger, or older. The primary issue in role model compatibility is whether clients can project themselves into a desirable character, seeing themselves as they have been, are today, or would like to become in the future.

Choosing a Role Model

One way to select a role model for a client is to conceptualize an ideal mentor, then choose a film that features such a character. For a discouraged middle-aged physician wrestling with managed care and questioning the wisdom of having given up research, we might offer Doc Graham from *Field of Dreams,* a film not only about dreams but also about regrets. Doc Graham left behind his first dream of playing major league baseball to treat generations of appreciative patients. In the end, he decided he had made the right choice. Our physician might take heart from sharing Doc Graham's journey and might see more value in his or her own career.

We recommend film role models who struggle with and overcome the same issues that our clients do, because we believe that clients will learn from a role model's experience. Fictional characters have their ups and downs, their dead ends as well as their successes. They make mistakes, as we all do, but they almost always learn from them. Clients benefit from film characters' lessons.

Guarding against Undesired Effects

Clients may be influenced by a fictional role model's negative traits as well as the positive ones. How does a therapist help them appropriate the positive aspects of a film role model while neutralizing the negative? In *Ferris Bueller's Day Off,* a film about adolescents trying to find themselves, Ferris Bueller is a free-spirited teen who will probably grow up to be a fine adult. But he is also sneaky with authorities and shows a blatant disregard for reasonable limits. How can adolescent clients borrow Ferris's spirit of independence without also adopting his oppositionalism?

In some cases, a therapist can inoculate a client against inappropriate identifications by cautioning what *not* to take from a character, for instance, "I am not suggesting that you should drive your automobile as fast or as recklessly as Ferris Bueller does." In other cases, the therapist might emphasize differences between the client and the movie character and stress that a movie character would not, unmodified, thrive in the client's world. Of course, if the client is an oppositional adolescent, neither of those approaches are likely to weaken an unhealthy identification. A better tactic in that case might be to talk about the pros and cons of a character, about desirable as well as objectionable aspects, then encourage the client to consider how those qualities would improve or hurt the client. With focused discussion of the good as well as the bad, there is less likelihood that a client will adopt the role model uncritically and that role models picked by therapists for one purpose will be derailed into another. The chart on page 48 shows how a client might sum up Ferris Bueller.

When Role Models Don't Work

We want clients to see the failures of a character and avoid those failures in their own lives. But clients may get an entirely different impression from what we had in mind. *An Officer and A Gentleman,* in which a narcissistic Marine learns about commitment and responsibility, was assigned

47

Ferris's Good Points:	**Ferris's Bad Points:**
1. He's got spunk.	1. He tells lies.
2. Everybody likes him.	2. He's conceited.
3. He's good with computers.	3. He's manipulative.
4. He has a great girlfriend.	4. He makes fun of people.
5. He's a good person.	5. He burns bridges with people he might need.
6. He takes care of his friends.	6. He's a little spoiled.

to a 22-year-old whose parents had guarded him from natural consequences. The intention was to reinforce the idea that there are limits in the real world and that he needed to live by the ground rules. Unfortunately, he saw in the protagonist only a clever fellow who was one step ahead of "all the suckers." In the follow-up interview then, we discussed how the Marine's unhealthy strategy had contributed to a very unhappy life and how the film dramatized the hard lessons he had to learn. The client eventually saw that he too needed to accept reasonable limits.

Ideally, role models should present better options for behavior than the strategies that clients are presently using. This result need not be dramatized in a happily-ever-after fashion, but the role model should emerge at the end at least sadder but wiser. For example, *The Doctor,* a movie about a physician who learns compassion when he becomes a patient, was assigned to a middle-aged banker who was having difficulty managing his employees. The client reported that he was often angry with his subordinates and complained that they were not producing the quality of work he expected from them. As he described his staff and their problems, he appeared not to appreciate his employees' concerns and feelings. So we hoped that in *The Doctor,* he would meet another professional who becomes more sensitive after seeing things from the customer's point of view.

The banker, a kind man who had simply grown to take his position too seriously, had no trouble making the connection. He related the doctor's haughty attitude to his own and saw how his attitude had been antagonizing his employees. He resolved to soften his approach and take his subordinates' problems more seriously. Our client learned the lesson he needed to learn by watching a role model learn his.

We began this discussion by suggesting that when clients do not have good role models in real life, film characters can be an effective substitute. But in fact, dramatic role models can sometimes be preferable. Real-life mentors often disappoint their protégés when they display human limitations. But role models in films almost always fall from grace, then work their way back. What clients learn is that true heros profit from their mistakes, and that they can too.

MATCH CONTENT TO THERAPEUTIC ISSUES

Therapeutic films should correspond to clients' narratives as closely as possible in terms of chronological age, socioeconomic background, education, values, and subject matter. Close correspondence is more necessary for some than for others. Clients who abstract easily, who are imaginative and tolerant of other opinions and lifestyles, can benefit from a wider range of films than those who identify exclusively with films and characters that reflect familiar environments. Ordinarily, however, films should mirror the client in as many ways as possible.

Content can be matched to therapy issues analogically as well as concretely. Not all adolescent clients face problems similar to those of the young basketball players from an inner city in *Hoop Dreams,* but many adolescents can share those players' confusion over immediate versus delayed rewards, goals for the future, and pressures from adults to succeed according to the adults' standards. Likewise, few couples are as literally combative as the caricatures Oliver and Barbara Rose in the film *War of the Roses,* but many divorcing couples act as if they are in a vicious battle. Films can express the spirit of a client's problem while being very different in the particulars.

Familiar Lifestyles

Clinicians should select films that feature lifestyles comparable to those of their clients. An archconservative attorney with a CPA spouse will probably relate more easily to the middle-class couple played by Jo Ann Woodward and Paul Newman in *Mr. and Mrs. Bridge* than to the flighty young couple in *When Harry Met Sally.* And conversely, graduate student couples will more likely appreciate the latter film.

We have found that films assigned to adolescent clients, for instance, are more successful when they feature adolescents who are similar in many respects—same social groups, same dress, same standing in relation to peers. Even slight deviations can make the film irrelevant. *Sixteen Candles,* a coming-of-age film, was assigned to a young woman who worried about many of the same issues as the protagonist—boyfriends, quarrels with friends, physical appearance. There was, however, a difference that proved critical: the protagonist's family was intact while the parents of the client were divorced. The client was unable to make an ideal connection. Although several points of comparison eventually proved fruitful for discussion, the client continued to see the film as remote from her own situation. VideoWork will be more successful when characters fit clients in as many ways as possible.

Holding Values in Common

The values shared between the film and the client are even more critical than the demographics. Although the ethical standards of the filmmaker need not exactly match those of the client, they should not raise serious moral objections. Mismatches may occur when therapists make film assignments that reflect their own values rather than those of clients. To prevent that mismatch from happening, therapists should bear in mind regional standards and should discuss potentially offensive aspects of a film (use of language, sexual situations, extramarital affairs and violence) before making an assignment. Failing to do so may interfere with therapeutic progress.

For example, I (Jan) assigned to a women's support group the film *Working Girl,* a movie about a secretary who uses brains and ingenuity to rise to the top of the corporate ladder. I suggested the film as a vehicle for discussing women's workplace issues. But two of the members reported the next week that they were unhappy with the homework. They explained that they attended fundamentalist churches and found the sexual content and language of the film offensive. This miscue on my part could have been avoided if I had prepared the group for the scenes in question and discussed their concerns. I should have been ready to suggest an alternative if objections to viewing *Working Girl* remained. A therapist who is concerned that a film will be offensive to a client is wise to discuss those concerns before rather than after an assignment.

One Film Impacts Many Problems

Ordinarily, the subject matter of a film should match the presenting problem of a client. We assign films about alcoholism to clients in recovery and films about parenting dilemmas to families with similar conflicts. But a film can serve more than one purpose. The film *When a Man Loves a Woman,* for instance, is about alcoholism. But we frequently recommend it to couples without substance abuse issues because the film effectively portrays relationship difficulties such as dependency, stereotypic male-female roles, and dysfunctional communication. A single film can be helpful to clients with several different concerns.

Therapists should conceptualize films as resources containing multiple issues, any one of which may be discussed in therapy. For example, *Fried Green Tomatoes,* a film about a woman's struggle for self-esteem, was assigned to a female client suffering from an eating disorder. The film is not about eating disorders per se, but focuses on a compulsive overeater named Evelyn who uses food to distract her from an unhappy marriage. The client was asked to described how Evelyn uses food, how Evelyn's interactions with her husband discourage her from losing weight (and encourage her to overeat), and the strategy by which Evelyn finally overcomes her problem. The movie has many other useful themes, but this theme was the most helpful for our client.

PICK FILMS CLIENTS ENJOY

Personal taste varies, and therapists should work with the films that clients prefer. Occasionally, clients will favor films that therapists do not. When we began using films with our clients, this problem accounted for periodic failures. We suggested films that we considered excellent works, films that were artistically well-constructed and offered many potentially useful insights. For some clients, our film choices did facilitate worthwhile discussions. But for others, the films were obviously irrelevant.

Clients often have strong preferences in the films they want to talk about and are not hesitant in asking us to see their films. For instance, many clients like *The Prince of Tides,* which we personally dislike for a number of reasons, not the least of which is that the film tacitly recommends romance between doctor and patient. Each time a client would talk about this film, we would try to redirect the conversation to a different film on abuse (one we liked better), but we often saw their enthusiasm wane. They might watch the film we preferred, but the follow-up discussion lacked spirit.

Eventually we realized that, in our film assignments, we were not speaking in the familiar language of our clients, but were instead expecting them to learn a foreign tongue—our movie preferences. At that point, we began asking our clients what films *they* enjoyed before we made suggestions of our own and then used the films they liked as often as possible. We found ways to caution against those aspects of films we thought might cause trouble (such as therapists falling in love with their clients), but we let the driving force of homework assignments be movies

---

Scoring with Movie Assignments

- Start with films that clients have already seen. Ask them to talk about a movie they like and listen nonjudgmentally.
- For the first assignment, choose a movie that is similar to the one they describe.
- Be sensitive to nuances. If a comedy is assigned, make sure clients don't feel discredited.
- Discuss scenes that might be offensive. Language, sex, nudity, and violence are hot points. Switch films if clients object to the one suggested.
- Clarify the intent when assigning a film in which a client might mistake the role identification.
- Tell clients that if they strongly dislike a film to turn it off. Admit inevitable mismatches quickly.
- Ask clients to be on the lookout for films that may be therapeutically useful. When possible, let clients suggest the films.

---

that they naturally enjoyed. And with that change, the hits started out-numbering the misses.

Clients Sometimes Know Best

Bill was an 18-year-old client with few friends and too many arguments at home. I (Jan) asked him to watch three coming-of-age films: *The Breakfast Club, Breaking Away,* and *My Bodyguard.* None really struck a chord, so I asked him to choose the next film. Bill chose *Can't Buy Me Love,* a film he called his "favorite of all time." During the following week, I also watched the film but did not share his enthusiasm. It is about an adolescent boy who pays a popular high school girl $1,000 to go out with him for a month, hoping she will improve his standing among peers. While the arrangement holds, he is more popular than before. But when his money runs out, so too does the popularity. The moral of the story is that money does not buy happiness.

For Bill, the film meant much more: it mirrored his high school with its emphasis on material success. His peers valued the cheerleader, the captain of the football squad, and the kid with a Corvette. In describing what he liked about the film, Bill said what he had previously not been able to put into words. Like the protagonist in the film, Bill too was in a no-win situation—his one success was nullified when he was cut from the basketball team. He saw no way to gain the respect of his peers. And his parents, he said, "didn't have a clue." Bill felt that *Can't Buy Me Love* was not just similar to his life, it *was* his life. So we worked with the film that meant most to Bill rather than films we may have preferred.

Hence the films that clients like the most may be unremarkable to therapists. Until clients begin to talk about what it is in a film that corresponds to the issues with which they are struggling, therapists cannot really know the value a film will have for a client. But the strategy that will improve the odds on making a good match is to work with films that clients appreciate.

SHOW CHARACTERS SOLVING PROBLEMS

Films are ideal metaphors for problem solving because they involve thesis, antithesis, and synthesis. A character experiences a crisis, tries out several unsuccessful responses, and ultimately finds a resolution. Although films rarely provide exact solutions that clients can imitate in their own lives, they frequently act metaphorically to generate new approaches. Ideally, clients identify with the major characters, test out options considered by those characters, and find points of agreement as well as disagreement with the resolution. In follow-up discussions, we reinforce the experience by making these impressions explicit, that is, by asking clients to describe which actions taken by the characters seemed to be the most helpful and how those same ideas might be utilized for clients' own problems.

One client, a woman in her early 40s, had just married into a blended family in which the three children, two of whom were hers and the third was her husband's, were experiencing setbacks in creating a new family. The client realized that the children were more sad than angry, but she was baffled in how to help them get past their grief. We assigned her *Fly Away Home,* a movie about a child's difficult adjustment in her divorced father's home following her mother's death.

In the film, the child is disconsolate and resistive to her father's attempts to help until she discovers a nest of abandoned goose eggs. She takes them home, hides them in the barn, and watches over them; after they hatch, she becomes the surrogate mother. Only through taking care of the goslings does she begin to have feelings of love once again. Finally she transfers those feelings to her new family.

The client readily identified with the frustrations of the adults in the movie over trying to deal with sad and angry children. Discussion focused on what the adults did in the film that was useful (listening when the child wanted to talk, supporting her in activities in which she showed interest, accepting her ambivalent feelings, and looking for occasions to demonstrate that she was in a safe and accepting environment). The discovery of the goose eggs may have been serendipitous, but it was the loving response of the adults to that discovery that made the difference. The solution in the film did not match the client's situation exactly, but she could solve her problem by borrowing skills from the movie characters that would be helpful with her new family.

Scale Down Characters to Real Life

Clients should critically evaluate the decisions made by characters in a film because a movie protagonist's choices may not be best for them.

When they begin to overidentify with a hero who throws caution to the wind, the therapist needs to celebrate the spirit while grounding the experience. In *Ruby in Paradise,* a young woman recalls how her mother trusted blindly in men and subsequently came to ruin. For that reason, her daughter avoids all dependence on men, even to the extent of temporary poverty. The film is powerful in its message to, as Joseph Campbell said, "follow your bliss," but it pays insufficient attention to the necessity of compromise in the real world.

Potential solutions from films always require careful consideration and modification to fit a client's situation. When clients tell us they have been moved by a film and "now know exactly what to do," we typically respond by asking them to describe the negative outcomes that might have occurred in the movie. Then we ask them to modify the initial idea to fit better with their real circumstances.

A client decided abruptly after having watched *Rudy* that she was going to quit her job and open an arts and crafts store. I (Jan) congratulated her on the idea, but asked her to compare her situation to Rudy's: he was a college student, had no other responsibilities, and could go to work with his family if playing football at Notre Dame did not work out. In contrast, she was a single parent supporting two children with modest child support from her ex-husband. Although over the years friends had encouraged her to start a business, she was not in a financial position to do so immediately. Her compromise was to rent a booth at an arts and crafts cooperative on Saturdays and to save her money. After a year, she had loyal customers and a nest egg, so she could pursue her dream full-time. Inspirations from films are valuable. But they must stand up to thoughtful analysis.

UTILIZE POWERFUL INDIRECT EFFECTS

An indirect effect is the impression that a client takes from an incidental aspect of a film, an impression not dependent on the film's major theme. The effect lingers long after the client sees the film and may be out of proportion to its narrative intent because of the psychological needs of the client at the time of viewing.

One of us (John) admits that he finally learned to ride a bicycle after watching a movie in the second grade about a motorcycle cop. Completely incidental to the plot, the officer did tricks with his bike and exhibited not a shred of concern for his safety. In contrast to the patrolman, the boy had fallen from his bike many times and was frightened to try again. After watching the movie, he went home, got on his bike, and rode off merrily without a single fall. In the boy's imagination, he was now in the California Highway Patrol, where fear was not an issue and ability was taken for granted.

Many therapists have used instructional videotapes that address issues such as parent-child relations, social skills training, and couples communication. These tapes have enjoyed success because of their effectiveness in providing not only didactic information about the issue, but also models with whom clients identify. We suspect that Hollywood films are potentially more useful because they approach therapy issues indirectly. After all, Hollywood films are not *about* those issues at all. Although they address many of the same topics as do prepared therapy videos, the teaching is embedded in the context of an unrelated story. Because resistance is not potentiated, the indirect message may be more powerful than straightforward instruction.

A therapist can use this indirectness to an advantage by paying attention to the images in a film that might appeal to a client or that might serve as cues for goals the client has discussed. I (John) once recommended *Top Gun,* a film about a young jet pilot's lesson in teamwork, to a professor in his early 50s who was bored with his academic job and had difficulties getting along with departmental colleagues. The direct theme to which I asked him to attend was teamwork in organizations, but the film elicited from him a need for greater variety in his life. It seemed to me as he described his impressions of the film that his new desire for adventure had been triggered by jet aircraft screaming across the skies and a soundtrack that pulsed with young life. When he scaled that desire down to reality, the client found ways to broaden his routine to include more novelty and challenge in his everyday life.

Each time a film is assigned, clients receive this indirect message: This film displays how your therapist sees you at this time. Most clients in our practice are flattered by our film assignments because our selections imply that we believe they, like the protagonists of the films, are capable of good choices and decisive action. But fragile clients may be confused about our intentions. We counter that by reassuring such a client prior to the viewing: "Susan, I'd like for you to pay particular attention to the character of Beth, who faces a problem at her job that's similar to your own." The therapist must ensure that clients do not think the therapist is comparing them to an objectionable character. That misunderstanding can be prevented if the therapist defines clearly why a film is being assigned.

EVOKE INSPIRATIONAL MOODS

We choose certain films not so much because they contain characters who are role models or because their themes are similar to clients' problems, but because the film as a whole offers a healing experience. In that sense, the film is similar to music used for stress reduction or to relieve depressed moods. Watching the film brings about a better frame of mind, a sense of being connected with the universe, and renewed hope.

Many people already use films in this way with or without therapists. Clients in intake interviews often say that they manage their sad moods by watching a favorite film. One elderly client, isolated in a small, inner-city apartment, said that when she was feeling blue she watched the film *On Golden Pond*. The majestic trees, the cries of loons, and the lapping of water in a quiet lake helped her recall a happy childhood spent in rural Massachusetts. The film, she said, usually made her feel better.

Such clients are placing themselves in predictable situations in which a familiar story will lift their moods. When we assign a film for the purpose of evoking inspirational moods, we may not even follow up the assignment with a lengthy discussion. Poetic films such as *A River Runs Through It* and *Jonathan Livingston Seagull* reconnect the viewer with a feeling of peacefulness from which analytical discussion may even detract. Although such films can provide discussions of specific interactions, they are more often suggested for the healing moods they facilitate.

This aspect is difficult to quantify; what is inspiring and healing for one viewer may be maudlin for another. The best rule of thumb we can offer for mood evocation is that therapists should recommend films that have facilitated such moods in themselves. For us, films such as *Field of Dreams, It's a Wonderful Life, Strangers in Good Company, Shadowlands, Rudy, The Shawshank Redemption, Fly Away Home,* and *Apollo 13* create an effect that goes beyond rational discussion and provide us with a feeling that everything will be okay in the end. These films imply that we are all more resilient than we believe ourselves to be and that hope and faith still have a place. Interestingly, we have found that when we feel inspired by a particular film, our clients often feel that way too. Mood evocation begins with a therapist's description of a film to a client.

Chapter **4**

Putting Video Work into Action

The majority of our VideoWork assignments are unstructured. We identify the film we would like clients to watch, offer viewing suggestions, and assure them that we will discuss the experience fully in a debriefing session. But we place little emphasis on what we think they should take from a film; thus most assignments are specific on procedure but open to potential meanings. These instructions tend to envelop the assignment with an aura of mystery and encourage clients to search for similarities to their own situations.

However, therapists sometimes fail to give *enough* information about how clients are expected to do assignments, so the assignment contains not so much mystery as confusion. Clients assume that the homework is not important, and they respond either by not carrying out the assignment or by watching the film with the wrong expectations. Although some clients follow any suggestion a therapist makes, the majority will not. Casually mentioning a film at the end of a session will probably not motivate clients to rent and watch that movie.

Tips for a Winning VideoWork Assignment

- Normalize the exercise. Reassure clients that film homework has been used with other clients and that results have been positive.
- Provide a rationale for why a particular film is being assigned. What clinical issues will the film address? Why assign the film now?
- Describe the characters that a client should note. What are some of the similarities between the client and a character?
- Discuss completely any scenes that might be problematic for a client (language, sexual situations, affairs, violence). Choose an alternate film if client's concerns are not resolved.
- Assure the client that the exercise will be thoroughly processed in a debriefing session.

A therapist should make an assignment expecting it to work. Let the client know why a film is being recommended and a few of the lessons to take from it. The film need not be so completely discussed prior to viewing that the surprises are spoiled or that the client's interpretations are preempted. The therapist should, however, tell about the story, identify characters to consider, and describe how the film exercise will be used in therapy. This information may sound like a lot of ground to cover in a session, but it can be done in five minutes or less.

MAKING THE FIRST ASSIGNMENT

In the first VideoWork exercise, therapists should give thorough instruction. It is important to establish the therapeutic context with a brief rationale for using films in therapy, a description of why a particular film has been selected, and assurance that the exercise will be processed in therapy. A typical film assignment begins something like this:

THERAPIST: Susan, I often ask therapy clients to rent movies and watch them. It is helpful to watch how characters handle the problems they are facing, even when the details are somewhat different. Most people enjoy finding connections with films. And they usually get new ideas that can be applied to their own problems.

I'd like to tell you about a movie that reminds me of your family; it's called *The Turning Point*. I don't mean to say that your family is exactly like the family in the film, but there are similarities, particularly in the relationship between the mother and the daughter. You may find it familiar to the way things were when you were a teenager, or you may see something else. In any case, I would appreciate your watching the film so that we can talk about how it might relate to you.

Would you be willing to rent the movie sometime during the next week? I'll be eager to talk about it in our next session and hear your ideas.

This method of introducing the film emphasizes that the suggestion should be taken seriously, that other clients have done similar work, and that a follow-up will definitely take place. We have not told the client how to interpret the film, but we have provided a reason for the assignment.

At this point, the client might have concerns about the assignment, but our experience is that they usually are willing to try it. Clients may say that they have already seen the film we mention, but we assure them that this time they should watch it in a very different way.

THERAPIST: Before you watch the film, I'd like you to spend just a few moments thinking about your own situation—the problems we've talked about and the goals you've set for yourself. Recall why you entered therapy, what was most important to you then. You might think about your problem as a puzzle to be solved. Imagine that this movie will relate to you in some special way. The film might offer new ideas or might seem very comforting. Of course, I don't know how or even if it will connect to your circumstances, but just be open to ways that the film might speak to you. If for any reason you want to stop the movie and think about things or replay parts, that's okay too.

Viewing Suggestions for Clients

- Keep notes if you wish.
- Stop the film when you have an insight. Think about how the film applies to your situation.
- Replay important scenes.
- If you are watching with a partner, pause to discuss important aspects or agree to discuss them at the end.
- Note characters you particularly like as well as ones you dislike. Make a note about why.
- At the close of the film, write down the main points you want to discuss in therapy.

FILMS AS PUZZLES FOR CLIENTS TO SOLVE

Clients are faced with a creative problem when given a film assignment by a therapist. They realize that the therapist believes the film is related to their problem. Although the therapist has made a suggestion about how they *might* connect to the film, the exact nature of that connection is up to them. So the assignment is a puzzle they will attempt to solve.

Our working assumption is that clients will extract from the viewing that which is most important to them. Films are multifaceted and draw from clients those aspects that are most salient at a particular time. We are indeed curious about which connections, of all the possible connections clients might make with a film, will stand out to them. As therapists, we have our ideas about what conclusions clients will come to. But clients almost always surprise us with their unique solutions to the puzzle.

WHEN CONNECTIONS FAIL

Almost all clients resonate with a character or theme from the assigned film, which leads to fruitful discussion. But in some cases, clients return with an interpretation that is at sharp variance with a therapist's basic assumptions about how film and client would relate. "I know you wanted me to watch that film because you think I have the same hang-ups as that guy," a client might announce. "But I don't think I do, and now I'm wondering if that's the way you see me." Film assignments sometimes reveal true differences in perception between client and therapist that had been limiting progress. Discussing those differences may get the discussion back on track.

Differences in interpretation between therapist and client can also lead to productive insights. One client watched the film *Matilda* and returned to say that she thought it was a complete mismatch. The parents in the film, she explained, were completely devoted to each other. They might be bad people, but at least they were together—it was Matilda who was out of step. But the client said her family was different. "Those parents get along fine, mine hated each other. I don't see that Matilda's family is at all like my own family."

I (John) was taken by surprise by her interpretation and told her so. This client was the first one to whom I had assigned that film who described Matilda's family in such a positive light. Most clients see that Matilda's parents get along because they are cheaters, liars, and child abusers. I did not criticize the client's interpretation but did express interest in her viewpoint. But a week later she came back and immediately started crying. She had rented the film again, fearing that she had missed something the first time.

The second time she saw a different movie. Now the client realized that Matilda was abandoned by her parents, and she saw many more similarities to herself. As with Matilda, no one had protected *her*, no one had appreciated *her*, and *her* childhood had been very sad. She had not recognized how isolated she had been, how her parents had made her believe she was "stupid and wrong." And she admitted that, ironically, she had always defended them. But the film caused her to doubt her misplaced loyalty. While watching Matilda rebel successfully against her parents, this client questioned the wisdom of never having done so herself.

The power of VideoWork is in the interplay between therapist and client. A film has many potential interpretations and many more connections to a client's situation. Clients who say they did not connect with a film usually mean that they did not get from the film what they believed the therapist wanted. We view this mismatch as a starting point. When clients do not make the connections we make, we ask: What do they see? And how might their interpretation change the course of therapy?

Remedies for Bad Connections

---

1. Ask why. What were they looking for and what did they see?
2. Find out if some element in the film violated important values.
3. Ask how the story was different from their own experience. Explore the dissimilarities thoroughly.
4. Consider denial as a possibility. If a client is strongly aversive to a character the therapist had suggested as a possible match, does the client's dislike arise from a mistaken identity or from too close an identity?
5. Look for basic differences in perception. If the film appeared useful to the therapist but the client didn't agree, review the client's main concerns as well as therapy objectives. Perhaps this disagreement points to more fundamental ones.
6. Have the client suggest another film. "Because the film I assigned doesn't describe your situation, let's talk about one you've seen that might."

FINAL STEPS IN MAKING THE ASSIGNMENT

The next step in assigning a film is to tell the client where to find the film and make plans for the follow-up.

THERAPIST: I don't know where you usually rent films, Susan, but I've seen this one at Video World. I believe it was in the drama section. If you have any trouble locating it, give me a call and I'll see if I can help you find it. Why don't we plan to begin our next meeting by talking about your impressions of the film.

Generally, we do not hand out written questions for the client to answer in conjunction with a film, but some clients choose to record their impressions during or after viewing. These notes reinforce the thoughts clients have while watching a film and lessen the chances of forgetting those impressions. Other clients find that writing down notes detracts from the experience. We offer both options as a choice a client can make.

When we suspect a film might be difficult emotionally for a particular client, we add a caution:

THERAPIST: *The Great Santini* is about a military family. The father was a Marine with a particular way of doing things, and he was very hard on his children. There are several places in this film that seem to arouse strong feelings for people who grew up in homes like that. I don't think those feelings will be a problem for you, but if for any reason you become uncomfortable, just turn off the movie and we'll talk about it. It's not important that you watch the entire film; watch only as much as is comfortable. If you still feel uneasy after you stop the film, give me a call right then.

As mentioned in chapter 3, if we suspect that the film contains significant conflicts with the value system of a client, we also discuss that problem. The film's rating is of limited usefulness because the goodness-of-fit between ratings and community standards varies. We prefer to talk specifically about the film's language and its treatment of sex and violence.

SUBSEQUENT FILM ASSIGNMENTS

Like other homework, VideoWork builds on previous assignments, addressing concerns as they arise in ongoing therapy. Clients who have a good experience with an initial film will be eager to receive new film assignments that correspond specifically to emerging issues. Therapists should assign follow-up films that target, through a character or a theme, an issue that has become central in therapy. Therapists may find that eventually they are not assigning films as much as discussing films that clients have watched on their own initiative. Clients arrive for therapy eager to talk about a film they watched that "hits the nail on the head."

A young female client who had survived cervical cancer had been having trouble articulating why she was unhappy after her doctors said she was cancer-free. "There's something missing," she said. "But I don't know what it is." She had watched several films as homework. Then, on her own, she rented *My Life,* a movie about a young man diagnosed with inoperative gastrointestinal cancer. She came to therapy the next week with new insights into her problem. "I realized I had been just like him. Before the cancer, I was a workaholic—I threw myself into every project. But now I don't care as much as I used to. I can't gear up for the things that meant something before; I don't think I'll ever be able to again. The problem is, I don't know what I should be doing—maybe paying more attention to my family and friends. That's what the guy in the movie did when he found out he was dying. Anyway, I know what's missing now: it's my purpose. I've lost my purpose."

Once clients learn that films speak to therapy issues, they make more connections with any films they see, assigned or not. We find that clients soon look for films that address their problems and are delighted to present us with their discoveries, which, because of the ownership involved, can have more impact than those films we suggest. Clients' experience with assigned films and formal discussions show them how to pick relevant films and watch those films in a new way. Training in VideoWork changes mere entertainment into a productive therapeutic exercise.

Now that we have explained the format we follow in making film assignments, we illustrate the process by presenting examples of Video-Work in two different circumstances. The first client had never before received a VideoWork film assignment. The second client had watched many films in therapy, but was finally moved to decisive action by a children's movie he merely happened to see. The first example shows what often happens in VideoWork, the second shows what sometimes can.

PHYSICAL ABUSE AND THE MOVIES

Thirty-seven-year-old Ted, referred by his family doctor for treatment of depression, had grown up in a New England family, the son of an immigrant father, now deceased, who drank heavily. On nights when the father was drunk, he lectured his five children for hours, ending the tirade by beating one of the children. The victim often was Ted, the oldest. When he talked about his father, Ted's voice was overcontrolled and analytical. "I can't explain it. I was always afraid of him, but it was more than that. Sometimes I didn't think there was any *me* when he was there, just him. I didn't know where he stopped and I began."

Ted had been in therapy for two months and was responding well to an antidepressant his physician had prescribed. He often brought up the subject of his father, but would quickly retreat into unproductive intellectualization. I (John) decided to recommend a film to help him articulate his vague feelings and encourage him to work toward closure with his father. I briefly described several abuse-related films: *The Prince of Tides, This Boy's Life,* and *Radio Flyer.* He chose to watch *Radio Flyer.*

I introduced the assignment by telling Ted that although the film was about childhood abuse, it was by no means the same as the abuse that he had suffered in his home. I also said that he might or might not identify with the characters. If he did feel compatible to a character, I told him, I would like to know which one he most identified with and in what ways. I expressed curiosity about how he framed the strategies of the film's two children in surviving an abusive stepfather and how those strategies compared to his own. I assured Ted that I did not anticipate any difficulties in his watching the film. If there were, he should turn the film off and call to discuss his feelings. Whether he kept notes was up to him. Ted said he understood the assignment, and he agreed to rent the film.

When we met again a week later, Ted reported that the film had touched him deeply. It was the first time, he said, that he had experienced feelings similar to those he felt as a child. The feelings, though strong, were manageable. He watched the movie the first time by himself and cried through much of it. The next evening, he asked his wife to watch it with him. "I told her, 'This is what I went through, this is really the way it was at my house.' " The two talked for a long time afterward, and Ted said he believed his wife understood at last what he had been wanting to tell her for many years.

For Ted, the film's escape fantasies (a souped-up Radio Flyer wagon) were comparable to his own fantasies. "I had weirder thoughts than that. When he was hurting me, I imagined that God would magically take me where he couldn't get to me anymore." Ted's interpretation of this personally meaningful film was more positive than what movie critics had written about it (one called the movie "child abuse meets Peter Pan.") As Ted described his reactions to the film, his overcontrol dissipated. He trembled when he related how Bobby, the younger child and victim, stared at the ceiling while waiting for his stepfather to enter his bedroom.

Ted said he knew how helpless Bobby felt, how isolated he was because there was no adult to turn to for help. The abuse was different, but the terror was the same.

In the sessions that followed, Ted was willing to reexperience his feelings rather than analyze them. Before he watched *Radio Flyer,* Ted had believed he was fated to be like his father and so had avoided situations that might lead to conflict. When his children acted out, Ted left the house rather than risk becoming enraged, but that action meant he was emotionally unavailable to his family. Now, Ted recognized that he was not identical to his father. As he separated from his father emotionally and gained control over his feelings, he started to trust himself to respond appropriately to circumstances as they arose—to discipline his sons appropriately when necessary. The film transformed Ted's therapy from an intellectual exercise to a healing integration of thought and feeling.

FROM THE MOUTHS OF BABES

Ben was a psychologist caught up in a batch of legal problems. He was separated from his wife and heading for divorce. He had allowed his successful practice to deteriorate. Ben spent most of his time blaming either himself or "the times." Although he promised he would never take his own life, Ben was committing a slow suicide of guilt and self-neglect.

Over the course of several weeks, Ben had watched films and discussed them in therapy, but none had led to appreciable improvement. Then, one Saturday afternoon, Ben took his two children to see *The Lion King.* Watching that film improved Ben's life suddenly and unexpectedly. Because his description is typical of the way clients talk about films when VideoWork has an impact, we have paraphrased Ben's remarks at some length:

BEN: I don't remember the first part of the movie. Something about a young lion named Simba who runs away from the pride after his father is killed. My kids were laughing and enjoying themselves. I drifted off to sleep, thankful that I was, for the moment, a reasonably good father. But suddenly I woke up and was glued to the screen.

Simba was hiding away with his pals, a warthog and a meerkat, when his old girlfriend from the pride showed up. She told him that after he'd run away (his father had been killed by an evil uncle who lied and blamed Simba), the whole kingdom had fallen apart. She said the pride's only hope was for him to go back home and rescue them. Naturally, that was the last thing Simba wanted to do. But that night he looked up at the stars and had a vision of his father, who scolded him for forgetting who he really was. Simba was a king, his father's successor, and his father told him he needed to go back home and start acting like a king. The father also told Simba that he shouldn't be afraid, that he would never be alone. His father would always be there for him.

For some reason, that scene really hit me where I live and the tears started to well up. I remembered *my* father and how I once believed nobody on earth was as wise. I thought about how much I'd missed him since he died, and how much I'd like him to tell me how to get out of this jam. I don't really know what Simba's father was saying to him because I was listening to my father talk to me: "You're selling out, Ben. Because of your fear, you've forgotten who you are. *Your* kingdom is in ruins. And you've got to do something before it's too late."

Then the dam holding back my feelings burst and tears rolled down my cheeks. That young lion was me, and I was taking the easy way out by running away from my troubles. I looked at my kids and wondered what they were learning from me. Was I teaching them to be cowards, to hide from their problems? I couldn't go on like that. It wasn't fair to them and it wasn't fair to me. I had to start fighting back.

Then the moment was over as quickly as it had started, but something had changed inside. I knew at that moment it was all going to be okay, though I couldn't begin to say how. My life was still in shambles, but my problems had nothing to do with lawsuits or my wife or "the times." Everything depended on what I would do. I could fight or I could run away. For the first time, I knew I had to go back home and clean up the mess I'd made, whatever the cost.

Of course, this film is open to many other interpretations. But for Ben, who had turned away from his responsibilities, *The Lion King* contained the clear message that he needed to reclaim his strengths and leave behind unproductive self-doubts. Therapy in the weeks to come focused on identifying the steps Ben could take in regaining control of his practice and in working out the marital difficulties that had developed. Ben's new focus was feasible because the film convinced him on an emotional level that his retreat into safety was not in synch with the person he knew himself to be. Before watching *The Lion King,* Ben had been unwilling to confront his problems, but afterward, they seemed manageable.

Ben's response to the film was unusual. Most clients do not grasp the personal significance of a film as readily as he did, nor do they as quickly translate that insight into action steps. The majority of clients require careful discussion with a therapist before converting their viewing experiences into blueprints for change.

INTEGRATING THE STORY INTO THERAPY

When we conduct follow-up discussions with clients, we begin with open-ended questions that reflect our curiosity about a client's impressions of the film. We ask questions such as:

- What did you find useful about the film?
- How did the film strike you?
- Of what value would this particular film be for someone in your situation?

Usually clients respond with a "thumbs-up, thumbs-down" assessment, which is a reasonable but not completely reliable indication of whether the film has relevance for them. Clients who find useful connections will value a film assignment more highly than those who do not. But even those who dislike a film sometimes add a note of promise: "It was hard to take because it hit too close to home."

Most film assignments should be followed by therapeutic conversation for maximum effect. For learning to occur, the therapist must take these raw materials and mine them for didactic value. Occasionally, however, clients watch films and make desired behavioral changes while discounting the movie. We don't insist on discussion in those cases, but encourage such clients to take full credit for positive change. The therapeutic rule that therapists give credit for positive changes to clients also applies in VideoWork. If clients watch films and their lives improve, film discussion is elective.

To illustrate how films can occasionally bring about change unmediated by discussion, we have included here conversations with therapist Foster W. Cline, M.D., as he describes his rationale for assigning a film and what emerged from his client's reaction to the film (personal communication, April 1996).

DR. CLINE: I assigned the movie *The Shawshank Redemption* to a borderline client who complained unproductively of "never-ending pain" and who reasoned that "life is completely unfair." I thought he might get some perspective from the film's protagonist, Andy Dufresne, who copes effectively with an unjust and truly frightening state prison. Not that the situations were the same, but I wanted my client to learn two basic lessons: that life is indeed unfair and that we all have to take it as it comes and do our best. He watched the film, but I was not prepared for how *much* he got out of it. I started off the discussion by asking him what he thought about the movie, and from then on, I didn't have a chance to say much.

Dr. Cline then paraphrased his client's experience.

CLIENT: I hated the movie. It was hard to make myself sit through it, and I kept cursing you for making me watch it. But after it was over, I thought about it some more and it was right on target.

I know why you wanted me to watch this movie. You're telling me I've built my own prison, aren't you? I got more and more uneasy about *my* prison while I watched. Like old Brooks [a character in the film], I hate this prison I made for

71

myself, but I've gotten used to it and now I depend on it. Somebody said that without the prison, Brooks would just be a used-up old guy with arthritis in both hands. Well I'm like that too about this mental illness of mine. Without this to rely on, I don't know what I'd do—kill myself, maybe, like he did. I wouldn't kill myself because of the illness, but because I might be losing the illness and wouldn't have any other excuses to be stuck. I never realized that before, but every time I start to get better, I find a way to get worse. Every time I'm almost free, I get sicker.

You're right, Doc, I *am* just like old Brooks in a prison I made all by myself. I need to get over the fear of being on the outside. I don't want to be Brooks. Damnit, I know I can do better.

Dr. Cline added: "I would like to take credit for being so perceptive, but this client saw things I never would have guessed that he might. And he never even mentioned Andy Dufresne, the character I thought he might identify with—only Brooks. I really never thought about that connection myself, but the client sure did."

This illustration points out that a character therapists believe will appeal to clients is not always the character with whom clients identify. We usually begin follow-up conversations focusing on the character with whom a client has identified, which we believe represents the self-concept. But although we take the client's response as a starting point, we find it productive to create a dialogue between other film characters and the client. The client in this illustration saw himself as Brooks—burned out, sick, and accommodating himself to his "never-ending pain." But his therapist saw him as Andy Dufresne, a clever and resilient man who could find a way to escape from his prison. The next step, because the client was displeased about identifying with Brooks, would be to discuss how he could relate instead to Dufresne.

We also pay attention to characters clients dislike, and we ask whether these characters have counterparts in the real world. We question a client about how an antagonistic character represents an obstacle

---

Follow-Up Questions

- Which character did you most identify with?
- In what ways was that character similar to or different from you?
- What attributes would you like to take from that character? What aspects of that character would you avoid?
- Are there other characters in the film who present positive options? In what ways?
- Who were the antagonists, and what obstacles did they present? How are they similar to people or situations in your own world?
- How did the protagonist succeed in overcoming the challenges?
- How can you use a similar strategy to overcome your own challenges?

---

and how that obstacle was overcome. Then we discuss how the client might incorporate such an approach in solving problems.

The protagonist in the film *Ruby in Paradise* experiences a number of unfulfilling relationships with men. I (Jan) assigned this film to a client who saw a number of similarities to her own relationships with men. Like Ruby, she found that the men in her life often wanted to rescue her and so tried to keep her weak, presumably so they could be strong. For this client, as for Ruby, these men were an easy way out, helping her avoid her difficult problems but at the cost of her self-esteem and independence. She said she appreciated how Ruby rejected that false sense of security, and she also wanted to learn to stand on her own.

Antagonists in a film can represent internal threats as well as external ones. In the film *Star Wars*, Darth Vader is a villain against whom the hero Luke Skywalker wages a life-and-death battle. But Skywalker discovers that Darth Vader is his own father and that they share weaknesses as well as strengths. For Skywalker to emerge victorious, it is not enough to kill off the antagonist. He must recognize and transcend the "Darth Vader" aspects of himself. Likewise, clients often find that the obstacles to self-improvement are not in the circumstances and people about whom they complain, but within themselves. To improve, clients must own these parts of themselves and conquer them.

CONNECTING TO REAL LIFE

Action plans follow viewing experiences, and the final phase of Video-Work is to encourage clients to apply ideas derived from assigned films toward solving personal problems. Therapists can use these steps to help clients appropriate the material:

1. Identify the central problem of the film and determine how it was resolved.
2. Articulate and modify a client's basic concerns about using that approach.
3. Develop action steps that incorporate lessons from the film, customized to a client's personal situation.

IDENTIFICATION AND RESOLUTION OF THE CENTRAL PROBLEM

The central problem is defined as what the client sees as the issue or issues that the protagonist of a film must overcome. That issue may or may not be the film's major theme. Various themes in a film can elicit various responses from a client, depending on perception and psychological needs. A client abused as a child might see the central problem of *Matilda* as how a parentally rejected child survives her difficult childhood. A young couple viewing *Parenthood* might see the central problem as how parents balance conflicting demands of work and home. The problem that clients see as central in a film is a function of what is most important to them in their present life circumstances. Identifying the central problem leads to a discussion about how characters in a film prevailed over obstacles and how clients can prevail over their own obstacles.

In most films, characters resolve the central problem by using skills and resources that are familiar to clients but are underutilized in clients' own lives. Once these attributes are recognized, clients see that they already possess them or that they can readily learn them. For example, *On Golden Pond* depicts a painful resolution between a woman and her father, brought about slowly and awkwardly as each makes halting steps toward the other. Clients might learn from this film that atonement in a family is a matter of persistently chipping away at resentments rather than executing a grand gesture and that they too are capable of such persistence. Clients can also learn that it is necessary to listen carefully to another person, to see things from another's perspective, and to be willing to forgive.

To help identify useful problem-solving skills from a film, we ask clients to name a few action adjectives that enable characters to solve their problems. Clients might say that the daughter in *On Golden Pond* was assertive, persistent, forgiving, caring, loyal, independent, and hopeful. Then we ask clients how these adjectives, if applied to their own situations, would be useful. How would persistence improve strained relationships with parents? Or assertiveness? Or forgiveness? Do they see how borrowing these attributes from a film character could help resolve their problems?

Some clients make useful discoveries from these questions. But more often, when we ask clients to apply a film character's behavior to their own, they will remind us that this movie is, after all, only fiction. By contrast, their lives are real. "Of course Henry and Jane Fonda eventually worked things out," clients say. "It was in the script. But my life is more complicated than that." Fortunately, we have an answer to that objection.

HOW CONCERNS LEAD TO APPLICATIONS

We assume that clients will and indeed should find incongruity with the actions of film characters. Many films produced today present unrealistic conclusions that, if taken literally, would result in disaster. The protagonist of *Falling Down,* a film about a frustrated and angry man, may well express the frustrations we all feel in a fragmented society. But as therapists, we would not recommend to clients that they fight back with automatic weapons, as the film character does. The question is, how do clients extract the good from the bad? How can the movie be used to help clients get more out of life? Our response, when clients say "It's just a movie; it won't work for me," is to ask clients to name their basic concerns with the way film characters solved a problem. How was the solution untenable? Was it contrived? Did the characters have more resources than the client? Were the situations entirely different? Was the solution illegal? Or is the client's objection a matter of, "that's just not me?" If we can find

75

Turning Concerns into Action Plans

1. List adjectives that describe how characters solved the central problem.
2. Apply those adjectives to a client's situation. How would those qualities help a client reach therapy goals?
3. Determine if the client has a significant concern with how a film character solved the central problem. If so, what is the concern?
4. Find ways to modify the solution so that it works for the client.

---

ways around the objections, we may be able to help clients find creative solutions to their problems.

For example, although *Falling Down* is not a film we assign in Video-Work because of its violence, we could if necessary discuss it with a client. Its protagonist does, after all, solve a problem—though not in a way that is acceptable.

The story begins in a Los Angeles traffic jam, when the man who will become known to the police only by his license tags, "D-FENS," decides he has taken enough insults. He had lost his job to downsizing and his wife and his child to a divorce, and he believes he is living in a jungle. He leaves his car and treks through Los Angeles, arming himself along the way with an automatic weapon. But this film is no vengeance movie in which the bad guys get what they deserve. The people this character kills are bad, but they are minding their own business before he comes along. He goes out of his way to find trouble.

Here is how we would conduct the conversation if a client says he wants to talk about this film.

THERAPIST: Okay, I understand how he got to the point he did, but as you say, this is a very sick man who did some terrible things. Still, I wonder if there isn't something positive about the movie. Can you think of anything?

CLIENT: I suppose there are some good things about the movie. For one, he finally fought back. He'd been taking it up to

76

here—which was doing him no good—and he finally just got enough. I've been there myself. I understand these guys who walk into the post office and blow everybody away. The guy in the movie was like that. I'd like to fight back too, but not to that extreme. I'm not that far gone.

THERAPIST: So there's really nothing unusual these days about a person getting beaten down by what goes on—his divorce and the problems at his job. You know what that's like. And you like the way he stopped "taking it up to here," but if he could have figured out a way to strike back that was more . . .

CLIENT: . . . reasonable . . .

THERAPIST: . . . reasonable. If he could have fought back in a reasonable way so that nobody got hurt and yet he was still doing something about what was bothering him the most . . . Do you have any ideas what *you* might have done if you'd actually been in his situation? If you take away the gun, but find ways to hold on to the anger, find different ways to express it.

Our conversation has rewritten the script in a way that is less dramatic but more useful for the client. How might the character have better dealt with his stress? What other resources were available to him? How do some people manage to live productive lives in an alienated society while others come to tragic ends? And more specifically, how can this client learn to "fight back" against the sources of his own unhappiness, but do so nonviolently?

An assigned film begins new conversations in therapy. By itself, it offers few magic answers, but it spurs the client's imagination to be creative, to consider new ideas and modes of behavior, and to find novel solutions for wearisome problems. Films are like fresh air from outside a client's window. They are messages of hope or consolation, other voices outside the loop of family and friends. Films require serious work and do not come with packaged meanings. But when clients discover the connections between themselves and a movie and then alter their insights to fit the real world, they find that a film can lead them to new and better strategies for living.

WHERE TO BEGIN?

One operational problem in using films is having a sufficient repertoire of film titles at hand. It is often difficult to think of an appropriate movie when clients bring up issues that films might address. And in an era of more paperwork for therapists, there is less time to search for therapeutic gems among film reviews.

We have created an anthology in this book to assist therapists in finding useful films. We suggest that the clinician read through the anthology and pick out films that seem useful for clients. Therapists should rent the films and watch them before assigning them in order to discover those films that are most valuable, that lead to the best discussions. A therapist using VideoWork will find that some films result in more success than others. The objective is to construct a list that matches the needs of a practice.

VideoWork is, of course, only one of many homework-based approaches available to the clinician who works from an outcomes perspective with a brief therapy orientation. VideoWork should not be used exclusively; in fact, it does not work with every client. But we hope that this introduction has described the possibilities for growth through VideoWork, and we anticipate that therapists will find this way of working with clients a helpful tool in their practices.

PART **II**

An Anthology
of Therapeutic Films

Introduction

The following reviews, or anthologies, highlight therapeutically appropriate films for therapists to use in VideoWork. Some of the films, such as *This Boy's Life,* are applicable to the special interests of particular clients, whereas others, such as *Field of Dreams,* are for more general use. These films are examples of the more extensive inventory that follows in the indices.

We categorize films by therapeutic issue, but most films fit well in more than one category. *City Slickers,* for instance, involves family-of-origin issues, men's concerns, grief, and loss. Placing it under the category termed Friends/Support Systems means only that we see particular value in its application to that area. We indicate in the review this overlap of categories for each film.

The anthologies contain overviews of the films as well as memory tags to help pick a film quickly during therapy sessions. Each write-up lists major characters, precautions (such as profanity, violence, or sexual situations), a sample of clients who might benefit from watching the film, and several of the film's main lessons. We also include a brief synopsis and a commentary in which we suggest ways the film relates to therapy.

A word of caution. Although we have used these films successfully with our clients, the therapist should watch them carefully before using them. A film such as *Like Water for Chocolate* is liberally laced with erotic images and is not appropriate for every client. The only way therapists can become comfortable in making assignments is to watch films and decide which are appropriate for their own clients.

ABUSE (EMOTIONAL, PHYSICAL, SEXUAL)

Dolores Claiborne
Rated R • 131 min. • 1995

Quick Take

"Sometimes being a bitch is all a woman's got to hold on to." Dolores's husband physically abuses her and sexually molests her daughter. She stops him the only way she knows how.

Key Characters

Dolores Claiborne. She's worked hard for 15 years and has done her best to forgive a daughter who abandoned her. When Dolores is accused of the murder of her employer, she reveals the family's dark secrets of physical and sexual abuse.

Selena Claiborne. Angry since childhood, like many victims of sexual abuse, she blames the mother who tried to protect her and idealizes the father who molested her.

Precautions

- Profanity.
- Sexual situation that involves molesting a child.
- Violence.
- Drug and alcohol abuse.

Main Lessons

1. When parents remain in abusive relationships, the children suffer.
2. The effects of sexual abuse are carried into adulthood.
3. Subtlety rarely works with a violent abuser.
4. The more approachable parent is the target for a child's anger.
5. Women don't cause their husbands to abuse them.

Categories

Abuse (emotional, physical, sexual), adolescence, affairs, communication and conflict resolution, emotional and affective disorders, family-of-origin issues, friends and support systems, grief and loss, marriage, parent-child relationships, substance abuse, understanding severe emotional illness, women's issues.

Suggested Viewers

- Women in abusive relationships.
- Adults who were sexually abused.
- Mothers and adult daughters with conflicted relationships.

Setting the Scene

As the film begins, Dolores Claiborne, a crusty woman living on an isolated island off the coast of Maine, seems to be murdering her employer. At least from hearing the screams, we assume that the body that tumbles down the stairs was pushed. Most everybody else does, too, none with more fervor than local detective John Mackey. A quarter century before, he had investigated Dolores for the murder of her husband, and though the jury acquitted her, Mackey knows she did it. Now he wants justice to prevail.

Dolores's daughter, Selena, whom she has not seen in 15 years, learns of her mother's troubles and comes to help. She takes prescription pills by the handful, drinks and curses like a sailor, and uses her job as a newspaper reporter as a lifeline to sanity. She's also forgotten a lot of the details of what went on while she was growing up.

Dolores hasn't forgotten though, and she's not reluctant to share the memories with her daughter. She reminds Selena that her father, Joe St. George, was a mean drunk who once beat Dolores with a stick of firewood just to prove a point. He stole money saved for Selena's education. He called Dolores fat and ugly while reserving words of tenderness for his daughter. He beat Dolores often and eventually molested his daughter.

At first Selena doesn't believe what her mother says. In her mind, her mother is to blame for everything that's gone wrong since her childhood. She blames Dolores for her relationships with men that went nowhere, for her continuing depression, even for her substance abuse. By contrast,

Selena idealizes her father. She remembers that he treated her with kindness while her mother nagged him. What did he have to be happy about? Like her, he had good reasons to drink and be enraged.

But as the story unfolds, Selena finds it more difficult to hide from the truth. Eventually she remembers that her father sexually molested her and that her mother did what she had to do to save her. With that memory, her worst enemy becomes her best friend, and she places her anger where it belonged from the start, with her father. She and her mother are reconciled when Selena recognizes the strength, resolve, and love that her mother showed in keeping her as safe as possible from her father.

Scripting for Therapy

The dynamics of spouse abuse and sexual abuse of a child are illustrated realistically in this film. Joe St. George is a severe alcoholic who combines the worst traits of an abuser. He insults his wife in every interaction and calls her names that tear down her self-esteem. When she tries to lift the depressing mood with humor, he beats her and then asks innocently, "Why do you make me do these things?"

The story is disturbing because Dolores does her best to stop the abuse. On the one hand, when Joe hits her, she hits back. On the other, she placates him, tries self-improvement, and builds up his low self-esteem. Nothing works. She tries to keep her daughter safe, but he continues to sexually molest her. By the time Dolores decides to murder him, her actions seem justified. There is nowhere to go that he can't find them, no one will come to their defense, and he is not going to change. She takes the only step that she knows will save them.

The effects of sexual abuse are dramatized in Selena. Through flashbacks, we see her change from a happy child to a sullen teen. She is "Daddy's girl," and although her father insults her mother, he lavishes praise on Selena. He takes special delight in discrediting Dolores's parental authority. When Selena complains about her mother making her do homework, Joe tells her not to bother. As a result, her grades fall from As to Fs. Dolores confronts her daughter to find out what is wrong. She suspects drugs but learns that Joe has been molesting her. Selena becomes enraged when her mother confronts her. She loves her father yet knows what he is doing is wrong. As an adult, her drug use and self-destructive behavior are attempts to blot out memories from the past. She lets men use her, for a price. When relationships turn difficult, she runs away.

Another issue of interest concerns the relationship between Dolores and her obsessive-compulsive employer, Vera. Dolores works for Vera 25 years, and every day is hell. But the relationship goes deeper than that. In a unique way, Vera becomes Dolores's mentor, a free and assertive woman who is in charge of her own life. Vera is the only strong woman Dolores has ever known, and the only person she trusts. She appeals to Vera when she learns that Joe is sexually molesting Selena, and Vera encourages her to stop him however she must. Dolores and Vera love and respect each other, and in all likelihood, this relationship is the only healthy one either has had.

Like *Matilda,* this film is a parable in which a victim fights back against an oppressor by using extreme measures. The victims are women, the oppressors men. The women survive by sticking together, not turning on each other, and by acting forcibly. Although therapists obviously would not condone the methods used, they can reinforce the idea that decisive action is the only alternative when dealing with abuse of this magnitude. The abused spouse must get away from the abuser. A therapist might deal with the murder in the film by stressing the resources for assistance that make such a choice untenable. An abused woman can turn to a women's shelter, to the police, and to the courts. Therapists should stress that violence directed at the perpetrator is not an option.

Matilda

Rated PG • 100 min. • 1996

Quick Take

A young girl grows up in an abusive family but makes her dreams come true through self-reliance.

Key Characters

Matilda.   She thrives despite dysfunctional and self-centered parents.
Harry and Zinnia Wormwood.   They are Matilda's narcissistic and cruel parents.
Miss Honey.   A teacher becomes Matilda's mentor and shows her love.

Main Lessons

---

1. It is possible to overcome a history of abuse and become a healthy adult.
2. You must be willing to risk the unknown when in an unhealthy situation.
3. Child abuse includes neglect and verbal mistreatment, not just physical abuse.
4. When children are not valued by their parents, it is *never* the children's fault.
5. Children are resilient; one nurturing adult can make a difference.

Precautions

- Young children may be frightened by caricatures of child abuse.
- Clients from abusive backgrounds should be assured that in assigning this film, the therapist is neither minimizing their suffering nor suggesting that Matilda is more resourceful than they.

Categories

Abuse (emotional, physical, sexual), adoption and custody, family-of-origin issues, friends and support systems, grief and loss, parent–child relationships, stepparenting and blended families.

Suggested Viewers

- Clients with a history of child abuse.
- Clients who need to learn survival skills.
- Clients dealing with family-of-origin conflicts, with or without abuse.

Setting the Scene

Harry and Zinnia Wormwood arrive at home with their newborn daughter, Matilda, then forget to bring her inside. Harry is a sleazy car dealer; Zinnia wants a big-screen television for their tacky suburban home. But Matilda is a pint-sized genius. According to the narrator: "By the time Matilda was two, she'd learned what other people did in their 30s—how to take care of herself. Whatever she needed in the world, she'd have to get for herself."

Eventually Matilda says she wants to go to school, but her parents balk. Then Harry sells a car to a vicious woman named Trunchbull who runs a school "where kids get what's coming to them." He decides it's just the place for Matilda and enrolls her the next day. Although the school is a horror, her teacher, Miss Honey, is a dream. She takes a special liking to Matilda and soon invites her home, where she tells the story of how she came to teach at such a terrible school.

Miss Honey had once lived happily in the house in which Trunchbull now resides. Miss Honey's mother died, and her father asked Trunchbull to move in to take care of her. Shortly after that, her father killed himself (some say it was murder), and Trunchbull became the tyrant in charge. When she was old enough, Miss Honey left home. But she had to leave everything behind, even her favorite doll. From the day she left, she never went back, though she always longed for her treasures.

Miss Honey's story gives Matilda an idea that will bring about a successful resolution to both their problems. By the film's end, Miss Honey has reclaimed her inheritance, and Matilda's parents have signed adoption papers. In a new home they have made with each other, Miss Honey and Matilda *do* get what they richly deserve: a loving family. And the evil adults are banished forever.

Scripting for Therapy

Roald Dahl, on whose book this film is based, wrote children's stories that were satires aimed at adults. In his tales, children live in poverty and are mistreated by adults who are stupid and cruel. Fortunately, the children are smarter and far more resourceful. Unlike real life, they always find a way to bounce back.

Since this film was released, it has been hands-down our favorite film for clients with abusive backgrounds. As silly as the film is, clients say "*Matilda* is exactly like my childhood." One woman said, "My parents and I were as different as could be. I always suspected they'd gotten the wrong kid from the hospital."

For an emotionally vulnerable client for whom a more serious film might prove threatening, this parody reintroduces old hurts in a gentle way. Here are some of the manipulative and abusive parenting practices alluded to in the film:

- Matilda's parents make their values absolute, use shame as punishment, and encourage Matilda to belittle herself. They say that because she is different from them she is inferior. Abusive parents also make their children out to be bad when they disagree. And without access to adults who can point out how self-serving their parents' values are, children from such homes develop low self-esteem.

- The parents overtly challenge Matilda's reality orientation. When she tells them she wants to go to school, they say she is four years old when she is actually six. Abusive parents tell children blatant lies. To cover up their misdeeds, they demand that children doubt their own perceptions.

- The parents introduce a hopeless situation to the child, based on the child's powerlessness: "I'm smart, you're dumb. I'm big, you're little. I'm right, you're wrong. And there's nothing you can do about it." Matilda responds by finding ways to meet her own needs without parental support. Many abused children, however, become depressed or aggressive.

- The parents use the child to satisfy their own selfish needs; Matilda is kept out of school to serve her parents' purposes. Once again, abused children develop low self-esteem when their needs are deemed unimportant by their parents.

- Matilda's abilities are discounted. Trunchbull scoffs at her extraordinary capabilities in math: "A calculator can do the same." Without an adult to properly evaluate and encourage a child's skills and abilities, these assets can be lost.

- One caring adult or mentor makes a difference. Miss Honey's unconditional love overcomes much of the harm of Matilda's parents. "You were born into a family that doesn't always appreciate you. But one day things are going to be different." Children from abusive homes are helped when an emotionally healthy adult gives honest feedback, encouragement, and provides a reasonable context from which children can understand their parents' mistreatment.

The Prince of Tides
Rated R • 132 min. • 1991

Quick Take

A southern man works out family-of-origin issues that affect his ability to be an available husband and father.

Key Characters

Tom Wingo. His "southern way" means keeping his feelings hidden. His marriage is almost destroyed, but he's so afraid of what's inside that he'd sooner live an impaired existence than fight the ghosts of the past.
Dr. Lowenstein. She encourages Tom to speak honestly but crosses professional boundaries.

Precautions

- Sexual situations.
- Inappropriate therapist–client relationship.
- Profanity.
- Rape scene.
- Aftermath of a suicide attempt.
- Extramarital affairs.

Categories

Abuse (emotional, physical, sexual), affairs, emotional and affective disorders, family-of-origin issues, grief and loss, marriage, parent-child relationships, substance abuse, understanding severe emotional illness, values and ethics, vocational and work-related issues.

Suggested Viewers

- Couples with marital conflicts.
- Clients whose family-of-origin issues intrude.

Main Lessons

---

1. Childhood abuse often requires therapy before adults can enjoy successful mature relationships.
2. Family secrets that cause damage should be shared with trusted others who can set them into proper perspective.
3. Abusive families frequently include not only the abuser but also a silent partner, about whom an abused child can have mixed feelings.
4. Emotional repression severely limits intimacy.
5. Having a sexual relationship with a client is unethical. In many states, it is also illegal.

- Men needing to get in touch with their emotions.
- Men who were sexually abused as children.
- Therapists, in discussing professional ethics.

Setting the Scene

Tom Wingo travels to New York City from his home in South Carolina at the request of a psychiatrist after his twin sister Savannah makes a third suicide attempt. The psychiatrist, Dr. Lowenstein, hopes that Tom can help her understand the family history and shed light on his sister's self-destructiveness. But the summons opens up Pandora's box. Tom's own marriage is failing, and because he is a "southern man," he's learned to laugh rather than cry about things that matter. The resulting emotional vacuum has driven his physician-wife into the arms of a colleague, who is ironically a heart surgeon. So when Tom arrives in New York, he is a candidate for psychotherapy himself.

Wingo and Lowenstein are soon excavating the Dickensonian history of the Wingo family: a churlish, abusive father; a ruthlessly ambitious mother; and three hapless children at the mercy of self-centered adults. Tom cowered in fear of his father while Savannah retreated into flights of madness. Although he doesn't want to talk about his problems in the past, Tom is in need of healing. Dr. Lowenstein, perhaps inappropriately as it turns out, takes on the task.

The relationship quickly exceeds the boundaries of a doctor-patient relationship. Susan Lowenstein, it turns out, is *not* so happily married to a concert violinist who browbeats her and their teenage son into playing supporting roles to his career. So as she helps Tom heal, he helps her regain self-respect. They fall in love, consider a more permanent arrangement, but part when Tom's wife asks him to come back home.

Scripting for Therapy

Some therapists value this film but others find it problematic. The film shows the difficulty that adults abused as children face in making a successful transition to adult life. But it also features an unethical relationship between a doctor and her patient. In fact, we have used clips from the film in ethics seminars as illustrations of professional mistakes that have legal implications.

Most clients, however, relate to other issues in the film. It demonstrates for clients with a history of emotional, sexual, or physical abuse how these traumas lead to emotional repression and failure in adult relationships. Clients can focus on the film's depiction of therapy sessions in which Tom Wingo talks about his childhood experiences. They can note how one result of those experiences is that he denies his spouse access to his real feelings and thus limits their intimacy.

In addition to the abuse that the children suffered at the hands of their father, the children and their mother were attacked by escaped convicts who raped them. Tom's brother killed the men, but his mother insisted that they bury the bodies quickly and never tell anyone. This undisclosed event haunts the family and contributes to Tom's sexual difficulties as an adult. Clients can see from this episode the damage caused when parents demand that their children guard destructive secrets. The storyline is an effective metaphor for encouraging clients to share family secrets of their own that may be haunting them.

Tom's relationship with his mother is also a useful topic for discussion with clients from similar backgrounds. Her failure to protect him from his father led to his distrust of others, particularly women. With his mother, he is angry, cynical, and mocking. He blames her for leaving him at the mercy of his father but does not address his resentment openly. So the relationship is one of ineffective bickering and complaining. The conflicted relationship generalizes to his dealings with other women, most especially his wife.

Other issues include the relationship Tom has with his children and his need for control over his family as well as over others. As a father, he laughs and teases his children, but cannot touch on serious subjects that might quickly go beyond his comfort zone. His children love him, but because he is one-dimensional, he gives them less than they need. Because he cannot ensure his emotional safety in all situations, he isolates himself from anyone wanting more than a superficial relationship.

This Boy's Life
Rated R • 114 min. • 1993

Quick Take

True account of a boy's struggle with an abusive stepfather and a passive mother who finally takes him to safety.

Key Characters

Toby.   He tries to cope without his mother's emotional support. He must find ways to survive his stepfather's verbal and physical abuse.

Caroline.   She wants a husband and a father for her son so badly that she ignores the truth of what she sees.

Dwight.   He convinces Caroline he's the answer to her prayers. But he's a nightmare for her son.

Precautions

- Depicts physical, emotional, and verbal abuse realistically.
- Teen use of alcohol.
- Profanity.
- Sexuality.

Categories

Abuse (emotional, physical, sexual), adolescence, communication and conflict resolution, emotional and affective disorders, family-of-

---

Main Lessons

1. Parents must protect their children at whatever cost to their happiness.
2. Concerned adults should help children or teens in at-risk families find sources of support.
3. Warning signs during courtship should be heeded.
4. A child from an abusive family need not continue the abuse into the next generation.
5. For some children, education is a way out of a dysfunctional family.

---

origin issues, friends and support systems, grief and loss, marriage, parent–child relationship, stepparenting and blended families, substance abuse.

Suggested Viewers

- Parents who need to better protect their children or be more available to them emotionally.
- Families with abusive patterns.
- Children or adults with abuse in the family history.
- Clients in abusive relationships.

Setting the Scene

Dwight, a guy with a shady past, plays a white knight who wants to rescue a divorcee named Caroline, a woman who takes naps when life gets to be too much. For her, he is too good to be true. He lights her cigarettes with a flourish ("something I learned in the Navy"), offers her a home, and wants to be a "strong male influence" for her son Toby.

Even at the early stage of their relationship, Dwight's facade is peppered with inconsistencies. He sneers at the wrong times, stops just short of hysteria when he is angry, and has a fragile ego. On the day he takes Toby home "to get used to each other," he pulls out a bottle of booze and snarls menacingly: "Now I've *got* you. You won't forget me, boy." Dwight is self-absorbed and convinced of his own worthlessness, so he makes certain that nobody ever outshines him.

Toby begins pleading with his mother to leave. "Why do you stay with him? Let's get out!" But Caroline has made up her mind to stay the course. She wants Toby to have a father, and she believes the way to bring that about is to refuse to intervene. "I'm not going to stand between you and Dwight. I'm going to make this marriage work." Toby soon understands he must endure as well as he can. So he tries to comply with Dwight's inconsistent and sadistic rules. From then until his mother finally takes action, Toby is submitted to a steady diet of emotional and physical abuse.

Scripting for Therapy

This Boy's Life shows a destructive assault against self-image from the viewpoint of an adolescent, conveying the youth's helplessness and hopelessness. Until his death a few years ago, the author Tobias Wolff's stepfather lived in Concrete, Washington, where the story took place. Events allegedly happened as they are depicted on the screen. Toby survived his stepfather's abuse by fighting back with an intelligence that would ultimately be his salvation, and he came to terms with his history by writing about it. For clients in abusive relationships, the story provides an example of survival through individual effort and gives hope and a strategy for those who feel trapped.

Watching this film leads clients with abusive backgrounds to talk about how their childhoods were similar and different. Therapists can ask questions to help them pinpoint the comparisons. How do clients understand Toby's relationship with his mother? How do they feel about her delay in leaving the abusive stepfather? Do they accept her explanation for why she stayed? And how can Toby forgive her for standing by passively as he was being mistreated? Clients must deal with such questions when they seek therapy years after abuse has ended. Therapists also know that the overt anger toward an abusive parent or stepparent is often only the tip of an iceberg. Clients also feel intense anger against the passive and less obviously destructive parent, and resolution of *that* anger is frequently the more difficult therapeutic task.

If a client has an abusive partner, discussion may focus on the options that Caroline has—choices that she refuses to make until she is forced. Before she meets Dwight, she believes that she cannot manage her problems by herself. The same problems are there when she finally runs away, but now she is motivated to look to herself for answers. Clients who are in abusive environments can identify options available to them. Are they certain that they cannot take care of themselves? Clients can be encouraged by this woman's courage. If she did it, so can they.

The film also shows how children from abusive homes drift into delinquency. Toby is noncompliant at the beginning of this film. After his encounter with Dwight, he is far worse. Experiencing the uncontrolled rage of an adult is, for any child, frightening enough. But believing that the rage might be justified by one's own bad behavior does far more damage. When a stepfather is the abuser and a mother seemingly complies with the punishment he inflicts, the self-attribution "I am getting this because I deserve it" is hard to avoid. Because we tend to act consistently with self-attributions, the irony is that an abusing stepparent's words may eventually prove true. Through little fault of their own, such children frequently become bad.

***ADOLESCENCE AND TRANSITION
TO ADULTHOOD***

Breaking Away
Rated PG • 100 min. • 1979

Quick Take

Four high school buddies spend a summer deciding what to do with the rest of their lives.

Key Characters

Dave.   He dreams of joining the Cinzano Racing Team and leaving behind his blue-collar roots.

Dave's parents.   Since the quarry shut down, his father, a master stonecutter, sells used cars and is soured on life. His mother referees arguments between father and son.

Dave's friends.   Fated to stay in Bloomington, they see the future reflected in their parents' weary faces.

Precautions

- Profanity.
- Brief nudity.

Categories

Transition to adulthood, adolescence, communication and conflict resolution, family-of-origin issues, friends and support systems, intimate relationships.

Suggested Viewers

- Adolescents preparing to leave home; parents of those adolescents.
- Families with communication problems.
- Older adolescents with identity problems.

Main Lessons

1. The stress of an adolescent's leaving home increases family arguments and misunderstandings.
2. Transition to adulthood means separating from friends as well as family.
3. "Who I am" is more than "*not* my parents."
4. Fantasies should be connected to reality.
5. Families can argue and still be loving if they speak honestly and with compassion.

Setting the Scene

It's summertime in Bloomington, Indiana, and the Cutters, as these high school buddies call themselves, are enjoying a last fling before settling down to jobs and marriages. None has a serious summer job. Most of their time is spent swimming, bragging, and wishing. Mike, the handsomest and most athletic, has seen his glory come and go—a football hero not up to college standards. Cyril will take entrance exams at a nearby college, but he figures he will fail; his dad told him he would. Moocher is in love with a girl who is as short as he is, which is his major concern. And Dave is oddly obsessed with all things Italian but mostly international bike racing. He and his father argue all the time. His dad wants him to learn about the real world by working at his used car lot. Dave wants glory.

The title reveals the theme: The Cutters are all leaving home. But a feeling of doom hangs over these boys. They are blue-collar kids in a college town. They have grown up watching affluent students drive convertibles through the streets, and they know they can't compete. The Cutters are trying to accept that their best times are all behind them. And they are hanging on to each other for support.

The most interesting story happens at Dave's house, where his father is one step away from kicking his eccentric boy out the door. Dad is a World War II veteran who doesn't have good memories of the Italians, yet his son has even renamed the family dog Fellini. With his son only a summer away from leaving, the father realizes that he has lost all control. He lost his trade when the quarry closed, and now he is losing his son. Dad can't figure out what went wrong. But from Dave's point of view, the situation is simple. His dad just doesn't like the person Dave wants to be.

Scripting for Therapy

We use this film with families primarily for three purposes: (1) to explore the family dynamics of the protagonist, who is an adolescent trying to find himself in a family that stresses conformity, (2) to understand the difficulty the family has in letting go of their son and allowing him to enter adulthood, and (3) to gain an appreciation for the ambivalence the boy feels as he pulls away from childhood friends. *Breaking Away* is a coming of age and leaving home film, issues familiar to therapists who work with adolescents and their families.

This film appeals to adolescents and parents because it treats everybody with respect and humor. Dave's father is a scoundrel and a clown, but by the end of the film it's clear why. He loves his son even though he cannot understand him. Much of the father's anger and frustration is because Dave is growing up and the father is not ready for that.

We assigned the film to a mother and her 18-year-old son, who was in his senior year of high school. They complained about arguing over household rules "more than ever," and each accused the other of "not caring anymore." But graduation was approaching and neither of them was prepared for the son to move on. Naturally, he covered up his feelings with bravado, but he was an anxious child facing the unknown. The mother was more forthcoming in her sadness, but she masked her feelings through dire predictions: "He's not ready to be on his own. He won't last a month in an apartment. He'll never hold down a steady job."

We wanted to shift the focus away from a personality clash and onto the process of transition. We assigned *Breaking Away* so we could discuss the family situation in a context not as emotion laden as their relationship had become. The pair returned a week later eager to share their insights. The mother identified with Dave's father because she also interpreted her son's pulling away as rejection of her values. The boy identified with Dave because he was more confused and worried about the future than he let his mother see. After the two agreed that it was normal to be anxious about such an important transition, they started communicating more straightforwardly and working together instead of fighting over rules. They visited colleges, she taught him to cook, and they bought a new computer for him to take to school. They turned their grief into an investment in the future.

The tension among Dave and his friends in the face of change is another aspect of the film useful for therapy with older adolescents. Dave is more talented than his friends; he will go on to college, whereas they will take local jobs. But like most adolescents who grow up with a few close friends, he feels disloyal as his path begins to diverge. When Dave decorates his room with Italian memorabilia, it is his way of separating from Bloomington and his old friends. By choosing an interest so far from their own, he creates a barrier so his leaving will be easier. Dave's action illustrates one way that adolescents graduate from their peers. They find new interests and pursue new goals that are irrelevant to their old friends, who then drift away. Adolescents quickly find new friends who are more compatible with their new life. *Breaking Away* shows this natural aspect of growing up and shows that adolescents do not need to feel guilty about splitting off from the old crowd.

Hoop Dreams
Rated PG-13 • 165 min. • 1993

Quick Take

This documentary film is about two talented high school basketball players.

Key Characters

Arthur Agee and William Gates. These two young athletes exhibit courage and persistence in rising from impoverished backgrounds. Although they do not succeed completely, their story is inspiring and challenging.

Precautions

- Drug use.
- Profanity.

Main Lessons
1. Reaching a goal requires hard work.
2. Staying on the path of a goal means seeing the big picture.
3. Not falling off that path requires putting aside distractions.
4. Winners mobilize their support systems.
5. Children should play sports for enjoyment, not to satisfy adult expectations.

Categories

Adolescence, friends and support systems, parent–child relationships, substance abuse, transition to adulthood, values and ethics, vocational and work–related issues.

Suggested Viewers

- Discussion groups talking about school athletics.
- Parents who push their children too hard.
- Clients who have trouble sticking with their goals.

Setting the Scene

Arthur Agee and William Gates are eighth graders; Arthur is from the Cabrini Green Projects, and William lives on Chicago's South Side. They are already talented basketball players and they are ambitious. When a scout from the famed St. Joseph's High School (alma mater of the legendary Isaiah Thomas) offers them a partial scholarship, the boys and their parents quickly sign on the dotted line. But it's a very long way from home, geographically and otherwise.

Academically, Arthur is at a fourth-grade level, which doesn't concern him because he knows his job at school is to score baskets, not make As. Matters at home, however, are more precarious. Soon after he enters St. Joseph's, his father is jailed for theft and selling cocaine. His mother becomes head of the household; she is not only working at a job but also attending night school to get a nurse's aide certificate.

William's family, on the other hand, is relatively intact. According to William's freshman coach, he's got the confidence, personality, and skill to be a great player. Although initially his grades are no better than Arthur's, William works hard to bring them up. Everything is going his way. And at the end of the first year at St. Joseph's, he gets invited back.

Arthur continues to fall behind academically, and worse, he fails to meet his coach's expectations. At the end of the semester, school officials ask him to leave. Despite the setback, Arthur is undaunted. He still dreams of playing in the NBA. He enrolls in a public school and leads the team to the Chicago City Championship. Soon afterward, he is offered a scholarship to a small junior college.

Meanwhile William, arguably the more talented of the two, loses ground. A severe knee injury sidelines him in his second season. The surgery that follows keeps him out of the lineup during his junior year. When William returns in the fall, still not quite healed, the coach lets him decide whether to play. William knows that despite his coach's reassurance, the pressure is on him to perform. So he plays, but is reinjured almost immediately. This time he gives up and drops out of school.

Scripting for Therapy

Simple aphorisms pale in the light of actual events in this film. These kids work *hard*. They get up before dawn and come home late at night. They grapple on the court and even more in the classroom. But despite their effort, not much works out for them. They are young men with great talent who get lost on the way up. Is their failure to go the distance due to socioeconomic limitations, poor coaching, bad breaks—or is it their own fault? What might have turned things around for each of them?

How these boys accomplish as much as they do is a useful topic for therapists to discuss with clients. One factor is the considerable family support each enjoys. Arthur has an extended family that comes forward when his father leaves, and his mother is always on his side. William's mother and brother also encourage him at every step. Each boy lives in a family that assumes responsibility for each other. When family members go through bad times, others volunteer to help out. Therapists can cite this cohesiveness as an example when encouraging clients to enlist and employ support groups, whether family or friends.

Another useful theme of the film is perseverance in working toward a goal. Arthur's mother is a shining example of a person who sticks with an objective despite the odds. At one point she taunts the filmmakers, "Do you ever ask yourself how I get by on $268 a month?" It is a good question because as a single parent, she has many reasons to give up. But she stays on track, takes care of her children, and still finishes first in her nurse's aide class.

Discussion can also center on the ways that organized school athletics help and hurt young athletes. St. Joseph's recruited these young men at an early age and treated them as if they were pros. Their value to the school was limited to what they could accomplish on the basketball court. When they were no longer useful, they were let go. It seems apparent that their coaches and school administrators, who should have known better, failed them. When adolescents are pushed too fast by adults, they often perform for approval rather than for intrinsic pleasure.

We used this film once with a father who was concerned about his son's loss of interest in football. The father had been a professional player, and he believed that his son had even more talent. But the boy saw football as a mixed bag and was entangled in struggles with coaches and his dad. For him, the game was no longer fun. We asked the father to watch *Hoop Dreams* and to pay attention to the pressure that the coach and the school apply to each young man. After viewing the film, he talked with his son and admitted that he had been wrong to push so hard. The father told him that he could quit the team if he wished. The son was relieved that his dad was willing to compromise. He had believed that his father didn't care about his feelings or what he wanted. But the son decided not to quit. He *did* want to play at a level that was comfortable for him, and they agreed that was the way it would be. The next fall he had his best season.

The setting of *Hoop Dreams* may be unfamiliar to some clients but the dynamics are not. Many young people have talent and drive but fail to reach their goals. This film provides an opportunity to discuss why youthful dreams sometimes fail.

ADOPTION AND CUSTODY

The Good Mother
Rated R • 113 min. • 1988

Quick Take

A custody suit follows allegations of sexual molestation in the home of the custodial parent.

Key Characters

Anna Dunlap. She finds new life in a relationship with her lover, but must choose between him and her child.

Leo Cutter. He volunteers to "play the perpetrator" in court so that Anna can keep her daughter.

Precautions

- Nudity.
- Erotic scenes.
- Profanity.
- Sexual relations outside marriage.

Categories

Adoption and custody, abuse (emotional, physical, sexual), affairs, communication and conflict resolution, divorce, family-of-origin issues, friends and support systems, grief and loss, intimate relationships, marriage, parent-child relationships, prejudice, stepparenting and blended families, values and ethics, women's issues.

Suggested Viewers

- Clients dealing with divorce, custody, single parenting, allegations of sexual abuse.
- Clients dealing with family-of-origin issues involving sexuality.
- Divorcing couples who need to be reminded that a child's welfare is the highest priority.

Main Lessons

1. Once domestic disputes enter the legal system, commonsense solutions are unlikely.
2. Whenever possible, divorcing parents should resolve their disputes by communicating with each other.
3. The child's welfare is uppermost in a divorce.
4. A good divorce requires parents to communicate, coparent, and exercise a degree of trust.
5. Repressed sexuality is passed from one generation to another. Breaking free is difficult.

Setting the Scene

Anna Dunlap is born into a wealthy, conventional family. The one renegade in the family is her rebellious aunt, a young woman who becomes pregnant out of wedlock. The family quietly sends the aunt to Sweden to have and give up her baby for adoption, but Anna's friendship with her sets in motion a persistent sexual curiosity. Anna marries, however, a cold and insensitive attorney who mirrors her family. She tries to make the marriage work, but knows that a relationship should offer more than what she experiences with him. Eventually they divorce, and she gains custody of her five-year-old daughter, Molly, a child she adores. She turns down her father's offers of financial help, working instead as a lab assistant and a piano teacher.

In time she meets a free-spirited Irish sculptor named Leo Cutter and falls in love. He helps her become a more open, sexually responsive woman. He encourages her to express her artistic nature and inspires her to live life fully. But after Molly goes away for a weekend with her father, Anna's carefree lifestyle comes to an end. Appearing on her doorstep, her ex-husband informs her that he is keeping Molly at his home and that he is filing suit for custody. Molly had apparently described sexual incidents between Leo and Anna during which she had been present. He is charging her with being an unfit mother. Anna is stunned and contacts an attorney.

She and Leo tell the attorney that they can recall two such incidents. The first was one night when Molly had quietly entered the bedroom while they were making love. They stopped as soon as they saw her. Molly crawled into bed, hugged her mother, and went back to sleep. The couple had continued making love, knowing that Molly was asleep. The second incident was when Molly had walked into the bathroom just after Leo had stepped from the shower. She was curious about his penis and asked if she could touch it. He allowed her to, believing that her mother wanted Molly to be raised in an open and honest atmosphere.

A child psychologist interviews Anna and Molly and concludes that the child has suffered no harm. Furthermore, he believes that Molly is deeply attached to her mother but is ambivalent about her father. He recommends that no changes in custody be made. Nevertheless, Anna's lawyer has doubts about how the story will sound to the judge. The lawyer says that Anna must be willing to claim that Leo made a mistake in allowing Molly to touch him. Anna says she will not because it is not true, but the attorney is insistent. He warns her that lying may be the only way she can keep her daughter. Reluctantly she agrees to make Leo the scapegoat.

Scripting for Therapy

The Good Mother shows the charge of sexual molestation being used as a weapon by an ex-spouse in a continued battle after divorce. According to authorities, custody fights foster many false allegations of sexual abuse. Some therapists might argue that Leo and Anna indeed acted inappropriately. But whatever one's opinion, this honest film illustrates the emotional impact and misunderstandings that surround accusations of sexual misconduct.

The movie treats the problem of intimacy for single parents realistically. Divorced parents contend with many difficulties, but none is more troublesome than establishing a healthy sexual life for themselves while being sensitive to the feelings of their children. How do they deal with hostile and jealous feelings of ex-spouses? How do they make certain that what they consider to be innocent behavior is not misinterpreted and used against them? Divorced clients often say that such concerns keep them from resuming their sexual lives after a divorce.

As the film clearly shows, these concerns have merit. Sexual events are routinely taken out of context by a legal system that may show little mercy regarding unconventional sexuality. In discussing this film, clients—particularly married ones with toddlers—have noted that what Leo and Anna did when Molly entered their bedroom is not unusual. Nor is Molly's curiosity about Leo, nor even his response. But the difference is that Anna and Leo are not married. Single parents with angry ex-spouses should be mindful, therefore, that what they believe to be acceptable in their homes can appear quite different when described in court.

Another issue is Anna's attempt to end the sexual repression that had been a legacy in her family. In one scene, she talks with her grandmother and learns that for ten years of her marriage, her grandmother felt so unfulfilled that she longed for death. To combat such an inheritance, Anna reads children's sex education books to her daughter, teaches her to call genitals by the proper names, and tries to make her comfortable with nudity. But in light of the court's finding against her, clients might question how Anna's behavior toward her daughter will change. Will she continue to teach Molly to look on her body and on sex without guilt? These useful questions can be pursued with clients who have similar concerns.

Losing Isaiah

Rated R • 108 min. • 1995

Quick Take

A white social worker and her family adopt a black, crack-addicted baby. The birth mother undergoes rehabilitation and wants her child back.

Key Characters

Margaret. She falls in love with Isaiah and cannot bear to lose him.
Khaila. She made mistakes in the past and paid the price. Now she wants to make amends.

Precautions

- References to drugs.
- Profanity.
- Some clients may find that a scene in which a child is forcibly taken from the adopting family is too intense.

Main Lessons

---

1. Love is complex and sometimes means making hard decisions for the good of a child.
2. A child can never have too many loving people around.
3. Unusual custody arrangements work only when adults cooperate.
4. Emotional pain hurts as badly as physical pain.

Categories

Adoption and custody, communication and conflict resolution, friends and support systems, grief and loss, marriage, parent-child relationships, stepparenting and blended families, substance abuse, values and ethics.

Suggested Viewers

- Clients who are divorcing, in emphasizing the importance of loving compromises that will protect their children.
- Discussion groups, regarding adoption, custody and racial issues.

Setting the Scene

Margaret Lewin is a hospital-based social worker who routinely makes life-and-death decisions about society's castaways. But when Baby Isaiah turns up in the emergency room, she falls in love. She finds excuses to check on him, rocks him back to sleep when he cries, and begins to think of him maternally. After a few days, against the advice of her colleagues, she and her family take steps to legally adopt Isaiah.

The crack-addicted baby is a handful. The Lewins' teenage daughter, Hannah, feels neglected when her parents focus all their attention on him. She's embarrassed and angry when his tantrums spoil her performance in a school play. Margaret's husband Charles tries to be supportive, but he's not sure that he is up to the challenge. Nevertheless they gradually integrate Isaiah into the family and establish an effective bond with the toddler. At that point the birth mother, a black woman named Khaila, emerges from a drug rehabilitation program and files a lawsuit to reclaim her child.

The trial that follows turns up assets and liabilities on both sides of the dispute. At the time of his birth, Isaiah's mother had barely been able to manage her own life. In a drug stupor, she had left him in an alley and hadn't returned to search for him until the next day. But she has admitted her mistakes and has gotten her life back together. According to her lawyer, she is mentally and physically healthy and can give Isaiah what the Lewins never can: his racial heritage. And that, the attorney argues, is the point of the trial.

On the defendants' side, the Lewins' lawyer argues that Isaiah has bonded with a stable, healthy family that loves him and can provide material advantages his birth mother cannot. Some experts testify that he is a well-adjusted, happy little boy and that he belongs with his adoptive parents. Others side with Khaila's attorney in arguing that his racial heritage is more important. The judge finds in favor of the birth mother.

But the adjustment does not go smoothly. Isaiah is tearful and then becomes noncommunicative and explosive. His mother knows what he is feeling, having been shuffled herself from one foster home to another as a child. She does not want to cause him pain, so she asks her friends what she should do. They reassure her that it all will work out in time. But Isaiah gets worse instead of better. One night when Khaila finds him curled up asleep in a corner of the bathtub, she knows that something must change. She contacts Margaret and the two negotiate a custody arrangement they hope will work better for Isaiah.

Scripting for Therapy

Persons with expertise in family law may find this film simplistic, but court cases can turn out like this. When custody is involved, no one argument always eventuates in a consistent ruling. And although judges and juries reach decisions they view as being in the best interests of a child, heartbreak abounds on both sides. The chief value of this film is its strong point that regardless of what the courts decree, parents are responsible for doing the best for their children—even when that action is against their own interests.

This film represents many different view points about custody. Opposing arguments are provided by attorneys on both sides; clients can see not only the logic but the feelings of the litigants behind these positions. On the one hand, Isaiah has bonded with his adoptive family. But the

108

birth mother's attorney argues that his race is a more important factor. The film tries to be fair to both these positions.

Clients can see how easy it is to become polarized into a fixed point of view when emotions are involved. Throughout the trial, the parents are contentious and absorbed in winning the dispute. Neither side sees value in the opposing view, neither seems concerned with what the child needs. When the parents finally focus on what Isaiah needs rather than on their legal rights, they find a solution that works for everyone.

Clients who face custody questions need not adopt the solution that these characters do, but they should be encouraged to look for loving compromises that work best for the children. We believe this film is valuable for encouraging clients to act humanely with respect to their children.

 ***AGING***

Strangers in Good Company

(Also known as *The Company of Strangers*) Not Rated • 100 min. • 1991

Quick Take

A docu-drama featuring a group of older women—actresses playing themselves—who share memories, hopes, and fears.

Key Characters

The strangers who become friends as they face adversity.

Precautions

Produced in Canada, this film may be difficult for clients in some locations to obtain. It is periodically aired on PBS and distributed by the National Film Board of Canada, 1251 Avenue of the Americas, 16th Floor, New York, NY 10020–1173.

Categories

Aging, chronic illness and disabilities, death and dying, family-of-origin issues, friends and support systems, grief and loss, women's issues.

Suggested Viewers

- Clients who need to better understand their older parents.
- Women, regarding the value of a social network.

Main Lessons

1. In any group, individual differences should be appreciated.
2. We usually can do what we have to do.
3. Compassionate listening is an essential element in healing.
4. It is never too late to try something new.
5. Optimism and risk taking are basic survival skills.

- All clients, in seeing how self-disclosure and compassionate listening facilitate healing.

Setting the Scene

A tour bus detours to a lake in rural Quebec, but the bus breaks down miles from the nearest town. The bus driver twists her ankle, so the seven passengers—women in their 70s and 80s—must fend for themselves. They pool what food they have and walk to an old, abandoned house. Inside they find materials for makeshift beds as well as a cache of stewpots, skillets, and eating utensils. For the next three days, as one of them tries to repair the bus engine, the others fish, gather mushrooms, and devise signals for help. They also play cards, gaze at stars, listen to birds sing, and share the stories of their lives.

Alice Diablo, a Mohawk Indian, and Catherine Roche, a nun, have the skills most needed to survive in the out-of-doors. Alice transforms a pair of panty hose into a trap for fish; Catherine knows how to repair combustible engines. The rest do what they are physically able: carry water, gather herbs and berries, lead calisthenics. They get swollen ankles and take their pills on schedule. Some can't sleep when others snore or when the noise of animals frighten them. They spend their days talking of death, children who have moved away, talents that went undeveloped when necessities crowded them aside, and young love.

Each reveals her character under the stress of the situation. Constance throws her pills away; she would rather die content than return home to a lonely old age. By contrast, Cissy is delighted by the surprises each day brings, and so is Winifred, a belly dancer in her youth. Some confess secrets and are quickly pardoned. When Mary tells Cissy she is a lesbian, Cissy laughs and replies mischievously, "Oh, that's good." A big-hearted bus driver, Michelle, coaxes a timid and self-conscious Beth to remove the wig that covers her balding and gray head. "But you're beautiful!" she says.

Catherine, arthritic in her feet and ankles, must eventually walk the 20 miles to town for help. In the meantime we are privileged to share the reflections of very special women who challenge the stereotypes of old age. At the close of the film, we regret that we met them so late and for such a brief time.

111

Scripting for Therapy

This film is deeply respectful. These women tell what probably are true stories about their own lives and offer to therapists a wonderful film about old age to use with clients. There is no attempt to make these ladies look spry and cute. When they go for water, they trudge along slowly; when they complain their feet hurt, they display swollen bunions. Some are feisty and optimistic, but at least one is significantly depressed. They tell their stories simply: the death of a child, a young love that turned bad, the slow recovery after a stroke. They do not offer easy advice to each other, but merely note with compassion, "Yes, that's very sad."

They talk of death often throughout the film. They admit they are afraid, but frankly they seem more curious, wondering what lies ahead. Some believe in an afterlife, others do not. But what frightens them more is becoming destitute and dependent on others. They dread a decline of physical and mental abilities, which means to them the loss of control over their destinies.

The film has moments that crystalize differences in temperament. After attempts to repair the bus fail, several women agree that rescue is probably impossible. Constance says with resignation, "I'd rather die here than in a nursing home." But Alice responds more forcibly: "Well, *I'm* not going to die. *I'm* going to fish." And when Catherine volunteers to walk into town for help, Mary says she could not possibly do that herself. Catherine answers, "You could if you had to." These are insights into how some people stay young.

The women discuss intimate relationships candidly. Alice recalls her feelings as a young girl falling in love and mentions that she still feels excitement while watching young couples dance. She envies them and would like to be 16 once more. As she reminisces, the others tease her about still having sexual feelings. Coyly, she admits that she might be talked into a relationship with the right man. And from a quite different worldview, Catherine tells Michelle her strategy for living as a celibate nun: "You pray a lot."

With encouragement from each other, they begin to take small risks. They take off wigs, dance, and spear frogs. These actions lead to talk of bigger risks and future possibilities. Constance had been an artist in her youth, but when her children were born she stopped painting. She admires Mary's ability to do sketches of birds; Mary tells her she should try again. Beth is embarrassed that she never completed her education. She's always felt inferior but Michelle assures her that she could go back to school. The film's message is that it is never too late to try out new ideas or resume old interests and that nothing stands in the way of doing so but fear.

Several of the women are wonderful role models for clients. Catherine describes how she masters hard tasks by concentrating her attention on details and by pausing occasionally to do something pleasant. Winifred recommends keeping up physical skills, such as dance. Michelle, though younger than the others, displays a vibrancy and love of life that is contagious. Mary is forthright in describing her sexual preference. Alice is unwilling ever to give up. As a group, they show consideration for the needs of each person, a willingness to help, an acceptance of differences, and good humor and respect for the life experiences each woman brings.

The Trip to Bountiful

Rated PG • 102 min. • 1985

Quick Take

An aging woman seeks to return to her roots. Her son and daughter-in-law want her to let go of the past.

Key Characters

Mrs. Watts.   Cut off from the home she loves, she longs to see the place of her youth once more before she dies.

Ludie Watts.   For him, the past is filled with loss. He loves his mother, but visiting his childhood home is more pain than he can bear.

Jessie Mae Watts.   She resents her mother-in-law and demands that her husband make a choice.

Categories

Aging, communication and conflict resolution, family-of-origin issues, friends and support systems, grief and loss, parent-child relationships, values and ethics.

113

Main Lessons

1. Revisiting the past is a way of resolving fears about the future.
2. Older persons need social outlets and connections to people who care.
3. Generation gaps do not exist where compassion thrives.
4. A sense of control over one's life is essential.
5. Aging brings with it a deeper appreciation of people and places that younger people may take for granted.
6. For people, belief in something or someone greater than oneself gives life a richer meaning.

Suggested Viewers

- Clients dealing with loss.
- Adult children of aging parents.
- Couples with difficulties in communication.

Setting the Scene

Relationships are difficult for many of us because we insist on believing that everybody else should find value in what we do. But the things that are important to us are not nearly so important for others, and that discrepancy is magnified across the lines of generations. What seems trivial to the young can be of great consequence to older people. And vice versa.

Times are hard. The elder Mrs. Watts lives in a cramped apartment with her son, Ludie, and his wife, Jessie Mae. They live together because they have no choice. Their east Texas farm played out years before, and they moved to the city so that Ludie could find work. Jessie Mae despises living with her mother-in-law, but she depends on Mrs. Watts's social security check. Ludie is caught in the middle of their bickering. He begs them to try and get along, but they barely tolerate each other.

Mrs. Watts wants to keep the past alive. The present is almost unbearable except for memories of her home in Bountiful, which she evokes by singing hymns she learned as a child. But Jessie Mae, a woman who lives entirely in the present, nags her to "stop singing about the sweet bye and bye." Ludie doesn't think much of the past either, because it reminds him of everything he has lost. Bountiful is where his father died and where he promised an uncle he would name a son after him. Now Ludie knows he is never going to have that son and that the past had best be forgotten.

But Mrs. Watts is feisty and clever and bent on getting back home. So after weeks of planning, she fakes a "sinking spell" and sneaks off to the bus station. After a narrow escape from Ludie and Jessie Mae who come looking for her, she is on her way to Harrison, the nearest town to Bountiful on the bus route. Sitting next to her is a sensitive young woman named Thelma, who is going home to live with her parents while her husband is in the army. The two women talk about how difficult it is to be in love with a person who is out of reach. Although she is so much younger, Thelma understands why getting back to Bountiful is important to Mrs. Watts.

Nobody else sees much purpose in her going there. In Harrison, the station master almost gleefully tells her that her old friends are either dead or moved away. Her home is gone, he says, why not just go back to the city? Meanwhile, Ludie and Jessie Mae keep drawing closer. When the local sheriff tells Mrs. Watts that he's supposed to hold her in custody until they arrive, she pleads her case passionately:

> It's my will to die in Bountiful, don't you understand? Suffering, I don't mind. I didn't protest once, not even when my babies died. But these fifteen years of bickering, it's made me like Jessie Mae sees me—ugly. And I will not be that way. I want to go home.

The sheriff takes pity, and Mrs. Watts reaches Bountiful. When Jessie Mae finally sees what the fuss was about, she is unsympathetic: "Why it's nothing but a swamp." But for Mrs. Watts, the scene brings back memories of "sitting on the front porch after supper on cool summer evenings with red birds singing in the trees." She can almost see her parents step through the doorway of the worn-down clapboard house.

Scripting for Therapy

The characters in this film, with the exception of Mrs. Watts and Thelma, are isolated and no longer have a sense of community. They have lost hope in the future, and their past is filled with broken dreams. They are disappointed in themselves, angry over events that have befallen them, and vicious toward people who still believe in something larger than themselves. Mrs. Watts's cheerfulness contrasts with their emptiness, and they resent her optimistic outlook. The hymns she sings, filled with promises and reassurances, are repulsive to her daughter-in-law who no longer believes in anything. The hymns remind Jessie Mae of a simple faith that led to disillusionment. The only way Jessie Mae can deal with her own disappointment is to make her mother-in-law out to be a fool.

The film touches on the issue of conflict between generations. But it is more concerned with visions that enrich life as opposed to those that diminish and how those visions relate to aging. Do we gradually lose touch with reality as we age, or do we come into a deeper appreciation of life around us? Is Mrs. Watts too old to see what is obvious to others, or does she see what they cannot? It is a matter of perception. Her daughter-in-law views her as senile, but her traveling companion, Thelma, envisions her as wise.

The film can be helpful for clients who are trying to understand aging parents. Some clients complain that their parents ignore practical realities that seem apparent to everybody else. Parents may want to stay in their own homes alone when logic dictates that they should move to a safer and more convenient retirement home. But the most thoughtfully designed retirement facility is demoralizing when compared to a person's home with its special artifacts that give meaning to life. The film illustrates that the concerns an older person has can be more important than the ones younger people consider essential. To find out what those concerns are, children should allow older parents to speak freely. Children should also let parents make choices for themselves for as long as possible.

The film's theme of revisiting home is a familiar one to therapists. One of our clients took her aging mother and an aunt who was in the early stages of Alzheimer's on a trip back to the old homestead. As they traveled together, the aunt became vivacious and told many stories the others had never heard. In a place that had meant so much to her, she went back in time. The two other women glimpsed for a moment a person they had enjoyed so much in years past. The trip brought them all closer together, and our client said that she and her mother felt a sense of closure with the aunt that had been missing before their journey.

CHRONIC ILLNESS AND DISABILITIES

Lorenzo's Oil

Rated PG-13 • 135 min. • 1992

Quick Take

A true story about a child diagnosed with an incurable illness and the parents who refuse to let him go.

Key Characters

Augusto and Michaela Odone. They are resourceful but have no medical training. Nevertheless, when scientists do not follow the leads they discover, they devote themselves to finding a cure.

Precautions

- This film may be too intense for families who have recently experienced the death of a child or for families of a terminally ill child.
- The film may be interpreted as endorsing alternative medical treatments. Clients should be cautioned about such risks.
- Highly emotional film—may be upsetting to depressed or anxious clients.
- Rapid-fire technical language.

Categories

Chronic illness and disabilities, death and dying, friends and support systems, grief and loss, inspiration, marriage, parent-child relationships.

Suggested Viewers

- Clients who need assurance that their efforts can bring about results.
- Clients who must maintain optimism in contending with challenges.

<table>
<tr></tr>
</table>

Main Lessons
1. Much can be accomplished when people refuse to give up.
2. Disagreements handled with respect are no threat to a healthy relationship.
3. Experts are not always right. Lay persons are not always wrong.
4. When couples work as a team, they are powerful.
5. Love sometimes *does* conquer all.

- Couples needing a model of how to work together in overcoming problems.

Setting the Scene

At the time that Augusto and Michaela Odone's five-year-old son, Lorenzo, was diagnosed with adrenoleukodystrophy (ALD), medical science offered only distant and improbable hopes. The Odones were told that the disease was rare, that it struck only boys, and that victims died after losing all sensory functions. Treatments were experimental and had not been successful. No child had ever survived the disease. Yet in spite of the dismal prognosis, the parents steadfastly refused to accept the inevitability of their son's death. Their race to find a cure served as the model for this film.

The film begins as Lorenzo shows vague symptoms, then is diagnosed with the disease. The Odones consult a specialist, Professor Nikolais, who is the acknowledged expert. He enrolls the boy in a high-risk program, but even with treatment, the disease continues to progress rapidly. Lorenzo's parents, though untrained in medicine, figure out that one problem is an absence of systematic knowledge. So they organize an international symposium, bringing together researchers as well as parents of ALD boys to share what they have all learned.

In the time that remains, Augusto combs the medical library for clues that might have been overlooked, becoming in the process a competent researcher. Michaela stays by her son's side, reading continually to him and refusing to let his mind grow weak. The couple is strained emotionally. They fight with each other and dismiss aides who cannot match their enthusiasm. Gradually, through their determined search, improbable possibilities begin to fall into place. They connect theories that to the experts appear unrelated, and finally they connect the right two theories. The answer, they discover, is in ordinary olive oil.

The doctors see scientific merit in the Odones' discovery, but are cautious and recommend further study. They know the Odones are desperate to save Lorenzo, but the doctors do not believe that this simple idea can lead to a real cure. False hopes, they warn the Odones, can be harmful. But the parents insist that their son should be treated with the new procedure. And against all odds, Lorenzo lives.

Scripting for Therapy

This film encourages clients to persist in their battles. And as a parable of empowerment, it teaches that lay persons may occasionally succeed where experts fail. Other parents of ALD children confront the Odones, criticizing them for questioning the scientists' findings. But the Odones argue that even if the slower paced medical researchers were to find a cure, it would be too late for their son. Because they are willing to risk censure by others, the Odones are ultimately successful.

One couple we saw in therapy had been told by teachers and counselors that their son, diagnosed with attention deficit hyperactive disorder, would never be scholastically successful. But, like the Odones, the parents continued to search for the right combination of medication, behavioral programs, and gifted teachers. They refused to accept the findings of the educators, focusing instead on achieving the right combination for their child. When particular teachers suggested that his limitations were unchangeable, the parents insisted on plans to deal with specific problems. They requested teacher conferences on a regular basis and asked that teachers call them if trouble arose. Although these clients gained a reputation as "pushy parents," their son's grades improved steadily with the hands-on involvement. Other parents, not so assertive, watched their children slip through the cracks of the system.

The film also illustrates the concept of teamwork applied to a marriage and specifically the ability to focus on an objective problem. We know little of the couple's relationship before their son is diagnosed, but once they begin searching for answers, they divide and conquer. He works with librarians, she with home health care professionals. Yet he also offers suggestions for the problems at home, and she gives feedback to his research findings. They argue between themselves vigorously, but they are always focused on a common objective. We see this film as an effective model for couples experiencing stress. Through watching the Odones, clients can learn to externalize problems and direct their energies at finding solutions rather than engaging in interpersonal attacks.

Philadelphia
Rated PG-13 • 119 min. • 1994

Quick Take

A young Philadelphia attorney sues his law firm when he is fired for being gay and having AIDS.

Key Characters

Andrew Beckett.   He spends his remaining days fighting for justice.
Joe Miller.   This attorney wants to help Andy, but to do so, he must deal with the seeds of prejudice in himself.

Precautions

- Graphic depiction of AIDS symptoms.
- Suggestions of sexuality.
- Profanity.

Categories

Chronic illness and disabilities, communication and conflict resolution, death and dying, family-of-origin issues, friends and support systems, grief and loss, intimate relationships, marriage, parent-child relationships, prejudice, values and ethics, vocational and work-related issues.

Suggested Viewers

- Clients who need to feel empathy for victims.
- Parents with difficulty in accepting family members who are gay.

Main Lessons

1. Prejudice, to some degree, affects everybody.
2. Prejudice comes in many forms, some obvious, most subtle.
3. Beyond the differences, all people are fundamentally the same and deserve compassion.
4. Families should represent the main source of strength for a dying person.
5. The process of dying can be dignified by keeping alive the qualities that make life worthwhile.

■ Clients who are the target of prejudice.

■ Clients with family members or friends who have AIDS.

Setting the Scene

Andrew Beckett is a bright young attorney on his way up; the prestigious Philadelphia law firm at which he is employed figures him for a star. But in a meeting in which Andy is assigned the most important client the firm has ever landed, a partner discovers a lesion on Andy's face that he knows to be symptomatic of AIDS. Two weeks later, after a report that Andy had prepared mysteriously disappears, he is fired. His bosses accuse him of gross incompetence, but he suspects, rightfully, that he was fired because they discovered he was ill. He files a lawsuit, charging the firm with wrongful termination due to his medical condition, and he searches Philadelphia for legal representation.

Andy talks with nine lawyers who won't touch his case before he consults a black attorney named Joe Miller. At first Miller, too, declines because he is intimidated by the old-line law firm and because he is prejudiced against gays. But when he sees Andy cruelly insulted by a clerk in a law library, Joe has a change of heart. He still doesn't like gays, but he dislikes prejudice even more. He takes on the case.

Just prior to the trial, Andy and his partner, Miguel, meet with his family to talk about what is to come. The two warn the family that things may get messy and ask for their opinion in whether to proceed. The family rallies without a dissenting vote. They pledge their love and support through whatever is to come. His mother says, "I didn't raise my children to ride in the back of the bus."

The trial takes place while Andy's condition is worsening. As plaintiff, he is seeking to show that the partners fired him because he had AIDS. The partners argue that they were unaware of his condition and that they let him go because he did not live up to their expectations. But what also is on trial is prejudice. Joe and Andy focus the jury on the two main issues: irrational fears about AIDS and prejudice against homosexuals.

The opposing attorney accuses Andy of hiding his disease from his employers. He counters that he was fully within his legal rights to have done so. The law firm's lawyer says the partners could not possibly have known that Andy had AIDS merely from seeing "an insignificant mark" on his head. But Andy removes his shirt and displays telltale skin cancers that are impossible not to recognize. Finally one of the partners admits that he had suspicions for a year and that he doubts the others were unaware that Andy was sick. The jury has heard all they need to hear.

Scripting for Therapy

Philadelphia is a film about AIDS. It is equally about prejudice and about dying with dignity. It illustrates how it feels to be the target of prejudice, how deeply it hurts to suffer a terrible disease and to be told that one has little worth, that one's death is inconsequential. It is about homophobia and fearing people who are different.

Before *Philadelphia* was released, one of our clients learned that his 23-year-old son was gay. The client was confused about what to do; he hated homosexuals, but he loved his son. Was it possible, he wondered, to put his son in therapy (against the son's will) to "get rid of this thing?" We advised him that therapy would not bring about the results he was seeking, and that in any case, we would not see his son for such an agenda. "But shouldn't I do something? His life is going to be so hard. Is there nothing I can do?" Had this film been available at that time, we would have suggested it to him as a way of helping him deal with his fear of gays and as a role model for how caring families show support to each other.

Andy's family, in contrast to his law firm, is a model of a loving, nurturing family that sticks with their son through hard times. During a humiliating court case and the publicity they knew would follow, the family is always on Andy's side. They had accepted his sexual orientation, and the relationship they have with him is based on Andy as a person, not as a homosexual. They accept Andy's partner as readily as they accept the heterosexual partners of his siblings. Thus the film is valuable for parents who have difficulty with a child's sexual orientation, but who are open to playing a more supportive role.

The film contains a number of touching scenes that succeed in showing the person beneath a label, making identification easier. One happens after Joe turns down the case. Andy stands outside his office building, depressed and frightened. As tears come to his eyes, the viewer knows the frustration and panic he must feel. Another occurs when Joe hears Andy's moving interpretation of an operatic aria. He doesn't care for opera, but as Andy expresses the feelings it arouses in him, Joe is touched in a new way. He leaves Andy's home and goes back to his own, where he embraces his newborn infant and his wife. He realizes that, aside from their sexual orientations, he and Andy have more similarities than differences.

Although prejudice is not a diagnosable mental disease, it creates situations that facilitate helplessness and hopelessness in the victim. Films such as *Philadelphia* show what it is like to be on the other end.

The Waterdance

Rated R • 106 min. • 1992

Quick Take

Autobiographical film based on the ordeals of the screenwriter after a hiking accident leaves him paralyzed.

Key Characters

Joel Garcia. In fighting back from his injury, he must deal with loss, grief, and anger.
Anna. She wants to be supportive, but Joel keeps pushing her away.
Raymond. In his rehabilitation, he must finally tell the truth about himself.
Bloss. Prejudice stands in the way of his physical and emotional recovery.

Main Lessons

1. Absolute control of one's life is an illusion.
2. Life can change in an instant, then one must cope.
3. Empathy for others must sometimes be learned the hard way.
4. Going through life changes with a support group eases the pain.
5. In adjusting to physical trauma, managing one's feelings counts a lot.
6. As human beings, we are far more similar than different.

Precautions

- Sexual situations.
- Profanity.
- Frank discussion regarding physical and sexual adjustments.

Categories

Chronic illness and disabilities, communication and conflict resolution, friends and support systems, grief and loss, intimate relationships, men's issues, prejudice, values and ethics.

Suggested Viewers

- Clients needing to develop empathy for others.
- Persons experiencing unwanted life change.
- Clients dealing with grief and loss.
- Clients dealing with guilt that prevents needed change.

Setting the Scene

Joel Garcia stares up at a succession of ceiling tiles as he is wheeled on a gurney through the hospital that will become his new home. He is confined to intensive care in a multiethnic ward after having been injured in a hiking accident. Reality has not yet sunk in. A journalist who boasts that he can write as well in traction, he will soon discover all that he has lost.

Joel isolates himself from the other patients, whom he sees as beneath him. He is educated, has a good job, and a woman who cares. *They* live only to grate on each other's nerves like bickering families. One head injury patient screams continually for pain medication, while a motorcycle gang type named Bloss tells him to shut up. Bloss hates everybody who's not white, but he singles out an African American ladies' man named Raymond for special treatment. Raymond returns the favor by casting doubt on Bloss's virility and by filling the ward with tales of his romantic conquests.

Joel's married lover is Anna, who is still devoted to him after the accident. They try to pretend that nothing has changed. But his paralysis and emotional difficulties cause them to reconsider her plans for a divorce. Joel soon starts picking fights. He is angry because she can walk out after their visits, but he cannot. She has a working spinal cord. Still, he refuses help from professionals who might make things better. When a psychiatrist questions whether he is as well-adjusted as he claims, he is dismissive: "Not as depressed as I should be? I've got depression penciled into my calendar for next week."

As the film progresses, Joel and his fellow patients must face their losses. The illusions and pipe dreams begin to fade. Bloss learns that his mother had wasted her money on a shyster lawyer and that a financial settlement that would make him rich is not going to materialize. Raymond discovers that he cannot escape into one-night-stands that had bolstered his ego in the past. His wife shows up to tell him he has failed at being a husband and father, and he can't find an argument that will prove her wrong. And Joel discovers that his greatest enemy is not the physical trauma he suffered but the anger that is in his heart. As each man faces failed expectations and new reality, they discover how much they need each other.

Scripting for Therapy

The Waterdance is a forthright and compassionate account of physical and emotional rehabilitation. It confronts specific problems such as impaired bladder control and how to cope with sexual needs. It deals with these issues directly, maturely, and without false sentimentality.

When we assign the film to physically challenged clients, we stress that the film represents the writer's rehabilitation but not necessarily their own. We ask them to compare their feelings and the stages of their recovery to Joel's. One client to whom we recommended the film was a woman who had been injured in a fall and who had developed secondary infections leading to total disability. She saw in Joel's irritation with his able-bodied lover a mirror image of her own feelings about the people around her. "It's impossible to tell somebody who hasn't been there what you go through. You get furious when a doctor talks about the ski trip he went on with his family. You want to tell him you don't give a damn whether his kids had a good time. See, my life stopped but his kept going. It seems unfair that he should be happy when I'm so miserable. Then I feel bad that I'm being such a bitch. It's not his fault."

We also assign the film to clients who share the psychological states, if not the degree of disability, that the protagonist does: chronic pain patients, clients who have experienced losses, and clients who must deal with radically altered body images in themselves or in those they love. We use the film as well to encourage empathy in caretakers, helping them to understand the frustrations of a person who is unable to function as before. The film illustrates how people adapt to any permanent change that entails significant physical loss and a basic reformulation of self-concept.

Finally, the film addresses the issue of grief. Joel undergoes the classic stages: denial, anger, bargaining, despair, and acceptance. He denies the gravity of his situation by maintaining that nothing important has changed. He imagines that his love affair with Anna will continue as before and that his career will not suffer. But when reality sets in, he is outraged. Why did this happen to him in particular? Like other people dealing with grief, he turns this anger against the person who is closest to him. But eventually he accepts his condition and sees past the rage. When he releases Anna as a lover and embraces her as a friend, the cycle is complete.

COMMUNICATION AND CONFLICT RESOLUTION

The Accidental Tourist
Rated PG • 121 min. • 1988

Quick Take

A couple separates after the death of their son. He meets a woman who encourages him to come to terms with his repressed feelings.

Key Characters

Macon Leary. He finds comfort in ritual and threat in change. When his 10-year-old son is killed, he turns away from his grief.

Sarah Leary. She wants support from her husband and wants him to share her emotional pain.

Muriel Pritchett. She is the single mother of a demanding child. She is looking for a "strong male role model."

Precautions

- This film may be too intense for parents who have recently lost a child.
- The story features an extramarital affair that leads to a man's choosing to divorce his wife. Some marriage partners might be unduly influenced.

Categories

Communication and conflict resolution, affairs, death and dying, divorce, family-of-origin issues, friends and support systems, grief and loss, intimate relationships, marriage, parent–child relationships, stepparenting and blended families.

Suggested Viewers

- Couples with communication difficulties.
- Clients recovering from loss.

Main Lessons

1. Relationships need time and attention in healing from tragedies.
2. In stressful times we reach for what is most familiar. But solutions may lie in the unknown.
3. When things get bad, healthy families talk.
4. Leftover family-of-origin problems sabotage adult relationships.
5. Men and women can have different parenting styles and still work together as a team.

- Obsessive–compulsive clients.
- Groups, in facilitating victim empathy.
- Stepparents.

Setting the Scene

Macon and Sarah Leary lose their young son, Ethan, to a holdup man's bullet in a fast-food restaurant. Macon shuts down emotionally. He gives Ethan's possessions away to other children, figuring that will put the loss behind him. But he cannot get over the tragedy, and he refuses to talk with his wife about their loss. She feels abandoned, and after a year of silence, she leaves him.

Macon returns to his family home to live with his unmarried brothers and sister and to lose himself in family rituals. His work helps him avoid thoughts of the tragedy. He writes a book series titled "The Accidental Tourist," guidebooks for the reluctant business traveler who wishes to avoid all unnecessary human contact and surprise. Novelty and spontaneity for Macon mean discomfort in travel as well as in everyday life.

Ironically, it is Ethan's dog Edward (Ethan's one possession that Macon had not given away) that brings him out of his shell. When he takes the dog to a kennel to board while he travels, he meets Muriel, a self-taught animal trainer. She offers to train the unruly dog while he is away. But Muriel, a single mother of a problem child, is interested in far more than Edward's improved behavior.

Although Macon is quite standoffish, Muriel pursues him with determination. Macon, who hates surprises, surprises himself by falling in love. But when he leaves his siblings to move in with Muriel, his wife

Sarah's interests are suddenly rekindled. Soon he must choose between a renewed delight in life with Muriel and a retreat back into a stilted emotional existence with Sarah. Once again, his choice surprises no one so much as himself.

Scripting for Therapy

This powerful story is told with gentle humor. The dramatic examination of the foibles of each character could have deteriorated into cheap satire, but instead the characters are treated with respect. We use the film frequently with couples because of the following teaching points:

- The Learys have not learned to manage their differences constructively. Like many clients, they confuse an absence of verbalized conflict with a good relationship. Hence the Learys' experience parallels what must be learned in therapy about effective communication in relationships.
- The film offers an effective portrayal of how tragedy disrupts a marriage through driving partners apart. For traumatized clients who believe they should feel closer to each other but do not, the film helps normalize their feelings.
- The film dramatizes the tension between the apparent but illusory safety of the past and the vibrancy of the future. When Macon feels most threatened, he retreats to the familiarity of his ancestral home. But once there, he discovers that he "cannot go home again."

The Learys' response to the death of their child is typical of couples who experience severe loss. At a time when they need to be together, they grow apart—partly through difficulties in communication. In this film, Sarah needs to talk, but Macon wants to be left alone. Both come to view the other as a source of unhappiness. Ethan's death brings to light problems that had been developing for years before tragedy struck. Macon had chosen a spouse whose personality made it unlikely that he would grow beyond his family-of-origin. In one way, he valued her for that; it was safe. But he also resented her. Sarah too had been held back by Macon's overwhelming fear of risk taking.

Couples with similar dynamics are frequently seen in marital therapy. We worked with a couple whose son had recently died in a motorcycle accident. The husband said he was "handling it fine," but he was not communicating with anybody. The wife said she had tried to initiate conversation but that her husband was unresponsive. Although the couple denied having had serious conflicts before their son's death, the event surfaced many complaints. The husband began drinking heavily and had an affair. The wife withdrew and became depressed. Neither related their marital problems to the tragedy. Their therapy involved putting aside the list of complaints compiled against each other and focusing on their loss. Only when the husband was able to grieve openly for his lost son—as Macon Leary does eventually in this film—was the marital dissatisfaction put into perspective.

Macon's obsessive-compulsive personality is caricatured in his siblings, whose fear of change far surpasses his own. The family is functionally incapacitated in their dependence on ritual. When Macon's sister Rose marries, she cannot deal with the demands of intimacy and quickly finds excuses for returning home to her brothers. Macon too is pulled toward his family but also attracted to a life of more risk taking. His choice of Muriel over Sarah at the conclusion of the film reflects his resolution of this tension. His willingness to risk more engagement with life demonstrates that even personalities as restricted as his can change. Some clients have become convinced that they always must be cautious to the point of immobility. But as this film illustrates, one can choose to act in a different way than one has in the past.

Macon is a role model for new stepparents in his interactions with Muriel's son Alexander. Stepparents must decide how much responsibility they will take for disciplining a child, what the nature of their relationship will be (friend, surrogate parent, "uncle" or "aunt"), and how much affection they will show their partners in the presence of a child. Macon chooses the role of good friend. He lets Alexander know that he wants to help with Alexander's problems and even provides a useful counterpoint to Muriel's overprotectiveness. Macon encourages Alexander to toughen up in a way that is not demeaning to the child but based on what he perceives Alexander to be capable of doing. And Macon's interactions with Muriel about her son acknowledge her concern, support her authority, and do not come across as an attempt at rescue. For her part, Muriel allows Macon to take these steps with her son and thus establishes their relationship as a team.

Terms of Endearment
Rated PG • 129 min. • 1983

Quick Take

A film about a complex relationship between a mother and daughter and about the daughter's death from cancer.

Key Characters

Emma.   She must contend with an overbearing mother and an unfaithful husband, but she is filled with character and drive.
Aurora.   In her mind, there are no boundaries between her and her daughter.
Flap.   He thinks he wants to be a husband and a father but discovers that he is not up to the task.

Precautions

- Profanity.
- Death of a young woman from cancer.
- Extramarital affairs.
- Sexual situations.
- Drunk driving treated casually.

Categories

Communication and conflict resolution, affairs, chronic illness and disabilities, death and dying, emotional and affective disorders, family-of-origin issues, friends and support systems, grief and loss, marriage, parent-child relationships, substance abuse, women's issues.

Suggested Viewers

- Clients with family-of-origin issues.
- Parents, regarding appropriate and inappropriate involvement in their children's lives.

Main Lessons

1. Personal strengths often overcome psychopathology.
2. Forgiveness is necessary for relationships to last.
3. Good relationships have boundaries and effective consequences for unacceptable behavior.
4. Families survive a loved one's death by pulling together. The needs of a child at such times are paramount.
5. Life goes on in spite of inevitable failures.

- Couples, regarding boundaries and limit setting.
- Clients facing illnesses in their families.

Setting the Scene

A young Aurora Greenway crawls into her baby's crib to make sure she is okay. When the baby starts to wail, her mother says, "Now that's better," then goes back to sleep. Throughout Emma's childhood and adolescence, her life will be much like that scene. Her mother, Aurora, is a pest. Aurora adjusts Emma's bra strap when she goes on dates, passes judgment on her friends, and when Emma marries against her wishes, she refuses to go to the wedding: "I am totally convinced that if you marry Flap Horton tomorrow, it will be a mistake of such gigantic proportions it will ruin your life and make wretched your destiny."

Aurora hovers not so much because she is concerned for her daughter's welfare but because it is a way to manage her own anxiety. Still, mother and daughter are best friends. When Flap takes a teaching job in a city far away, the two women talk every day by telephone. Aurora insists that her daughter put everything aside the moment she calls, and although Emma knows how disturbed her mother is, she usually complies. Partly as a result, Emma's husband drifts away.

Emma and Flap have a child almost immediately and then two more. He becomes involved in the first of many extramarital affairs with students. Emma puts up with it and raises their three children by herself. Meanwhile her repressed mother becomes romantically embroiled with a neighbor she's known for fifteen years—a former astronaut named

Breedlove with an enormous belly and an eye for young women. Breedlove drinks too much and tells Aurora she should drink also "to make yourself into a real woman." Their personalities are far apart, but Aurora falls in love because Breedlove reintroduces sexual intimacy into her life.

Tragedy strikes when a doctor discovers two suspicious lumps under Emma's right arm. The biopsy comes back positive—the lumps are malignant. Emma's health goes downhill fast and soon the family is gathering to say goodbye and to make hard decisions about where the children will go. Flap is their father, but he hardly knows them. It's no time for mincing words, and true to her strong character, Emma does not.

Scripting for Therapy

This film is terrific, but it illustrates the difference between judging a film on its own merits and using it therapeutically with clients. In *Terms of Endearment,* unlike in real life, dysfunctional relationships somehow endure. But we use the film to show what usually does not work in families: that an absence of boundaries between parent and child contributes to an absence of boundaries in a child's marriage; that relationships suffer when partners do not confront serious problems early on; and that children are frequently neglected when their parents are preoccupied with personal problems.

Many problematic parent–child relationships produce children who leave home in anger or maintain a highly conflicted relationship with their parents. Aurora and Emma illustrate the latter. Aurora is a selfish and insensitive mother; she knows no limits when dealing with her daughter. Emma's overattachment damages her development as an adult and is a factor in the destruction of her marriage. Because she had never stopped her mother from encroachments, she is predisposed to accept those of her husband too. Clients should understand that parents such as Aurora must be confronted forcibly and early. As adults, clients should not allow their parents to interfere in their marriages or make decisions for them.

The film addresses the issue of marital infidelity. Emma fails to effectively confront her husband's indiscretions and so they continue. She is upset when she learns about his first affair, but she returns to him with no clear agreements about the future. In the same way that she had complained ineffectually about her mother's overinvolvement, she nags Flap about his marital infidelities. She does nothing, however, to stop them; her only response is to have one herself. Therapists might discuss with their clients what steps Emma could have taken early in the marriage to stop the affairs from becoming a pattern.

The film is also useful in discussing death and dying issues, both from the standpoint of what is helpful in such situations and what is not. The family makes mistakes in handling Emma's dying. Neither Aurora nor Flap helps the children cope with their mother's death. In one scene, Aurora slaps an older child for speaking out angrily against his mother. Therapists can point out better ways of preparing a child for the death of a loved one: normalizing the mixed feelings that a child expresses, providing assurances that the child will be cared for, and treating compassionately but realistically the wishes of the child regarding future living arrangements. However, the film beautifully depicts a family picking up the pieces and going on after a loved one's death. It sends a powerful message that people who love each other, even imperfectly, can pull together and survive terrible pain.

 **DEATH AND DYING**

My Life

Rated PG-13 • 112 min. • 1993

Quick Take

A successful but narcissistic young executive is dying from cancer and must come to terms with his past.

Key Characters

Bob Jones. A husband and soon-to-be father, he learns the difference between a medical cure and genuine healing.

Gail Jones. She wants to become closer to her husband to garner strength for his passing and the baby's coming.

Bob's parents. Well-intentioned toward their children, they are more than supportive at the end.

Precautions

- Fairly graphic scenes that show side effects of chemotherapy.
- Profanity.

Main Lessons

1. Exploring feelings in intimate relationships is painful but productive.
2. Leftover resentments against parents must be processed, accepted, and transcended for mature love relationships to bloom.
3. In the final days of life, relationships become paramount.
4. Support sometimes means forcing a person out of his or her emotional shell.
5. Not everyone can be cured, but all can be healed.

Categories

Death and dying, aging, chronic illness and disabilities, communication and conflict resolution, family-of-origin issues, friends and support systems, grief and loss, marriage, parent-child relationships.

Suggested Viewers

- Adult children who remain angry with their parents.
- Adults disconnected to their feelings.
- Couples, in stressing the need for emotional openness and communication.

Setting the Scene

How would you handle a diagnosis of incurable cancer? Would you curse the fates, sue the doctor, explore alternative medicine? Because there is no protocol for such situations, it seems fitting that public relations whiz Bob Jones sets up a video camera and rehearses his parting lines after learning that he has inoperable kidney cancer that has metastasized to his lungs. With gallows humor, he videotapes greetings, instructions, and farewells to a child he will probably never meet. He also uses the camera to block out feelings that might overwhelm him and to keep others— primarily his wife Gail—at an emotionally safe distance.

The tape is mostly wry advice, such as his comments on shaving: "There are basically two approaches: up or down. Not sideways. Never sideways." Only occasionally does a more serious topic emerge. Once he tells his child not to be too upset if his mother decides to remarry. When Gail sees the clip, she is furious. "Why can't you tell me what you tell that stupid machine?" But Bob has trouble speaking the truth to anybody when the truth is from his heart.

As his condition worsens, Bob is invited to his younger brother Paul's wedding in Detroit. He doesn't want to go, but Gail tells him it is time to work things out with his family. Bob had cut them off years before and has had no contact except for occasional phone calls. Because he is dying and his wife insists, he agrees to go. But he swears her to secrecy regarding his illness.

From the time he enters his parents' home, Bob hides behind a camera and cracks jokes. Facing a table that groans with delicacies, he quips:

"I have two words to say: 'Weight Watchers.' " After the wedding, he and his brother try to patch up old quarrels. Years before, Paul had visited him and Bob had offered him a high-paying job. But Paul missed his family and friends in Detroit and returned home to work for his father, which made him a loser in Bob's eyes. The two men see their father very differently. "You hated him because he was a junk man," Paul says, "but I loved him because he was a hard worker."

Back in California, conventional treatments fail and Bob reluctantly consults a Chinese spiritual healer recommended by a friend. The healer diagnoses a bad case of harbored resentments. Bob storms out. "He said I was angry, the sonofabitch!" But he returns hat-in-hand a few weeks later. After a few treatments, the spiritualist says that he cannot cure Bob's medical disease, but tells him what he must do to heal. "You must forgive," he says.

Scripting for Therapy

Clients react to this film in many ways. Some wonder what they would do if they were given a death sentence. One client said, "I hated the way I felt when I watched it, but the film really did get under my skin. I can't imagine what it's like to anticipate death. There's a guy at the office my own age who just found out he's got cancer. The movie helped me understand what he's going through. Now I'm not so afraid to talk with him." For such clients, the film is valuable in coming to terms with the death of a friend or relative and in thinking about their own mortality.

Some clients are struck by how Bob reorders his priorities once he finds out he is dying. His interests rapidly shift from his job to exploring the relationships that matter to him, from making money to achieving peace. As he becomes worse physically, he becomes better psychologically and spiritually. He asks deeper questions and is more open. Clients can recognize that these possibilities were always available to Bob, and they can learn from his example while they still have time to make changes for the better.

Other clients identify with Bob's rage against his family but see that many of his complaints against them are self-serving and shallow. After watching the film, they question whether their own complaints against families are as exaggerated as his. We have recommended this film to clients who blame their parents for failures they have experienced as adults. We ask them to focus on the different interpretations Bob and his brother Paul have of their parents.

Still other clients for whom the film is helpful are "workaholics" who ignore their family's needs. Bob faulted his father for being consumed by work, but Bob is far worse. His father had worked to provide for the basic necessities; Bob works to enhance his self-image. In the end, Bob regrets that he had not taken more time for the people he loves. For a client in the prime of life, a person who neglects spouse and children for work, this film is an eye-opener.

Shadowlands

Rated PG • 130 min. • 1993

Quick Take

A marriage late in life and a wife's terminal illness teach a repressed intellectual how to love.

Key Characters

C. S. Lewis ("Jack"). He's an aging bachelor whose emotions are unavailable. His world is tidy until an American woman finds the key to his heart.

Joy Gresham. She's a divorced writer, open to new adventures. She loves Jack but she can't break through his shell.

Precautions

- Graphic depiction of suffering that precedes a death.
- Emotionally wrenching scene in which a young boy talks about his mother's death.

Categories

Death and dying, chronic illness and disabilities, communication and conflict resolution, friends and support systems, grief and loss, inspiration, marriage, parent-child relationships, stepparenting and blended families.

Main Lessons

1. Loving another person means confronting your personal weaknesses.
2. Thinking your way through life is not enough.
3. Sharing emotional pain with another accelerates healing.
4. Commitment to another requires a willingness to change.
5. Spirituality is no guarantee that tragedy will be more manageable, but it offers the possibility that a tragedy will be more meaningful.

Suggested Viewers

- Couples with communication difficulties
- Women who want to understand men who fear their emotions.
- Adults dealing with the death of a parent.
- Clients with repressed emotions.

Setting the Scene

This wonderful film, an adaptation of the stage play by William Nicholson, is a dramatic account of the love affair and marriage of the British writer C. S. Lewis and a feisty American poet, Joy Gresham. Jack, a middle-aged bachelor prone to intellectualization, lives with his brother Warnie and enjoys the comfortable security of an Oxford don. He grants an interview to Gresham, who presents herself by letter as an admirer of his work. But as he awaits her arrival in a restaurant with Warnie, he has second thoughts. Just then she walks confidently into the room and abruptly shatters the silence: "Anybody here named Lewis?"

Her refreshing and disarming honesty quickly wins Jack's heart, but because he is a stranger to romantic love, he doesn't realize how much he cares. She returns to America, but visits him again in a few months, this time accompanied by her 8-year-old son, Douglas. Douglas is thrilled to meet the author of *The Lion, the Witch, and the Wardrobe,* but is disappointed to learn that the wardrobe in the attic is not magic.

Joy's first marriage has failed, and with Jack's encouragement, she decides to remain in England. In the months that follow, they grow to care for each other as friends. Then Joy's visa expires, and she cannot stay unless she is married to a British citizen. Jack quickly volunteers to be the spouse of record. It is a mere formality, he reasons; the least he can do for a good friend.

Once married, they go their separate ways, living apart and meeting occasionally. But Joy begins to exert a subtle pressure on Jack. She challenges him to be less emotionally distant, more vulnerable. So sure of himself in his writings and public lectures, he is ill at ease when not in control of his environment. On the rare occasions when students challenge his authority, Jack relies on a sharp intellect to quash their critiques. Joy tells him plainly that he has surrounded himself with people he can easily overcome.

"I like a good fight," says Jack.

"That's great," says Joy. "But when's the last time you lost?"

Then Joy discovers that she has bone cancer. A pivotal moment occurs in their relationship, more so for him than for her. He had, after all, married her as a courtesy. She assures him he need not stay with her now that she is ill. But her illness forces Jack to confront his real feelings for her. He must decide if he will be her husband in reality or back away from involvement. He decides to stay.

Joy suffers a protracted and painful illness that challenges Jack's comfortable religious beliefs. When a clerical friend says that her illness is part of God's plan, reassurance that Jack himself might have offered others before, Jack is outraged. He prays more than ever, he says, but does not hope that his prayers will save his wife. "I pray because I can't help myself. I pray because I'm helpless. I pray because the need flows out of me all the time, waking and sleeping. It doesn't change God, it changes me." But when Joy dies at last, Jack's faith experiences its greatest challenge.

After Joy's death, her son grieves silently and alone. Jack avoids him for a long time, not knowing how to help. But when he finally does counsel the boy, he speaks from his heart rather than from his head. Not offering false hopes or simplistic explanations, Jack merely shares the grief. It is a moment of enormous pain and courage. As the two weep together, their emotional recovery begins.

Scripting for Therapy

Therapists may be struck by how different Jack and Joy's marriage is from many couples they see in therapy. Marital partners often approach with immature, romantic beliefs the decision of whether to stay together. They compare their marriage to what it was like when they dated, remembering novelty and the associated high. They ask themselves whether sex is frequent enough and as enjoyable as before, whether they are as esteemed by their partners as they think they should be. And they question whether their prospects for happiness are greater with the spouse than with another or even alone. Partners who divorce because their needs are not being met feel justified. But Jack's commitment to Joy was irrevocable. Her grave illness did nothing to alter his resolve. The film is a reminder that partners in marriage must accept the bad with the good and must play fair with the other person. Commitments are made without knowing what the future brings.

The film also shows how commitment must be based on a willingness to confront emotional pain courageously. Jack is reluctant to recognize his ambivalent feelings for Joy because, as a child, those feelings had overwhelmed him. But she teaches him that the love they share is in proportion to their willingness to accept losses that will inevitably follow: "We can't have the happiness of yesterday without the pain of today. That's the deal." Through Joy's dying, Jack learns to accept the pain as well as the pleasures of his emotions—a new intimacy made possible through being vulnerable to another.

Clients who enter into relationships based on an assumption that things will always remain the same set themselves up for bitter surprises. As long as they have no tragedies, the couple believes their relationship is strong. But that belief is cast in doubt when something goes wrong. Severe illness, loss of a job, the death of a child—these events can reveal a weak relationship. Such couples find that their foundations had been built on shaky ground. The added stress of devastating events is too much to bear.

How Jack manages his disturbing feelings throughout Joy's illness is a study in surviving loss—an illustration of the stages of grief. At first, Jack denies the reality of Joy's condition by emotionally distancing himself, settling into familiar routines. When her cancer is in remission, he pretends that nothing has changed and imagines that she will recover. But as her symptoms reappear, he bargains with God, offering to take on the suffering if she can be spared. When Joy steadily grows worse, Jack is angry that God has not accepted his offer. He feels hopeless and depressed when nothing he does makes a difference. But in her death, he accepts the loss and realizes what her life had meant to him. And in helping her son deal with his grief, Jack overcomes his own emotionally repressed past.

In a fundamental sense, the film is religious. It deals with prayer, the silence of God, and sorrow as a stage in redemption. It shows the relationship between intimacy and spirituality, teaching that marriages are not merely interpersonal balance sheets. Jack's marriage was a field test of faith, an opportunity to integrate his love for God with devotion to another human being. By deciding to remain with his wife throughout her illness, Jack learns that, in marriage, it is necessary to love fully and accept gratefully whatever comes to pass. And this acceptance, according to the beliefs by which Jack lived his life, is the condition of faith.

C. S. Lewis's own account of Joy's death is found in his book, *A Grief Observed*.

 **DIVORCE**

Bye, Bye Love

Rated PG-13 • 106 min. • 1995

Quick Take

Divorced dads juggle their kids' needs and their own.

Key Characters

Dave.   He wants to satisfy them all but ends up antagonizing everybody.
Vic.   Furious with his ex-wife, he is soured on women in general.
Donny.   He is still in love with his ex-wife.

Precautions

- Mildly sexual situations.
- Profanity.
- Alcohol use by adolescents.

Categories

Divorce, adoption and custody, affairs, communication and conflict resolution, friends and support systems, grief and loss, intimate relationships, marriage, men's issues, parent-child relationships, stepparenting and blended families, women's issues.

Main Lessons

1. Divorce is a difficult adjustment for parents and children alike.
2. Children's emotional needs take precedence over those of adults.
3. Acting out anger toward an ex-spouse resolves nothing.
4. When a marriage is over, it is better to accept the new reality and move on.
5. Friends are essential in coping with loss.

Suggested Viewers

- Divorced clients, particularly men.
- Parents preparing for a divorce.
- Exasperated single parents.

Setting the Scene

Dave, Vic, and Donny are three dads trying to contend with life after divorce. The film begins at McDonald's, where their ex-wives bring the kids for the weekend exchange. After an acerbic remark or two ("Your girlfriend is too blond and too young"), the fathers and their children hit the amusement park trail, cramming as much fun into one day as they can.

Each of the men is stuck between his past and future. Dave wants a new partner, but his priorities are all confused. His girlfriend seethes when soccer moms show up at his house with freshly baked bread; these divorced mothers are looking to replace the fathers their own children have lost. Dave's problem is that the women who drop by are his children's type, whereas his girlfriend is *his* type. In one scene, the girlfriend has prepared an elegant dinner that Dave's son hates. She offers to make him a hot dog, but he hates that too. Dave tries to smooth things over but only traumatizes his son and makes his girlfriend angry. He wants the children to care for her as much as he does, but the kids will have no part of it.

Vic is the angriest of the trio. His ex-wife is supporting an unemployed lover, and it galls Vic to see the guy sunning on the deck of his old home. He listens each morning to a radio therapist who talks about divorce as an opportunity for personal growth. He scoffs at the easy advice but tunes in because he doesn't know what else to do. His friends encourage him to begin dating, but when he finally does, the date is a disaster.

Donny still pines for his ex-wife. He is so hung up on her that he has trouble connecting with a teenage daughter who blames him for disrupting her life. Their conversations at the dinner table are awkward. He wants to go on being her dad as if nothing has happened, but she misses her friends on weekends and resents the court-ordered visits with her father.

All this hovering between past and future sets the stage for a variety of misadventures and mysteries. Will Dave commit to his girlfriend? Will Vic make peace with the past? Will Donny get over the woman he has lost? More important, will the children cope with these confused adults? It is a tough agenda, as anybody who has gone through a divorce can testify.

Scripting for Therapy

Don't expect the quality of *Parenthood* in this film. All the right elements are here, but *Bye, Bye Love* is neither as funny nor as poignant. What the film does well, however, is open up for discussion the problems about which divorced clients with children often complain: how to manage limited time, how to manage the children's variable emotions, how to manage one's own feelings about an ex-spouse who is with someone new.

The film fails to reflect the terrible pain that children face in divorce as well as the significant investment that divorced parents must make in helping children cope with loss. These kids are angry with their parents for breaking up their families, but the heart-to-heart talks between parents and their children depicted here are not likely to solve any problems. Therapists can point out what actions might have worked better for the children, such as addressing their feelings without criticism, allowing time to pass before introducing new girlfriends, and simply having more unstructured time together.

The three major characters present different reactions to the needs of their children. Dave wants his kids to like his girlfriend, but quite naturally, they don't. He might have handled the problem of "but she's not mom" by addressing the anger his son feels without letting his own frustrations get in the way. Dave wants to make everybody happy but nobody cooperates, and he does not understand why. Unfortunately, his strategy of demanding cooperation from his children and glossing over their feelings is not unusual. Clients complain that their children are "just not trying." They can be asked how this father might have eased his son's pain and how to apply that knowledge to themselves.

Vic's problems are also familiar in real-life settings. Ex-spouses continue their marital arguments into divorce, particularly when jealous of the ex-spouse's new lover. Clients might be asked if they see how Vic's destroying a deck he had built misses the point. How could Vic have better handled his conflicted feelings?

Vic's blind date will be a familiar scenario to divorced clients who have reentered the dating world. His date talks throughout the evening about what a scoundrel her ex is and bristles with mistrust of men. The evening is evidence to Vic that beginning again with someone new is not going to work, but actually the date only validates the saying, "You have to kiss a lot of frogs before you find a prince." Clients who are starting to date after a divorce need to realize that when they date people with post-divorce problems of their own, there will be more mismatches than connections.

Although divorce severs the legal ties, love does not always end so easily. Donny wants to get back with his ex-wife, and so he has trouble letting go. He has difficulty relating to his daughter in the context of her new family. At his daughter's graduation reception, given by her stepfather, she dotes on her new dad. Donny is crushed when she pointedly ignores him. He still wants to play the role of dad in her life. But Donny must face reality in order to move on and to allow his daughter to do the same.

Don't expect role models for clients from this film. And don't look for a sensitive treatment of the conflict between divorced parents and their children. A better film would confront the hard issues with more candor, but this movie is a nod in the right direction. Clients will identify with the problems these men face. With guidance, clients can find better ways to resolve these problems in their own lives.

Kramer vs. Kramer

Rated PG • 106 min. • 1979

Quick Take

A father discovers the joys of parenthood only after his wife leaves and he assumes care for their child. Then she comes back and sues for custody.

Key Characters

Ted Kramer. Too busy to be a husband and a father, he rises to the occasion when he must. But the suffering does not begin until he loses the child he has come to love.

146

Main Lessons

1. Parents who divorce should honor their children's rights and help them heal.
2. Divorce is never painless. All parties get hurt.
3. Bonding happens with a child in the course of activities, not just brief conversations.
4. When bosses ask for everything, everything else gets lost. An employee has a right to set limits.
5. Marriage counselors should be consulted before attorneys are.

Joanna Kramer.   She leaves because she does not know what else to do. After she resolves her problems, she returns for her child.

Precautions

- Profanity.
- May be emotionally too intense for clients who have recently lost a child through a custody hearing.

Categories

Divorce, adoption and custody, communication and conflict resolution, grief and loss, marriage, parent–child relationships, values and ethics, vocational and work-related issues.

Suggested Viewers

- Divorcing clients, in keeping uppermost the welfare of a child.
- Clients from divorced homes.
- Parents with intact relationships, in emphasizing how time actively spent with a child intensifies the relationship.

Setting the Scene

Ted Kramer is an ambitious art director who drinks with his boss long into the night and calls the office for an update the moment he gets home. One night his wife Joanna is standing at the door with her suitcase. She is leaving him and their five-year-old son, Billy. "It's not you," she tells Ted, "it's me." The next morning, father and son stumble through making French toast and getting ready for school and work. It is only temporary, Ted explains to his son. "Mommy is coming back."

But Joanna does not come back. Instead she sends Billy a goodbye letter in which she tells him that she will always be his mommy but that she has to go away. Billy pouts and won't talk about the situation, but his father is panic-stricken. Ted does not know how to juggle work and full-time parenting. When he appeals to his boss for help, the boss just tells him to find somebody who will take his son. Looking more confident than he feels, Ted assures his boss that he is on top of it all.

He is not, of course. He doesn't know anything about taking care of a child or even himself. Billy has to point out which dishwashing detergent to buy. And Ted has trouble convincing his boss that he is still the go-getter he was before. For a while, Ted doesn't do either job very well, and the frustrations begin to boil over. Gradually father and son get the routine down, and Ted starts enjoying his child for the first time. He laughs more, listens better, and becomes a great dad. About that time, two events halt his progress: Joanna comes back for her son, and he loses his job.

The lost job is the easier of the two to repair. The divorce proceedings, however, are bitter and cruel. Once lawyers are involved, any hope of a painless solution is futile. Joanna's attorney calls Ted an unfit parent; his attorney calls her unstable. In the end, the court rules in Joanna's favor and instructs Ted to relinquish custody of his son. But after a week of soul-searching, the Kramers reach a different decision on their own.

Scripting for Therapy

Billy is devastated when his mother leaves. He sulks, cries, won't eat, and sleeps all the time. But his father is obsessed with his own worries and neglects his child's feelings. Ted gets angry when Billy will not cooperate, and he shows how out of touch he had been as a husband and father. A workaholic who had left child rearing to his wife, he now sees that he is unprepared for parenting. When he takes Billy to school on the first morning after Joanna leaves, Ted has to ask Billy which grade he is in and who his teacher is. But after the initial shock, Ted rises to the occasion. Eventually he becomes a competent parent.

Clients, particularly men, might discuss how the relationship between father and son improves as Ted does more things with his son. Children value a parent who does things with and for them, and for a child, love is related to activity. The positive changes that Ted makes in his relationship result from his taking a more hands-on approach to fathering.

In discussing the film, clients often express a need to determine who is right and wrong in the divorce. Clients make arguments on both sides. The more productive topic for discussion, however, is how both the Kramers act for the good of their child. They exhibit an awareness that their disagreements with each other are not as important as helping Billy deal with the divorce.

For instance, once Joanna is awarded custody, Ted reassures Billy that they will visit often and that he will be happy living with his mother. When Ted's attorney tells him that filing an appeal will mean greater suffering for the child, Ted quickly declines to proceed. And when Joanna gives Billy back to her ex-husband, she does so because she believes that taking Billy away would be harmful. Additionally, when referring to the ex-spouse in front of their child, they are respectful toward each other. The parents know that, although they no longer love each other, Billy loves them both. This film is a good model for clients who are divorcing, because it demonstrates how couples can disagree yet still be mindful of the needs of their child.

We want to make this observation about Ted's relationship with his boss. For the boss, work is everything. It means staying late into the evening drinking and chatting, not necessarily about work-related subjects. Only when Ted says he is going home does the boss bring up an important business topic to discuss. So when Ted finally loses his job, it is not because he is incompetent but because he is no longer exclusively committed to the job. In his boss's opinion, Ted spends too much time with his son, and his stories about Billy are obviously tiresome. Ted is fired because his priorities have changed.

Clients with supervisors who demand that they socialize with clients or staff to the neglect of family might want to discuss this issue. Therapists may note that one reason Ted's boss sees a significant difference in his behavior before and after the marital separation is that Ted had set himself up for an unfortunate comparison. Before he assumed responsibility for his son, Ted had complied with his boss's every request and had set no limits. That person was the employee his boss wanted, not the person that Ted became. So when circumstances changed, the boss let him go. Clients might consider ways that Ted could have established a more balanced approach to work and home and ways that they can, too.

The War of the Roses

Rated R • 116 min. • 1989

Quick Take

A divorce battle from which literally no one walks away.

Key Characters

Oliver Rose.　He is an up-and-coming attorney who neglects his marriage and ignores the seeds of destruction.

Barbara Rose.　She is okay with the house and the trimmings, but she wants more from a husband. When he becomes combative, she matches him blow for blow.

Precautions

- Nudity.
- Strong language.
- Sexual situation.

Main Lessons

1. Small neglects evolve into big problems.
2. Relationships must be founded on more than materialism.
3. When couples stop talking about things that matter, they lose what means the most.
4. Domestic violence proceeds from verbal to physical abuse.
5. Love isn't about keeping score or hurting one another.
6. It is possible to divorce and still be humane.

- Because of the violence of this film, it should *always* be accompanied by detailed explanation regarding a therapist's specific purpose in assigning it and followed up with comprehensive discussion. Therapists might also recommend *The Verbally Abusive Relationship,* a book on domestic violence by Patricia Evans.

Categories

Divorce, abuse (emotional, physical, sexual), communication and conflict resolution, grief and loss, marriage, values and ethics.

Suggested Viewers

- Couples who are seeking to improve their relationship or are considering divorce but who are open to options.
- Couples in premarital counseling.

Setting the Scene

Oliver Rose is a pushy graduate of Harvard Law School who aspires to senior partner in a big-name firm. He is not really a bad guy, but his narcissistic priorities are clear from the start. Barbara is beautiful, witty, and generous, and she is willing to go along with Oliver's plans. When they marry, it is for love. All the rest, they assume, will follow.

At the beginning, their marriage is ecstatic. She buys him a sports car, he buys her French crystal. Sex is naturally great. But soon Oliver starts taking Barbara for granted. He is polite but not affectionate, preoccupied with the problems at work. When she tries to make light conversation, he ignores her. After their two children are born, he has little interest in the family. And he begins to show a cruel streak she had not seen before. During a dinner party for his boss, he insults her by correcting her speech and finishing for her a story she is telling. In short, he becomes a snob, ashamed of his wife in the new surroundings. Their polite conversations grow less polite and more bitter. Eventually they do not talk except to handle the business of the day.

Years pass and so does what remains of their love. Oliver makes senior partner and is at the office more than at home. They cordon off their dream house into territories: it is his dog, her cat; his son, her daughter. She starts a business for something to do, but more important, to have money that he cannot touch. When he has an onset of indigestion that is first thought to be a heart attack, she doesn't go to the hospital. Later she tells him what worried her while he was away. "I realized what it would be like to be alone in this house. And I got scared because I was happy!" She asks for a divorce; he is incredulous: "What have I done wrong?"

Scripting for Therapy

In practice, we suggest this film primarily to couples trying to improve relationships that are only slightly impaired, not to couples in the heat of a divorce. But almost all troubled couples can identify themselves at points along the path taken by the Roses. Their problems are relatively mild in the beginning, but become more serious as time goes on.

Couples can see where neglect and a lack of respect lead. Oliver quickly begins to make decisions for Barbara. He prioritizes his work over their home and abdicates responsibility for their children. He seems cheerless after they have been married only a short time. As he concentrates more on his ambition, he smiles less, jokes less, has little patience for the light moments that had been important before. By contrast, when he is with his law partners or trying to capture a new client, he turns on the charm. Barbara's love for him fades as she becomes aware of this growing discrepancy.

Clients should also notice how the language used between the Roses changes with time. At the beginning, their words are kind; they listen patiently and give thoughtful feedback. But soon their conversations are more acerbic and, finally, cruel as barriers to verbal abuse are removed. The point we stress to clients is that the Roses "talk tough" before they "act tough." Their language sets the tone for actions that follow. Thus clients can learn that the language they use with each other is important. Like the Roses, when partners abuse each other verbally, physical abuse may not be far behind.

The dynamics of abuse often involve economic inequality between partners, which is true for the Roses. Barbara has no income apart from what Oliver gives her. So she takes his insults and hopes that if she can be "good enough" at making a home he will once again become the man she married. She begins to fight back after she starts her own business and it becomes successful. But by that time, she is so angry that her power is destructive. Therapists can discuss with clients how power issues impact a relationship.

Clients may be asked to consider how the Roses responded to changes in their relationship and how their responses were instrumental in leading to further marital distress. What actions could Oliver or Barbara have taken to turn things around? Clients may compare their own marriage and themselves to the Roses. How are they similar or different? Have they also ritualized certain patterns of conflict? How could their communications be improved through changes in attitudes and behaviors? And if they have become verbally abusive, as the Roses became early in their marriage, can they contract to stop verbal abuse before it escalates?

Used in premarital counseling, the film shows what *not* to do. In the film, common mistakes increase until it is too late to save the relationship. Caught early, those mistakes might be corrected before they reach a point at which change is more difficult.

EMOTIONAL AND AFFECTIVE DISORDERS

Dead Poets Society
Rated PG • 128 min. • 1989

Quick Take

A teacher encourages a student to pursue his passion against his father's wishes. The adolescent commits suicide and the father blames the teacher.

Key Characters

John Keating. A master teacher motivates students to love poetry. He encourages them to spread their wings, but cannot protect them from their falls.

Precautions

- This film portrays an adolescent's suicide. Parents who have experienced a child's death may find this too intense.
- Depicts alcohol use among teens.
- Not suitable for at–risk adolescents.
- Profanity.

Main Lessons

1. Commonsense advice may not be in an adolescent's best interests. Adolescents feel intensely and take advice literally.
2. To guide an adolescent well requires listening skills more than charisma.
3. Mentors of teens should recognize their responsibility.
4. Adolescents may think of suicide as a magical solution. Counselors should take any mention of suicide seriously.
5. Where feasible, therapists should always include an adolescent's family in treatment.

Categories

Emotional and affective disorders, adolescence, communication and conflict resolution, death and dying, family-of-origin issues, friends and support systems, grief and loss, inspiration, men's issues, parent-child relationships, transition to adulthood, values and ethics, vocational and work-related issues.

Suggested Viewers

- Professionals who work with adolescents, such as teachers, counselors, clergy, and physicians.
- Parents of adolescents who need to better understand developmental needs.
- Therapists in training.

Setting the Scene

John Keating is a charismatic teacher who returns to Welton Academy, a boy's prep school, to teach poetry. Welton is long on tradition and discipline, and John has little patience for what he regards as stodgy conformity. In his first meeting with the class, he displays old class photographs. "You know what they are now?" he asks. "Food for worms. Listen to what they are saying to you: *Carpe diem,* seize the day."

The boys revive a club called The Dead Poets Society, which John himself had formed while a student at Welton. They gather in a cave at night to read poems, smoke their pipes, and entertain town girls. Gradually the club meetings create a spirit of rebellion among the boys. Having been content in the past to follow Welton's rules, they now begin to experiment with breaking them.

For the most part, John brings forth the best from his students. A stuttering and frightened boy creates a poem from the heart in front of the class, urged on by John's infectious enthusiasm. Another shy lad works up the courage to pursue the girl of his dreams, competing successfully against the captain of a football team. But from the start there is a dark seed of calamity looming in John's iconoclastic teaching style. It flowers in the best student of the class, Neil Perry, who discovers that his passion is acting. Neil's father is furious when he learns of his son's plans to participate in a school play. He orders him to give up "this frivolous pursuit" and plan on going to Harvard, where he will become a doctor.

Neil tells John that he will have to drop out of the play. John advises Neil that he *must* talk with his father and assures him that his father will be supportive. Neil agrees to talk with his father but is too frightened to do so. On the night of the play, his father unexpectedly attends the performance. He takes Neil home immediately, intending to move him from Welton to a military academy. Late that night, Neil kills himself. The blame, of course, is laid squarely on John.

Scripting for Therapy

Increasingly, therapists are asked to consult with professionals such as teachers, clergy, and school counselors regarding decisions that have psychological overtones. What is the best way to handle a situation such as that represented in this film, in which the interests of an adolescent are pitted against the express wishes of a parent? Should the mentor support the student against the parent or proceed along a different course altogether? We think that for professionals who deal with adolescents, this film is an illustration of what *not* to do.

John errs in his advice of how Neil should handle his father's objections to acting. Neil goes to John for support rather than advice; he has already decided to resign from the play and follow his father's orders. But with little understanding of the effect his charisma has on his students, John offers a double bind that can only end sadly. He gives Neil a piece of unsolicited advice: "You must tell your father how you feel about acting." But John does not know Neil's father, is unaware of the family dynamics, and has no understanding that he is putting Neil in a dangerous situation. John puts the burden of action on a confused student.

Therapists should be familiar with this dilemma because they too treat adolescents struggling with the demands of parents who may be insensitive to their feelings. But therapists need to realize that adolescents must continue to live with their parents. Therapists can offer support, understanding, and a reasonable game plan, even survival skills for living in a troubled family. But they should not position a child against the parents.

John, however, sets up a tragic confrontation for his student without a thoughtful plan for how the student can resolve his difficulties.

Furthermore, some educators have argued that John's educational style, while colorful, does not serve his students well. In one scene, he tells his class to rip out a chapter on poetry written by an academic authority he does not respect. A mature teacher might have helped the boys think through the essay critically. John encourages free thinking in his students, which naturally leads them to experiment with rebellion. But John himself is a rebel only to a point. He tries to explain this discrepancy to his class when he chastises one student for a stunt that turned sour. John's political realism, however, is not nearly so attractive as his "seize the day" lectures.

What is missing from the warm relationship that John establishes with his students is effective follow-up. He throws out challenges without awareness of the consequences that may occur. On the one hand, he understands the powerful effects he has on his students and even encourages them to idolize him ("You may call me 'my captain.'") On the other, he does not recognize the thin line that separates a charismatic teacher from a demagogue.

What's Eating Gilbert Grape?
Rated PG–13 • 117 min. • 1994

Quick Take

A family that defies diagnosis, the Grapes love each other and accept their eccentricities. The father dies, the mother gains weight and quits life, a brother is mentally retarded, and Gilbert tries to manage their lives and his.

Key Characters

Gilbert Grape. Stuck in a small town, he is waiting for something to happen.
Mama Grape. She gave up on her life when her husband died. Now she must let her children go on with their own.
Becky. She's the stranger whose arrival brings a crisis to the Grapes.

Main Lessons

1. Families do not have to be perfect to be loving.
2. There is a fine line between codependency and caring for the people one loves.
3. Finding one's adult partner means leaving the family-of-origin.
4. Local communities help isolated individuals by making them a part of community life.
5. Healing happens when one stops clinging to the past.

Precautions

- Nudity.
- Profanity.
- Sexual situations.

Categories

Emotional and affective disorders, chronic illness and disabilities, family-of-origin issues, friends and support systems, intimate relationships, parent-child relationships, transition to adulthood, understanding severe emotional illness.

Suggested Viewers

- Clients with dysfunctional family histories.
- Caretakers who have trouble setting limits.
- Clients, in understanding physical and emotional challenges.

Setting the Scene

What's Eating Gilbert Grape? is a delightful film for anybody with a heart. The armchair analyst will enjoy diagnosing the colorful characters who make up the family Grape. First is Mama, weighing more than 500 pounds. The family literally revolves around her, taking meals in the living room at a table they bring from the kitchen. Next is Arnie, retarded and "not supposed to live until his 18th birthday." He loves to climb the town's water tower and watch the people below. Sisters Amy and Ellen are in their early teens, embarrassed by their strange family and hypersensitive around friends. And watching over them all is Gilbert—a sweet kid who has graduated from high school but is hanging around waiting for life to begin. He bides his time working in a grocery store and drinking coffee with friends. But mostly he takes care of his family.

Gilbert has been the caretaker since his father committed suicide a number of years before. Gilbert's salary keeps them on the respectable side of poverty, and his supervision keeps Arnie out of an institution. Gilbert loves his whole family but at times he gets worn out. Every day is the same, with no sign that his life will improve. Gilbert's romantic life is confined to trysts with an attractive and lonely housewife to whom he delivers groceries and a little adventure.

Gilbert's life changes with the arrival in town of Becky, who is traveling with her grandmother in a snowbird caravan. Their RV breaks down, and while waiting for it to be repaired, Becky meets Gilbert and instantly falls in love. He likes her too. She is the first girl who has captivated his heart, and he starts to think about what he wants for the rest of his life. Becky genuinely cares for Gilbert's family, but Mama Grape knows what Becky's coming means. She knows that Gilbert has found a life of his own and that it is time for her to let go. So she takes a dramatic step that will set her children free.

Scripting for Therapy

This film is a reminder that internal strengths are more important than disabilities. The Grapes do not view themselves as tragic characters, nor do they ask for pity. They do what they must to solve problems as they arise. The Grapes have warm feelings for each other, sadness for the things that cannot be, and frustration, even irritability, with the day-to-day jams they get into. But they are genuinely fond of each other and forgiving of mistakes. The Grapes illustrate to clients that admittedly imperfect people can still love each other in a family.

The town looks with kindness on the Grapes, acting almost as an extended family. They demonstrate the value of a community that cares. For instance, when Arnie climbs a water tower, bystanders naturally gather below. But they gather out of concern, not because they are morbidly curious. After all, it is Arnie on the water tower, a boy they know and love and whose family they care about. As they chat among themselves while

Arnie is deciding whether to climb down, it is clear that the townspeople feel responsibility. They model how communities should help persons with physical and emotional challenges feel integrated into a wider social network.

Gilbert, in his role as the family caretaker, is committed by default to responsibilities for which he didn't ask. When his father died, he became the surrogate parent because he was the oldest and because his mother was depressed and unable to guide the family. There are no agencies for Gilbert to turn to nor relatives nearby. He is trapped but he bears his responsibility with dignity. His situation is similar to clients who find themselves caring for others without obvious alternatives. For clients in caretaking roles, the film shows the nobility in staying the course. It shows that with time, things sometimes change, albeit slowly.

The course of Mama Grape's depression, which leads to morbid obesity, is well illustrated in the film. In one clip she is shown prior to her husband's death, an attractive and vivacious woman. But after he commits suicide, she becomes isolated and starts gaining weight. She gives up almost entirely and lives vicariously through her children. She does not allow any of the siblings to separate from her or from each other. But when Gilbert falls in love with Becky, Mama Grape knows that she must let go. In a powerful scene, she leaves the living room in which she has lived for years and climbs the stairs to her bedroom. By doing so, she symbolically removes herself as an obstacle to her children. The gesture is an illustration of how one generation must loosen its grips on a younger one, how one parent finally accepts that her children have a right to independent lives. Mama Grape's decision to let go is an inspiration, a message to parents who cling too long to their children.

FAMILY-OF-ORIGIN ISSUES

Like Water for Chocolate

Rated R • 113 min. • 1993 (In Spanish with English subtitles)

Quick Take

A narcissistic mother tries to keep her daughter from growing up.

Key Characters

Tita. To become an adult, she must confront and overcome her pathologically self-centered mother. She weighs the demands of tradition against the desires of her heart.

Mama Elena. She cares nothing for the welfare of her youngest daughter and falls back on family tradition as justification for robbing Tita of full adulthood.

Precautions

- Nudity.
- Explicit sexual situations.
- The story is told in the Latin tradition of magical realism. Clients who prefer less abstract films may find its symbolism confusing rather than enlightening.

Categories

Family-of-origin issues, adolescence, communication and conflict resolution, emotional and affective disorders, friends and support systems, grief and loss, intimate relationships, marriage, parent–child relationships, transition to adulthood, understanding severe emotional illness, values and ethics, women's issues.

Suggested Viewers

- Clients dealing with family-of-origin concerns.
- Clients in relationships with narcissists.
- Couples with intimacy issues.

Main Lessons

---

1. Family traditions may interfere with appropriate developmental choices.
2. To break an unhealthy cycle, extreme measures must be employed.
3. To establish an intimate adult relationship, one leaves behind the exclusivity of a parent-child bond.
4. True love finds a way.

Setting the Scene

Family tradition demands that Tita, as the youngest daughter, remain unmarried and care for her mother for as long as she lives. When Tita falls in love with a boy named Pedro, her mother absolutely forbids the marriage. Pedro, however, marries Tita's sister, Rosaura, then whispers to Tita at his wedding that he is marrying to be near her. The birth of a son to Pedro and Rosaura only draws the lovers closer. Because Rosaura is too sickly to breast-feed her child, Tita becomes the wet nurse.

Mama Elena sends Pedro, Rosaura, and their newborn to San Antonio, hoping that by separating Pedro and Tita, she will destroy their passion. But without Tita, the child refuses to eat and soon perishes. Tita denounces her mother's decision to send them away, blaming the child's death on her. Mama Elena strikes her daughter and tells her she is an evil child. Tita climbs into the dovecote of the barn and stops speaking. After three days, Mama Elena sends her to an asylum.

The physician to whom Tita is sent, John Brown, refuses to place her in an institution, but takes her to his home. He accepts her silence and treats her with kindness; in caring for her, he also falls in love. Once she is well, he asks her to marry him. Tita loves him, but not as she loves Pedro. Yet she considers his proposal carefully. Her choice is between marriage to a man she respects but for whom she feels no passion and pining away for a lost love. Then the unthinkable changes everything. Mama Elena dies.

Tita returns to her home believing she is free, but the ghost of Mama Elena roams unbridled into her mind. As a spirit, her mother is even more powerful than she was in life. Tita despairs of ever separating herself from this bitter woman. Finally her desperation drives her to strike forcibly at her mother's spirit with an incantation that brings liberation.

> I know who I am! A person who has a perfect right to live her life as she pleases. Once and for all, leave me alone; I won't put up with you! I hate you! I've always hated you.

With those words, her mother's spirit fades into nothing. And Tita at last can become an adult and join her lover.

Scripting for Therapy

Two principles clash in *Like Water for Chocolate* with the angry force of mythological gods. First is the overwhelming power of life's insistence, pressing a child toward adulthood and toward a soulmate. Second is a parent's attempts to forestall death by stunting her child's development. Each is resolute, and compromise is not possible.

Although told from a distant magical culture, the film portrays suffering similar to what clients experience as they try to wrench free of narcissistic parents who refuse to let go. The message sent by the parents is "my life is more valuable than your life." In breaking away from such an irrational claim, simplistic strategies rarely work. Therapists advise their clients in such circumstances that they must get away from a toxic person however they can and at whatever the cost.

Commitment to an aging parent is good and honorable, but there must also be a recognition that older generations pass away as new ones come into being. Both parent and child must adhere to natural law. If the parent refuses to accept the inevitability of the process, the child must be willing to risk strong confrontations that will bring about release.

Yet even when clients do break free, the narcissistic parent can continue to stalk them. In reality or through perceived guilt, clients become their own jailers. Therapists may feel powerless to facilitate an effective separation. What frees Tita is her recognition that it is solely in her power to sever the relationship. She finally accepts her own power and dares to use it. And with that step, her mother's spirit is put to rest. Therapists can help clients translate that symbolic message into action that will be effective.

163

Of course the problem can and does exist in reversed order. One of our clients, a parent in her 50s, was distraught over her 28-year-old son who continued to come back home for financial and emotional assistance. "We told him he's not a child any longer. But he calls us selfish and says we should take care of him as long as he needs help." The connection between this parent and her adult child was every bit as destructive as that between the mother and daughter in the film. Our client broke the magical spell by presenting her son with a transition plan. She agreed to help him for several months while he got on his feet. But she also let him know that if he did not assume responsibility for himself, she was no longer going to rescue him.

FRIENDS AND SUPPORT SYSTEMS

Circle of Friends
Rated PG–13 • 112 min. • 1995

Quick Take

Three young Irish women explore friendship, first love, and sexuality.

Key Characters

Bennie, Eve, and Nan. In pursuing their dreams, the depth of their friendship is tested.

Precautions

- Teenage drinking.
- Brief nudity.
- Sexual situations.
- Frank discussion of budding sexuality.

Categories

Friends and support systems, adolescence, affairs, communication and conflict resolution, family-of-origin issues, grief and loss, intimate relationships, marriage, parent–child relationships, transition to adulthood, values and ethics, women's issues.

Main Lessons

1. Honesty and fairness keep friendships healthy.
2. Love relationships cannot include manipulation or subterfuge.
3. To forgive and forget requires time and consistently better behavior.
4. Mature love is founded on more than physical attractiveness.
5. Relationships should be viewed realistically, not misread in terms of one's fantasies.

Suggested Viewers

- Adolescents, in discussing issues of sexuality.
- Adults and adolescents, regarding honesty in relationships.
- Couples needing a model for starting over.

Setting the Scene

Nan, Eve, and Bennie, lifelong friends, attend Dublin's Trinity College, which is only a short distance from their small village but worlds away in other respects. Each girl knows what she wants from life. Nan is beautiful and seeks a rich man who will rescue her from working-class roots. Eve, an orphan raised by nuns in the local convent, is a gifted student who knows that education is her ticket to a better life. Bennie is a stereotypic plain girl with a terrific personality, possessor of a sharp wit and a no-nonsense awareness of self. She wants both a man and a better life, but on her terms.

The year is 1957, a time when children still obey their parents even when they find their demands unfair. Bennie travels each day to Trinity College by bus because her parents fear corruption in the city. Even her parents' vigilance, however, cannot shield her from falling in love with Jack Foley. He can have his pick of the girls; he invites all three to a dance because he cannot decide which one he prefers. Well aware that she is not as pretty as the others but at least as worthy, Bennie tells Jack: "I know I may look like a rhinoceros, but I'm quite thin-skinned, really. Don't mess me about. I'll flatten you." Jack insists he will not toy with her affections.

In her efforts to catch a rich husband, Nan is deflowered and then abandoned by a wealthy villain named Simon Westward. Now pregnant, she settles for less than she had hoped. She gets Jack drunk, coaxes him into sex, and a day or two later gives him the bad news. Naively Jack doesn't doubt that he is the father, so he resolves to do the right thing by Nan.

Bennie and Eve talk it over; neither blames Jack entirely. They figure Nan is smarter than he is, and both suspect there is more to the story than they know. When Nan shows up with Jack on her arm at a party, everybody desperately tries to let bygones be bygones—everybody but Eve, who suddenly figures it all out. She creates a scene, drives Nan away, and gets Bennie and Jack back together, though not without Bennie's asking, "Now exactly how do we just start over?" Jack patiently courts Bennie anew. After an appropriate probationary period, she allows herself to fall in love with him again.

Scripting for Therapy

Can adolescents in the United States understand the culture shock three young women from the country must have experienced in entering Dublin's Trinity College in 1957? These women adhere to rules of a society in which the Catholic Church dictates what is right and wrong, even when the rules seem heavy-handed. Such respect for authority may strike today's adolescents as naive at best. But what *is* relevant is the ambivalence that many adolescents still feel when sexual intimacy becomes a possibility; also relevant is the misguided notion that girls, not boys, are charged with the decision whether to "go all the way."

The plot centers on Bennie's relationship with Jack and the implication that this relationship is a mismatched pairing. It is unfortunate that we find remarkable a story in which the heroine, attractive but not beautiful, snags the handsome leading man. But perceived inequities do raise eyebrows, then as well as now. Jack does not articulate what he appreciates most about Bennie, but the viewer knows that this is one time when the more attractive member of a pair looks beyond what is only skin deep. Clients may infer that, although beauty may be the deciding factor in many romantic pairings, in the best of relationships it is not.

Clients may also see that friendship and loyalty to one's friends are important, the maintenance of which sometimes requires one to put aside personal goals. Of course one's own goals are important, but gaining those goals at the price of a friend is seldom worth the loss. In this story, if Nan had succeeded in deceiving Jack, someone would have no doubt discovered the truth. Nan sacrifices friendship for personal gain, and the sacrifice is a bad bargain.

Why did she do it? Nan probably would not have fallen to such depths if she had not misread Simon's intentions, brought about by her desire to escape a life she did not want to lead. He never suggests he will marry her, but Nan hears what she wants to in her imagination. Clients may see in this situation an illustration of the therapeutic truism that one should focus on what is real as opposed to what one would prefer to be real.

Finally, in the way that Bennie treats Jack after Nan's deception has been discovered, the film offers an excellent portrayal of how couples start over after significant breaches in a relationship. Bennie welcomes him back, but does not agree to pick up where they had left off. As she explains it to him, both he and she are not the persons they were before, so they will have to get to know each other again. Jack must be patient, allowing Bennie the time she needs to trust him again. Clients too are frequently in such quandaries. How do they repair the damage done when one partner falls astray? How is trust reclaimed? And what can the transgressor do to right the wrongs? This film offers a suggestion for how to proceed.

City Slickers
Rated PG-13 • 108 min. • 1991

Quick Take

Three friends in the midst of midlife crises find meaning on a cattle drive.

Key Characters

Mitch.   Burned out with his job, he doubts himself as a man. He tells great jokes that cover up an ailing self-image.

Phil.   He has been trapped for years at his father-in-law's grocery store. When a clerk turns up pregnant, his wife sends him packing.

Ed.   His father abandoned the family, and he has sworn not to make the same mistakes.

Curly.   The last of a dying breed, he has found the one thing he loves and is content to spend the rest of his life doing it.

Precautions

- Profanity.
- Several scenes involving animals in distress may be frightening to young children.

Main Lessons

1. Good friends are an asset in dealing with the ups and downs of life.
2. Lasting relationships require a heavy dose of commitment.
3. The remedy for burnout is to do one's job well and have varied interests.
4. Fathering is about doing positive activities together as well as having long talks.
5. Life is a series of "do-overs"—chances to try something once again and this time do it better.

Categories

Friends and support systems, affairs, aging, communication and conflict resolution, divorce, family-of-origin issues, grief and loss, intimate relationships, marriage, men's issues, parent-child relationships, transition to adulthood, values and ethics, vocational and work-related issues.

Suggested Viewers

- Clients experiencing burnout.
- Clients in midlife crisis.
- Male clients, in learning the value of same-sex friendships.
- Clients who have experienced significant loss.

Setting the Scene

At a show-and-tell presentation in his child's class, Mitch plays second string to a garbage collector who tells the kids about his job. Mitch tries to compete by exaggerating the importance of his work as a radio spot salesman. But when the kids start to doodle, he admits with weary resignation, "What I do is, I sell air." Each year Mitch and two buddies, Ed and Phil, take Outward Bound–like adventures to faraway places. They run with the bulls in Pamplona, play fantasy baseball in Florida, and trek to the North Pole. This year it is an authentic cattle drive from New Mexico to Colorado. The wives are glad to see their dissatisfied husbands leave. Mitch's wife tells her glum husband: "Go find your smile."

169

Driving cattle provides a lot of time to talk, and these guys talk about commitment, children, adultery, and electronics equipment. Naturally they have long discussions about sex and how to deal with temptation ("If she were a beautiful alien and nobody'd ever know, would you?"). They describe their best and worst days. Ed says his best *and* worst day was as a teenager when he kicked his philandering father out of the house. They even confess stereotypic male inadequacies—such as Phil's admitting he had never learned how to program a VCR. As they punch cattle, a guru in the guise of a trail boss named Curly tells Mitch the secret of life. Sitting tall in the saddle, Curly holds up one finger. "You've got to find that one thing," he says enigmatically. Mitch looks puzzled and asks, "What one thing?" Curly smiles broadly. "That's what you've got to find."

The crisis occurs when Curly dies and they have to bring the herd in by themselves. It is a moment of truth with no excuses. Before they reach home, they must fight drunken cowhands, ford swollen rivers, and overcome a number of city-bred phobias. But with the theme song from the television show *Bonanza* blaring forth, the men finally break into a gallop and "run them dogies into the corral."

Scripting for Therapy

This film is a buddy-movie for three, a male-bonding adventure in which existentialism is mixed with belly laughs. Clients, particularly males, can take heart from its lessons of how adults in their 30s cope with typical problems such as the following.

Father-Son Bonding. Phil says a shared interest in baseball bridged the gap between him and his father. "When I was 18, my dad and I couldn't communicate. But we could still talk about baseball." Mitch remembers his first trip to Yankee Stadium, when his father explained the intricacies of the game. It was his best moment from childhood. The disclosures illustrate how fathers bond with sons in the activities they do together as much as in the words that they speak.

Some fathers do not understand this concept in terms of their relationships with their sons. Feeling inadequate because they think they should be having deep talks with their sons, fathers overlook the possibilities in merely doing fun things together. The activity does not have to be a cattle drive or a trip to Pamplona. A camping trip for father and son of-fers the same opportunities for getting closer.

Commitment. Of the three, Ed has the biggest problem with com-mitment because his father had left Ed's mother for another woman when he was in his teens. Ed is afraid he will do the same so he avoids long-term relationships and having children. What Ed figures out during the cattle drive to Colorado is that his life is less than it might be because he will not make a stand. By the time he returns home, he decides to give life his best shot. He is a good role model for a male client who is still toying with adult life.

Effects of the Past. Another lesson of the film is how mistakes from the past control one's future. Phil has lost his wife, children, and job be-cause of a mistake he made. He believes that his life course is set. His bud-dies disagree, and they remind him of a rule that kids have when someone hits a ball into a tree. "It is a *do-over*," they tell him. "You just get the ball down and you start over again. Your life's like that, Phil—a do-over."

Clients in the middle of divorces or victims of corporate downsizing can do the same. They can start fresh from where they are. There are no rules that dictate they must let history determine their futures.

Parenting. The film gives parents an effective role model in the trail boss, Curly. He allows his neophytes to learn from their mistakes without nagging or bargaining with them. He says little and backs up his words with natural consequences. When Mitch brings a battery-operated coffee grinder onto the range, Curly tells him, "You're going to spook the cattle." He doesn't argue with Mitch. He simply makes his point by allowing the cattle to stampede. On another occasion, when a cow is struggling to deliver her calf, he orders Mitch to deliver the calf and won't accept his excuses. Furthermore, the advice he gives Mitch facili-tates an inner search for answers. Like a zen master offering a koan, Curly tells Mitch that what's important is to "figure out that one thing," which Mitch finally connects to the family he'd left back home. Clients can learn from Curly that good parenting involves natural consequences, de-vising learning experiences, and helping children discover answers on their own.

Friends and Support. As friends, the three men support each other through difficulties. They tease and bicker, and at times, threaten to leave. But they forgive and forget. And when one gets in trouble, the others come to his aid. They share their fears and their failures, and they encourage each other.

By contrast, many male clients complain that they have no friends and are not interested in cultivating any. Feeling competitive with other men, they hide what's real about themselves. But there is a value to same-sex friendships for which marriage is no substitute. When a married male client asks his spouse to be his best buddy as well as his wife, he may load up the marriage with more than it can bear. Men need friends as much as women do.

Steel Magnolias
Rated PG • 118 min. • 1989

Quick Take

A diabetic woman marries and gives birth to a child her doctor warned her not to have.

Key Characters

M'Lynn. She faces every parent's worst fear and survives, thanks to her strong character and good friends.
Shelby. She refuses to settle for the limitations of a physical disease.
Truvy, Quiser, Claree, Annelle. The "Steel Magnolias" gossip and support each other through many life changes.

Precautions

- Mild profanity.
- This film depicts a young mother's terminal illness. It may be too intense for clients who have experienced recent tragedies.

Categories

Friends and support systems, aging, chronic illness and disabilities, communication and conflict resolution, death and dying, grief and loss,

---

Main Lessons

1. Having close friends is an important asset in facing life changes.
2. A grieving person needs to express feelings without being criticized or given too much "good advice."
3. Those we love sometimes make life-altering decisions with which we must come to terms.
4. Partners cannot meet all the emotional needs of their spouses. The best marriages recognize that a couple should be involved in a wider community.
5. Forgiveness is essential in maintaining good relationships.

---

marriage, parent-child relationships, transition to adulthood, women's issues.

Suggested Viewers

- Isolated clients who need to learn the value of social support systems.
- Individuals or couples in grief.
- Persons adjusting to the limitations of disease or aging.

Setting the Scene

In small, southern towns, people go to beauty and barber shops to catch up on all the gossip. When this film begins, the regulars at Truvy's Beauty Shop have gathered to fawn over M'Lynn's daughter, Shelby, who is getting married. But in the middle of the celebration, Shelby suffers a diabetic seizure. Although she recovers quickly, the incident casts a pall over the happy event. Both she and her mother cannot help but recall what Shelby's doctor had said about the marriage: that Shelby should not plan on having children.

Other dramas take place at Truvy's. Annelle, a woman with a past, has just hired on as a beauty operator. The others cannot wait to pry into her secrets. Claree's husband recently died; she is trying to find ways to fill the gap he left behind. For the moment, she spends her time in squabbles with Quiser, the local eccentric. Quiser, in turn, devotes her attention to fighting with M'Lynn's husband over a tree that straddles their shared property line. All the while, Truvy does their hair and offers sage advice. But when the women leave, she faces a husband who is out of work and depressed.

Several months after the wedding, Shelby tells her mother she is pregnant. M'Lynn cannot be happy for her because she knows the risks. But when the baby boy arrives, M'Lynn is a delighted and proud grandmother. Then one day while at home with her child, Shelby collapses into a coma and does not recover. Only a few days later, the family must make a painful decision to discontinue the life support system.

Scripting for Therapy

Shelby's tragic death illustrates a message about the importance of friends in coping with inevitable trials. Friends are important, and reaching out to them brings healing. M'Lynn is able to deal with her daughter's passing because she is surrounded by people who love and care for her. But clients without close friends must often face grief alone. One of our clients, a middle-aged woman, lost her husband after he suffered a heart attack. Because she believed that as a widow she was now "different," she isolated herself from friends and extended family. Without social support, she became depressed and felt hopeless. She rebounded only when she responded to the overtures of old friends, who were relieved she would finally let them help.

The women in this film demonstrate flexibility in their daily interactions, recovering quickly when conflicts occur. They know each other so well that they are able to deliver barbs that strike to the root of their personality flaws. But they are forgiving, and they never cut each other off. The friends are in many respects closer to each other than to their husbands. This concept stands in contrast to the beliefs of some clients, who assume something is wrong if they highly value same-sex friends. But each relationship is fulfilling in its own way. Friends can sometimes say to each other what spouses cannot.

One of the functions of good friends is to accept a person's grief in its emotional variability. This film is helpful to clients who are grieving and who question if their feelings are appropriate. They know that sad feelings are normal, but they are not prepared for occasional moments of giddiness or fury that seem wrong. We have asked such clients to watch this film because it shows the array of emotions that people feel after a loved one dies. Sadness, anger, and even humor often exist concurrently.

A theme lightly touched on in the film is accepting the decisions of those we love when we do not agree with them. M'Lynn warns her daughter against having a child, and as it turned out, Shelby *was* too weak to bear children. But M'Lynn hears Shelby's point of view. ("I'd rather have 30 minutes of wonderful than years of nothing special") and accepts her decision. This theme applies to clients for whom a child's transition into adulthood brings no alteration in the relationship. They continue trying to exert parental influence and blame their children for refusing advice. For clients who cannot let go of their grown children, the scene in which M'Lynn learns of Shelby's pregnancy is a helpful focus for discussion.

 **GRIEF AND LOSS**

Ordinary People
Rated R • 125 min. • 1980

Quick Take

The death of a son in a boating accident throws a family out of balance. The son who survives becomes the scapegoat for their grief.

Key Characters

Conrad. He cannot forgive himself for surviving and attempts suicide after his brother's death.

Beth. She is unable to love the son who lives.

Calvin. He cares deeply for both his wife and son but cannot bring them together.

Precautions

- Depicts the death of a child. Not for parents who have recently suffered a similar tragedy.

Main Lessons

1. Nurturing adults must sometimes help children pull free from abusive parents.
2. Families should expect emotional turbulence after a traumatic loss.
3. Guilt is often a function of injustice, but must be overcome for growth.
4. The death or serious illness of child exacerbates existing family problems.
5. Emotional abuse is as serious as physical abuse.

- Caution advised in recommending the film to a parent who might overidentify with the repressed and emotionally abusive mother.
- Profanity.

Categories

Grief and loss, adolescence, communication and conflict resolution, death and dying, divorce, emotional and affective disorders, family-of-origin issues, friends and support systems, marriage, parent-child relationships, prejudice, understanding severe emotional illness, vocational and work-related issues.

Suggested Viewers

- Couples with communication problems.
- Individuals, regarding family-of-origin issues.
- Therapists, involving ethical issues and therapy with an adolescent.
- Clients with survivor's guilt.
- Therapists, regarding effective work with a depressed adolescent.

Setting the Scene

Conrad says he is not hungry; his father cajoles him good-naturedly. "You've got to have your breakfast, main meal of the day and all that." But his mother rolls her eyes and abruptly removes his plate. "If he says he's not hungry, he's not hungry. Let's drop it." The scene illustrates what is terribly wrong with the Jared family. Conrad is tentative, depressed, and withdrawing. His father is well-meaning but apprehensive. His mother barely contains her rage behind a smile cast in wrought iron. All three tacitly agree to maintain an icy standoff, never admitting the truth to themselves or each other. Secrecy, hidden emotions, suppressed feelings—these make up the facade that the family uses to maintain the illusion that everything is all right.

The family problems, of course, had existed for many years. But they came to light when an older son, Bucky, drowned in a sailing accident. Conrad was rescued, but he attempted suicide because he felt guilty as the survivor. When the film opens, he has just come home from a psychiatric hospital. It is a hard transition. The kids at school call him crazy, and his father treats him with kid gloves. His mother speaks to him only when she must. Conrad knows that as far as she is concerned, the wrong son perished.

Eventually he contacts a psychiatrist suggested by the hospital. Dr. Berger is straightforward and will not tolerate innuendoes and half-truths. He is neither impressed with nor frightened by the suicide attempt. When Conrad says that he blames himself for clinging to the boat while Bucky was swept away, Berger tells him, "Maybe you were the stronger one." It's the first time Conrad has considered that he might be superior in any way to his brother.

As Conrad gradually improves, his mother deteriorates. She maintains a cheerful front with her friends, but she turns away from light conversation with her son. Her anger is always just beneath the surface. When he quits the swim team, she is furious with him, worried about what her friends will say. And when he tries to hug her, she cannot bear his touch. She finally admits that she is embarrassed to have a son like Conrad, a son with emotional problems.

Scripting for Therapy

The dynamics present in the Jareds are similar to many dysfunctional families. They do not talk honestly, and they avoid sensitive subjects rather than confronting them. During this film, father and son change for the better in that regard. But the mother does not. The family's dysfunctional communication is conveyed subtly through glances and bits of behavior. They say one thing to each other, but their behavior sends a different message.

Many couples use the same poor communication patterns as the Jareds. They deny the important problems and focus on the ones that can be resolved with more ease. They nag about the house being untidy but avoid admitting that they have stopped caring for each other. Of course, the difficult problems do not go away. This film shows that when people do not face their critical issues directly, those problems will eventually destroy a relationship.

Because the Jareds' messages carry so much emotional weight, each encounter threatens to explode into a family argument. When the explosion finally does occur (ironically during a trip to Houston, where Beth has talked Calvin into getting away from their problematic son), it is catastrophic because of the years of accumulated hostilities. Calvin finally admits to himself that he is married to a selfish woman whose "niceness" is all on the surface. Beth is consistent to the end. When her husband tells her he wants a divorce, she turns silently to pack her bags.

The psychiatrist in *Ordinary People* demonstrates effective skills in helping troubled young people. He speaks candidly, focuses Conrad on problems that need to be resolved, yet provides a safety net if things go wrong. He asks questions that lead Conrad to make discoveries for himself. Dr. Berger helps Conrad see that he is damaging himself through negative self-attributions rather than putting the blame on his mother. And he is well aware of the risk his client poses. He makes it clear to Conrad that he can count on the doctor's support and establishes a safe environment to explore Conrad's troubled emotions. He leads Conrad to accept his mother's rejection as a fact of life. "Maybe she is unable to love you any more than she does." The implication is that the responsibility for their poor relationship lies more in his mother than in himself—a possibility Conrad had not considered before.

A River Runs through It
Rated PG • 123 min. • 1992

Quick Take

A family tries to understand its prodigal son's needless death.

Key Characters

Norman. He's the good son who follows in his father's footsteps.
Paul. He is drawn to intensity and the wrong crowd and is at peace only when he fishes the river.

Precautions

- Alcohol, gambling, sexual situations.
- Nudity.

Main Lessons

1. "We can love completely without complete understanding."
2. "Bad things happen to good people."
3. Mild but early conduct problems lead to more serious difficulties in adolescence and early adulthood.
4. There is a value in simplifying one's life.
5. One cannot help those who do not want to be helped.

- Profanity.
- Violence.

Categories

Grief and loss, death and dying, family-of-origin issues, friends and support systems, inspiration, parent-child relationships, substance abuse, transition to adulthood.

Suggested Viewers

- Parents of a self-destructive child.
- Parents of adolescents or young adults with conduct disorders.
- Adults searching for meaningful guidelines.

Setting the Scene

In the spirit of Izaak Walton's reflections on angling, *A River Runs through It* weaves fly-fishing instructions with observations about the nature of God and man. Near the Blackfoot River in western Montana shortly before World War I, Norman and Paul Maclean learn from their father that fly-fishing is one means by which God teaches the right use of creation. If you can fly fish correctly, the Rev. Maclean tells his sons, you are a long way toward knowing how the universe really works.

Norman leaves home to study literature at Dartmouth. Paul stays in Montana to study the Blackfoot River, where he learns to "think like a fish." His angling skills are soon celebrated, but everything else in his life falls into disarray. A sports reporter with a paper in Helena, Paul drinks on the job, carouses all night, and is an addicted gambler who makes enemies of the wrong people. When Norman returns for a visit after his graduation, he learns that Paul has run up a debt with the local mob, who are threatening to kill him. Norman offers to help, but Paul says he has everything under control.

Paul has one last idyllic day on the river, during which he comes as near to fly-fishing perfection as he will get. Then all his debts fall due. On hearing of his murder and that the fingers of his hand had been broken, his father asks, "Which hand, the left or the right?" They tell him it was the right, his fighting hand. As the family mourns its loss, Rev. Maclean asks Norman to write Paul's story in order to understand why Paul chose the path that he did.

Scripting for Therapy

This film is inspirational for clients and a resource for discussion. It celebrates the timelessness of nature, the healing power of love, and families who never stop caring for each other. It also contains themes related to the difficulties that families experience when dealing with a self-destructive child. We assign this film to clients who want to simplify their lives as well as to those who are trying to understand a person like Paul. Three lines from the film summarize its more important lessons.

"Why can't the people who need help the most take it?" Norman offers to help Paul break free from gambling. Later he tries to help his girlfriend's brother, a narcissist who pretends to be successful but is an obvious failure. Neither accepts his assistance; neither believes he has a problem. Both continue on their paths of self-destruction despite the efforts of people who love them.

Clients become frustrated when they cannot influence a family member or friend to make changes that will improve that person's life. Substance abusers, for instance, cannot be helped until they hit rock bottom. Before they reach that point, they deny having a problem and resent offers of help—as Paul does in this film. Family members may see tragedy approaching. But if the troubled person does not desire help and is unwilling to accept it when it is provided, the efforts of others are futile. Clients wrestling with this issue will identify with Paul's family, who care for him but cannot influence him to change.

"It is those we live with and love and should know who elude us." Even Paul's early childhood shows signs of trouble. At first he is merely obstinate. But as he grows older, he acts recklessly more often. He fights, steals, and associates with unsavory characters. He begins drinking and gambling at an early age. His father uses the same discipline that worked well with his other son, but with Paul, he is ineffective. His father sees Paul drifting toward destruction, but does not know how to stop him. He cannot understand his son, and in a time when there are no other resources, he cannot find someone who does.

Clients also find it difficult to grasp why a family member acts self-destructively. They feel guilty that they have not been able to help. We use this film to address those feelings and to illustrate how difficult it is for families to determine on their own what a troubled person really needs. Reaching out for professional help is often the most loving step a family can take.

"You can love completely without complete understanding." On the day that Norman returns home with his wife and children to hear his father preach his last sermon, his father summarizes how he has come to grips with the family tragedy. "We can love completely," he assures his congregation, "without complete understanding."

Clients sometimes do their best and tragedies still befall them. Good parenting is no guarantee that a child will become a successful adult. Caring families still have their lost souls. Even competent therapy has its percentage of failures. Yet knowing all that does not stop people who love each other from loving as much as ever.

Unconditional love is not the same as unconditional support—financial or otherwise. Clients should be encouraged to see the difference between loving a person and contributing to his or her pathology. The 12-step approach emphasizes this distinction in its admonition, "Let go and let God." Love is an orientation of unlimited positive regard. It should not be confused with unlimited involvement and misplaced responsibility.

 **INSPIRATION**

Field of Dreams
Rated PG • 107 min. • 1989

Quick Take

An Iowa farmer finds meaning by trusting his intuition and taking a risk. In the process, he learns to forgive his father.

Key Characters

Ray Kinsella. A man with a dream, he marches to his own drummer.
Annie. She's the wife who helps Ray see his vision through to the end.

Precautions

- Not for impulsive clients inclined to quit jobs or relationships.
- Profanity.

Categories

Inspiration, communication and conflict resolution, family-of-origin issues, friends and support systems, grief and loss, intimate relationships,

---

Main Lessons

1. Never stop dreaming. Dreams give spice to life.
2. Support for partners means taking their visions seriously even when they are not one's own.
3. Set goals and stick with them. Don't give up.
4. To forgive a parent, it is necessary to walk in their shoes.
5. Burnout may be a symptom of dwelling on mistakes.
6. Sometimes one has to act on information that is less than complete.
7. To reach one's goals, help others reach their own.

---

marriage, men's issues, parent-child relationships, transition to adulthood, values and ethics, vocational and work-related issues.

Suggested Viewers

- Young adults searching for identity.
- Couples needing role models who demonstrate support for a partner.
- Older individuals who are disillusioned, cynical, despondent.
- Estranged fathers and sons.

Setting the Scene

Ray Kinsella is an ex-radical from Berkeley who moved to Iowa to be a farmer. One day he hears a voice say, "If you build it, he will come." He somehow knows that "it" is a baseball diamond and that "he" is Shoeless Joe Jackson—a hero of Ray's deceased father. So after a talk with his wife, Annie, he mows down a section of the corn field and builds a ballpark. The other farmers gossip that he has gone over the edge. But weeks later his daughter, Karin, looks through a kitchen window, then turns to her father. "There's a man in your field." Sure enough, Shoeless Joe is in center field. "Is this heaven?" he asks. Ray smiles. "No, it's only Iowa."

Other voices soon follow. The first sends him to Chicago to meet Terence Mann, a disillusioned civil rights leader of the 1960s. According to Ray's intuition, he is to take Mann to a baseball game in Boston and wait for further instructions. Once they are seated behind first base, they see a picture of a Minnesota player named "Moonlight" Graham on the scoreboard and a message meant for them alone. "Go the distance," it says. So Ray and Terence head for Minnesota.

When they arrive, however, they learn that "Doc" Graham, whom everybody knows and loves, had died years before. This time, Ray figures, the voice must have made a mistake. But on a magical and foggy night on a deserted street, Doc reappears and tells Ray about his life as a country doctor. He has no regrets, but wishes he had been given a chance to bat just once in the major leagues. He had never really known how good he might have become, he said, and he could rest easier if he knew. Ray has just the place for him to find an answer.

Scripting for Therapy

Depending on their circumstances, clients identify with characters in the film who are experiencing developmental problems consistent with young adulthood, middle age, or old age. The film uses the metaphor of baseball to treat issues such as (1) being content with one's circumstances and valuing what has been achieved, (2) holding to a right course of action when others disapprove, (3) achieving a relationship characterized by mutual support, and (4) recognizing that dreaming (by which is meant the creative spirit) is potentially available at all times.

"If you build it, he will come," is a way of restating the adage "In order to see, you must first believe." Whether the goal is a new career, a more satisfying relationship, or a loving family, before it can be realized, it must capture the imagination. A goal's creative images organize thought and motivate change. Clients must think of their goals as inevitable and then take steps to make those visions come about.

The first message Ray hears implies that sometimes we must act on information that is less than complete. When clients gain insights from therapy, they naturally want to accumulate as much additional information as possible before taking action. But eventually they have to act on what amounts to a partial understanding. Ray Kinsella does not know at the outset what lies ahead. He hopes that his experience will lead to something worthwhile, but he has only a strong hunch and a few ambiguous words to guide him. Yet he trusts the process and forges ahead. Like Ray, clients too must act on therapeutic insights that can be ambiguous.

The second message, "Ease his pain," refers to Terence Mann, who is angry and disillusioned. He had hoped that through his efforts the world might become a better place. Now he is disappointed that he was not more effective. When Ray finds him, Terence is hiding from the world. Ray helps him become reenergized by engaging his curiosity in a quest that is larger than himself. The rejuvenated Terence Mann is a role model for clients who have given up on life. If they can expand their focus to concerns larger than themselves—stop dwelling on their regrets and on what they cannot change—they may again find their will to live. Therapists can use Terence Mann as an antidote to burnout, to offset a condition that is a function of small interests and self-focused vision.

The third message is "Go the distance." The voice says that once a journey is begun, it must be completed. Clients in therapy reach a point at which it is easier to stop than go forward. They are tempted to be satisfied with surface insights and changes that are manageable but not threatening. Therapists encourage clients to see that stage as an opportunity to redouble their efforts. After all, it takes less work to break through barriers when 80 percent of a job is finished than to start over another time. Clients who see a therapeutic quest through to the end are usually glad that they persevered.

The film also teaches us that we actualize our personal dreams while we help other people to actualize their own. Doc Graham turns away from professional baseball to be a small-town physician. And Terence Mann finds a new sense of purpose in helping Ray understand his strange voices. The dreams that are fulfilled in this film come to fruition because the dreamer concerns himself with other people. Therapists can encourage clients to see that their dreams are more likely to come true when they find ways to be of service to others.

The movie suggests that understanding and forgiving one's parents is a function of seeing things from their perspectives. Ray and his father were not speaking when his father died, and Ray regretted that they had never worked things out. He blamed his dad for not giving him more. But in the final frames of the film, his father appears as young ballplayer and they play a game of catch. It is the first time Ray has ever thought of his father as anything but an old man. His father is not bigger than life, not all-knowing, but just a young man doing his best. Ray's resentments melt when he sees that he and his father are fundamentally the same. His father had been the best father he knew how to be.

It's a Wonderful Life

Not Rated • 125 min. • 1946

Quick Take

Sentimental and adorable classic about a man rescued from self-doubt and despair by a cuddly angel.

Main Lessons

1. When families and neighbors stick together, they can beat the odds.
2. Relationships count more than money or success.
3. People have more positive influence on others than they believe.
4. "It's always darkest before the dawn." Before giving up, let time pass and wait for unpredictable events to unfold.
5. People don't realize how many resources there are for solving problems.

Key Characters

George Bailey. A good man in the midst of a scandal, he suddenly wonders if his life has been worthwhile.

Clarence. This angel wins his wings by showing George the meaning of his life.

Precautions

- The film depicts a man who considers suicide and decides to live only after recognizing his worth. Therapists should help clients understand how they too have touched others in positive ways, even if not as obviously as the protagonist.

Categories

Inspiration, friends and support systems, grief and loss, marriage, parent-child relationships, transition to adulthood, values and ethics, vocational and work-related issues.

Suggested Viewers

- Clients who question whether their efforts have merit.
- Older clients who regret the loss of youthful dreams.
- Clients in need of hope.

Setting the Scene

George Bailey stands at the rail of a lonely bridge and stares at the swirling waters below. He can think of no reason to live. George had been an ambitious young man who yearned to see the world, but one thing after another stopped him from fulfilling his dreams. After his father died, George saved the family business from ruin. Then he passed up lucrative business offers to stay in Bedford Falls and help his neighbors. He fell in love and married a local beauty, and they were blessed with four delightful children. Of course he could have escaped from his responsibilities. But each time that he might have walked away, he chose duty over adventure. Now, after his sacrifices, he is deceived by his nemesis, the evil Mr. Potter, and faces disgrace and prison. So he targets a spot in the dark river and prepares to exit a disappointing world.

Just as George is preparing to jump, an angel named Clarence appears on the scene. Clarence temporarily transforms Bedford Falls into what the town and the townspeople might have been like without George and shows him the results. The picture is bleak: Without a clear-sighted young George Bailey to stop him, the local pharmacist accidentally switched a bottle of poison for medicine and killed a child. Unopposed by George, Mr. Potter reduced the town to crime and poverty. And in the face of despondency, the people of Bedford Falls became churlish and mean-spirited. Gradually, George realizes that although his life goals were not achieved, he is truly a success. He possesses what Mr. Potter with his wealth cannot buy—the respect, appreciation, and loyalty of friends and family.

Scripting for Therapy

Few clients achieve the goals that they set when they were young, but if they learn to value the objectives they have reached, they develop maturity. Therapists can use this film to encourage clients to reassess disappointments about the past. Like George, who eventually sees what his labors have wrought, clients too can put into perspective the gap between what they intended and what came about. Clients often say that if it were not for circumstances (the accidents and unwanted surprises), they would be much happier. But a realistic assessment reveals that these serendipitous events have also brought many of the blessings clients enjoy.

Troubled clients may take their relationships for granted. George has a supportive and loving family, but when faced with scandal, he begins to lose sight of their importance to him. Only after Clarence shows him a world without his loved ones does George set his priorities right. Like-wise, clients in stressful circumstances lose sight of how valuable their intimate relationships are. Therapists can ask clients to put themselves in George's place, to imagine that they are without family or friends. The problems that had overwhelmed them suddenly pale in comparison to the absence of the people they love. Then therapists can ask these clients to return to reality and see these people in a new light. As clients turn back to the problems they face, they may realize that although life is stressful, their loving relationships will sustain them.

Recognizing the strength of those relationships can lead clients to a sense of personal power and control. George feels that he has lost control entirely when his company's deposit is missing on the eve of a bank audit. Unless the money can be found, George will go to prison. Faced with what appears to be an unsolvable problem, he loses sight of the source of his real power—the network of friends in his community. It is that network that finally solves the problem by pooling its resources to make up the lost funds. Therapists can use this film to show clients how to tap into potential sources of power that they may have overlooked.

Perhaps the most important theme in the film is the strength that comes from people helping people. An angel helps George put his problems in perspective, but George's friends save the day. Fighting together against Mr. Potter, they show what can be achieved when people unite. That example is helpful for families who need to learn to stick together when times get tough. Although the tendency at such times may be to fragment, families that join together and ask each individual to contribute to a solution can prevail over obstacles.

We have used this film with couples in the midst of stresses to emphasize the importance of focusing on the problem to be solved, not on the faults of the partner. When couples contend with difficulties, they need to draw closer rather than drift apart, but too often they attack each other and lose sight of what might be accomplished by acting as a team. In this film, a group of people pool their resources to meet a challenge when no one person's contribution would have been sufficient by itself. Therapists can point out that the real power in this film comes from the unity those people achieve, not from the magic of an angel.

Rudy

Rated PG • 112 min. • 1993

Quick Take

A pint-sized athlete sets out to play college football against the advice of his family and friends.

Key Characters

Daniel "Rudy" Ruettiger, Jr. He is up against steep odds to make his dream come true but is willing to pay the price.

Fortune. The groundskeeper at Notre Dame, he becomes Rudy's mentor.

Daniel Ruettiger, Sr. Rudy's dad wants to keep his son from being disillusioned.

Precautions

- May be tedious for clients who are not sports fans.

Categories

Inspiration, friends and support systems, parent–child relationships, transition to adulthood, values and ethics, vocational and work–related issues.

Suggested Viewers

- Adolescent males without role models.
- Adolescents or adults who have trouble sticking with their goals.
- Families, in appreciating individual differences.
- Parents who overprotect their children.

Main Lessons

1. Persistence pays off.
2. Dreams can come true.
3. Families are for support.
4. Statistics aren't always relevant.
5. "It ain't over til it's over."

Setting the Scene

Rudy Ruettiger's dream from childhood is to play football for Notre Dame. On the surface, Rudy is not a good prospect. He is stocky but short, determined but dyslexic. After high school, he fails the Notre Dame entrance exam. So he spends the next two years at Holy Cross College, where he raises his grade point average and saves his money. He has but one goal: to make the Notre Dame practice squad and be in a regulation game for one play.

Only two people besides Rudy believe in his quest: a priest who thinks that with tutoring Rudy can make the grade, and a Notre Dame groundskeeper who believes Rudy can get on the team. Sure enough, after a lot of hard work, Rudy finally meets Notre Dame's academic requirements, and then he gets on the practice squad as a blocking dummy. But he is still miles away from his goal.

His family tells him he is crazy. His brothers say he should be satisfied working at the steel mill where they work. His father tells him to face facts: "Not everyone is meant to go to college." And the girlfriend back home in Joliet finally gets tired of waiting and marries a less ambitious man. Still Rudy persists in doing all he knows how to do to reach his goals. He asks himself only one question: "Am I doing everything I can?"

Along the way, the Notre Dame players become his primary cheering section. These giants who use him for target practice cannot believe that he can take their punishment and more. Rudy is a curiosity on the team at first, but then he starts to symbolize the Notre Dame spirit for them all. Even a highly skeptical coach finally tells his team that they should all have Rudy's courage and spirit. From that point, Rudy is only one step away from his dream.

Scripting for Therapy

Organized sports are adolescent rites of passage in some parts of the country, and football is arguably the highest rite. People who disagree with the custom take potshots at football but miss the point. It is not the game itself, but giving one's best through inevitable disappointments that builds character and teaches life skills. The physical requirements are obvious, but the emotional investment is even more critical. To succeed, an athlete of modest ability must stand up to friends and family who offer rationales to quit. Kids who persist learn that they can handle whatever comes their way. Kids who quit have to learn the lesson of persistence when the stakes are higher and less forgiving. We use this film as a metaphor for the game of life to teach clients to persist in striving for their goals.

Sometimes clients have learned the lesson, but their children have not. One of our clients said he, too, had been too small to play high school football, but through dogged efforts he eventually made the team. His son, however, had quit sports, school, jobs, relationships—projects he would start with enthusiasm but quickly abandon. His father did not know how to help him: "How do I teach him that *everything* gets hard sooner or later, and that's when you have to knuckle down?" The father explained that conversations with his son usually ran aground when the boy would say, "Well, you're different." This client came for therapy before we used VideoWork, but were he in our practice today we would recommend *Rudy* as a way to get through to his son. The boy would not listen to his father, but he might listen to Rudy.

The film, as one reviewer claimed, is more about trying than about winning. We recommended the film to the parents of a boy who had stopped going to classes during his first semester in college. The boy was gifted academically, but in making the transition from high school he had been intimidated by the higher academic requirements. His father had finally withdrawn the boy from school after discovering that he had not gone to a class in more than two months. At the time the family came for therapy, the boy was living at home and playing video games on the Internet. His parents wanted him to get a job, but they were "afraid of traumatizing him."

After the parents watched the film, they discussed how Rudy grew stronger through facing adversity. No one, the parents pointed out, had protected him. Rudy's father —although no model of ideal parenting— had ironically forced Rudy to test himself and develop his skills. By contrast, these parents said they had done everything possible to make their son's life easy. They concluded that they had made a mistake in fighting his battles for him. And they decided that although they could not guarantee his success, they could at least stop contributing to his failure. The parents worked out a reasonable plan to place the burden of change where it logically should have been.

By taking an ordinary talent and making the best of it, Rudy is a strong male role model for adolescents transitioning into adulthood. But the film is inspirational to young and old alike; what works for Rudy is within reach of most of us. He demonstrates that when we are willing to pay the price, we can bring about good results.

The Shawshank Redemption
Rated R • 144 min. • 1994

Quick Take

Life inside a state prison in which natural consequences prevail.

Key Characters

Andy Dufresne. Imprisoned for a crime he did not commit, he must find ways to survive the system, his fellow inmates, and the slow passage of time.

"Red" Redding. He's a lifer in danger of becoming institutionalized.

Precautions

- Rape scene.
- Strong language.
- Nudity.
- Explicit sexuality.

Categories

Inspiration, communication and conflict resolution, friends and support systems, grief and loss.

Suggested Viewers

- Persons contending with overwhelming obstacles.
- Clients who feel trapped.
- Groups, regarding principles of leadership.
- Adolescents who feel wronged and want revenge.

Main Lessons

---

1. Seemingly hopeless situations can be improved through applying learned skills.
2. Complaining is wasted energy. Don't get mad, get even.
3. Empowerment happens when people assume personal responsibility for action.
4. Never give in to oppression. Survival is a right and is instinctual.
5. When planning an escape, the less said the better.

Setting the Scene

As the "new fish" parade in front of their prison cells, the old timers make bets on which ones will break first. Red Redding bets on Andy Dufresne, a lanky, fresh-faced, young man obviously out of his element. But Red loses the bet when Andy refuses to cry during the first night, and in coming weeks, Andy evidences an understated power not often seen at Shawshank Prison. No matter what he has to deal with, Andy finds a way to cope. He is not a violent man. But he will not accept abuse, and he fights back when he must.

Andy has skills that soon enhance his value in the prison system. An accountant, he begins doing the warden's books, helping the warden cover up shady dealings. Word spreads and other administrators line up for Andy's advice on investments and pension plans. That advice gives Andy the clout to, for instance, get cold beers on a hot day for inmate friends working on a roof. In prison, what counts among the inmates is who is strong and who is not, who can get things done. Andy is a guy who gets things done.

He and Red become good friends. Red has to go before the parole board every year and pitch his case. "It's been 10 (then 20, then 30) years. Do you think you're rehabilitated yet?" With the predictable rejections, Red is in danger of getting trapped by the system. One old lifer, who later commits suicide when released, explains the trap succinctly: "First you hate it, then you accept it, finally you come to need it." Andy, however, maintains his own agenda and never puts hope in the possibility of parole. Red draws strength from his friend's no-nonsense approach. But

Andy does not merely intend to make Shawshank a better place to live. A surprising conclusion reveals his long-secret strategy.

Scripting for Therapy

There are some situations that people cannot simply walk away from: jobs they hate but cannot leave, babies born before the parents are ready to have them, growing up in a mismatched family. Clients who are imprisoned in life circumstances they did not choose (or have come to dislike) face the same choices that Andy Dufresne does. His response, and what therapists can teach their clients, can be summed up in the following points.

- Andy makes himself needed. Although being in prison is a long way from working in a bank, he finds ways to apply his financial skills. Oftentimes when clients are stuck, they overlook the skills they have to make things better.
- Although imprisoned, Andy exerts what control he can. Some inmates let themselves be used sexually; he fights back every time he is attacked. The message he sends his attackers is that although they can overpower him, he will exact a heavy price. Clients say, "I'm tired of fighting," but they need to realize that if they stop fighting, things probably will get worse.
- Andy does not complain uselessly. Although innocent of the crime that sent him to Shawshank, he doesn't try to convince people who can do nothing to change the situation. In contrast, clients expend energy on useless complaints that create a climate of despair in which effective action is unlikely. They should learn to make their efforts count, know what they want and go for it, and play politics when it's the right thing to do. Anger is not a strategy.
- Andy keeps his own counsel. He doesn't share his *real* plan with anybody. If he had, it probably would have failed. Effective plans always have some element that is undisclosed. There are times to talk with others, and times to remain silent. Clients should learn to recognize when each is appropriate. In certain situations (domestic abuse, for example), it is necessary for clients to trust themselves and their instincts.

- Andy bases hope on what he knows he can do. He does not believe in the parole system or in a sudden admission of guilt by the real killer. When therapists ask clients what would make their situations better, the answer may be, "If I win the lottery" or "If my partner stops being so selfish." But clients need to see that positive change happens only when they assume responsibility and take their own actions.

Another interesting theme in the film is the friendship between Red and Andy. Red is at first a mentor, the old timer who can help Andy adjust to life in the prison. But Red soon sees that Andy has unique gifts. The relationship that follows is highly adaptive, based on trust and abilities. Their friendship is the model of a flexible relationship in which the two change roles as the need arises. By contrast, clients describe relationships that are imbalanced: either they are dependent on others or they are the caretakers. Andy and Red are willing to be leader or follower as circumstances require.

INTIMATE RELATIONSHIPS

About Last Night
Rated R • 116 min. • 1986

Quick Take

Danny and Debbie discover the difference between dating and long-term relationships.

Key Characters

Danny. He wants intimacy with a woman but is afraid to be emotionally vulnerable and fully committed.

Debbie. She is tired of being single, but she will not settle for a relationship that is less than honest.

Bernie and Joan. They are the best friends who try to sabotage the relationship.

Precautions

- Nudity.
- Explicit sexuality.
- Strong language.
- Recreational drug use.

Categories

Intimate relations, communication and conflict resolution, friends and support systems, men's issues, transition to adulthood, women's issues.

Suggested Viewers

- Couples, regarding better communication of feelings.
- Individuals who fear commitment or who suppress their emotions.
- Young couples making a transition from the single life.

Main Lessons

1. In mature relationships, people know who they are apart from their partner.
2. Intimate relationships depend on honestly sharing feelings and concerns, not just sex.
3. Relationships suffer when friends or family become too involved. Clear limits should be set.
4. Couples should learn that sharing emotions need not lead to dependence. Confiding to another person that one hurts emotionally does not mean that one is asking for rescue.
5. Having a close relationship means confronting inevitable conflicts and not withdrawing.

Setting the Scene

It is love at first sight for Danny and Debbie. Although she has a rule of no sex on the first date, she breaks it for him. He phones her twice the next week. His friend Bernie says that means commitment and warns him to back off while there is still time. But Debbie's roommate, Joan, interprets two calls to mean that he was with somebody else. Nevertheless, true love somehow finds a way, and Danny and Debbie overcome the self-serving advice from their best friends. Soon they decide to share an apartment. But on moving day, Joan and Bernie, feeling abandoned, warn their friends that they are making a terrible mistake.

The real difficulties begin once they are living together, because they handle problems in different ways. Debbie is open; she shares the good as well as the bad. But Danny wants to keep his troubles to himself. The discrepancy surfaces the day Danny's boss orders him to stop doing business with an old customer who has fallen on hard times. Danny refuses and goes home in a bad mood. Debbie knows that something is wrong, and she invites him to confide in her. But he plays it cool, and although he is obviously upset, he denies that anything is bothering him. When she presses him to tell the truth, he explodes and pulls away. Eventually he explains what was going on, but their argument sets the pattern for how they will deal with conflict in the future.

Scripting for Therapy

The film highlights four important tasks in young relationships:

1. Drawing a distinction between one's identity as an individual and in a partnership: "Who am I" versus "who are we."
2. Becoming interdependent rather than dependent.
3. Communicating effectively.
4. Drawing boundaries with friends.

Who Am I? versus Who Are We? When they first meet, Danny and Debbie do not know what they want out of life, let alone who they are. Their jobs are not important; they skip work to play. The word "family" is mentioned only when Debbie is washing the dishes after a Thanksgiving feast and says to Joan, "I've just turned into my mother." Neither has a sense of vocation, a functioning set of ethics, or a meaningful heritage. Neither has, in short, an identity.

Therapists can use these characters to illustrate to clients the importance of developing self-identity before entering into long-term relationships. Like many clients, these characters travel quickly from their families-of-origin into adult relationships. They do not take the time to develop as individuals, but seek another to assist them in that task. They become a reflection of what the other person wants, which is not satisfactory to either. When clients try to be whom their partner wants them to be, they are not being true to themselves. Their first task is to establish their own identity, and that task requires time and experience. Many clients look for a short cut. Therapists can emphasize that two half-developed personalities do not make a whole and that an investment in finding one's identity is well worth the effort.

Becoming Interdependent Rather Than Dependent. Danny is afraid to share his problems with Debbie because his notion of being a man means not showing weakness; sad feelings mean he is weak. He fears that if she sees his imperfections, she will use that knowledge to hurt him. Furthermore, in his mind, revealing uncertainty means asking for rescue, which leads in turn to dependency. And he is afraid of becoming dependent on her.

Therapists often have clients who are either too dependent on others or too isolated. One person in a relationship clings while the other is distant. Neither viewpoint makes for a mature relationship. Young couples have to find a balance between these two extremes. Therapists should discuss ways that clients in relationships can help each other and still maintain autonomy.

Communicating Effectively in Intimate Relationships. In the singles lifestyle of the couple in this film, first impressions appear to be everything. Decisions about desirable prospects are made rapidly and based on superficial information. Danny and Debbie fall for each other initially because they are physically attracted to each other. But that attraction is not enough to carry them through the next stage of their intimacy. For that stage, they will have to genuinely listen to the other and respond with empathy.

Single clients who are most successful in attracting partners can be least successful in making the transition to long-term relationships. People who attract other people easily may do so because they sell the sizzle rather than the steak. Therapists can use this film to show clients that successful long-term relationships depend on a new set of communication skills based on honestly sharing their feelings. Intimacy grows when partners are willing to reveal their liabilities as well as their assets.

Drawing Boundaries with Friends. Joan is bitter, cynical, and self-defeating. Bernie is a womanizing alcoholic. But Danny and Debbie allow these friends to interfere in their relationship. Why? Having little sense of individual identity, the two lovers have not determined what roles friends should play. They are defenseless against the sabotage their friends carry out and do not see how self-serving their friends' advice really is.

Clients often describe the same situation. Friends or families have too much power to influence choices. Boundaries must be drawn. Clients need to determine in what areas they alone should make decisions. They may ask friends for advice, but should balance that advice against their own thoughts and against the usefulness of the advice of others in whom they confide.

Groundhog Day

Rated PG • 103 min. • 1993

Quick Take

A narcissistic young man grows up after time stops on Groundhog Day.

Key Characters

Phil Connors. He's a self-involved television meteorologist who is denied the love of his life.

Rita. She wants more than a superficial relationship.

Precautions

- Mild sexuality.
- Profanity.

Categories

Intimate relationships, communication and conflict resolution, men's issues, transition to adulthood, values and ethics, vocational and work-related issues.

Suggested Viewers

- Narcissists with a sense of humor.
- Couples, regarding communication.
- Individuals searching for personal identity.

Main Lessons

1. Others are not usually to blame for one's problems.
2. Positive growth comes from admitting one doesn't have all the answers.
3. Personal growth is a series of lessons mastered one by one.
4. Life is meaningless unless one learns from the process.
5. Good guys sometimes finish first!

Setting the Scene

The setting is Punxsutawney, Pennsylvania, where the town's beloved groundhog appears each February 2 to predict the arrival of spring. Phil Connors, a television meteorologist, is on hand with his crew to cover the event. He is planning to leave after picking up a sound-bite, but despite his forecast of sunny skies, Phil gets stuck in a blizzard and must lay over until the storm passes. Problem is, the storm is *never* going to pass for Phil. Like a space traveler in a time warp, he wakes each morning to Groundhog Day.

Phil consults a local psychologist, who is baffled and tells him ironically to come back the next day. Phil is miffed but tries to make the best of things. After all, he can do whatever he likes without worrying about consequences. So he eats jelly-filled doughnuts by the score, drinks himself into oblivion, and takes a dive from a church steeple just for laughs. In short, he lives out a narcissist's fantasy, having it his way all the time. But to Phil's chagrin, he finds that it's no use. The more he gets, the more he wants. And the more miserable he is.

So he decides that true happiness lies in seducing Rita, his producer. With the benefit of hindsight, he sets about the task systematically, noting each of her likes and dislikes. When she says she likes poetry, he appears the next evening with a book of her favorite poems. When she orders a special drink, the next day he orders it for her. But no matter what he tries with his time-travel hocus pocus, he doesn't succeed with Rita. She's not quite sure why, but she does not trust Phil.

Failing all else, Phil reverts to simple honesty. He rescues children who fall from trees, changes tires for stranded motorists, and offers a kind word to those in need. He stops laughing at the hicks and starts enjoying them. Most importantly, he gives up trying to trick Rita into loving him and settles instead for an appreciation of their time together. His evolution surprises no one so much as himself. "No matter what happens tomorrow or the rest of my life," he concludes, "I'm happy now." And with that conclusion, Phil's life falls back into place.

Scripting for Therapy

We like this film because it is an all-purpose, fail-safe VideoWork assignment, a comedy with a protagonist so repugnant that our clients know we are not identifying them with him. The story, however, is a perfect analogy for the frustrations that clients often describe. Waking each day to the same set of tiresome problems strikes a chord with many people. Events do seem to repeat themselves endlessly, and no matter what they try, things never seem to work out. After watching Phil go through all those stages before he finally instigates personal changes, clients are encouraged to reframe their own problems from "one damned thing after another" to learning to cope and moving on to fresh challenges.

Phil's confinement in Punxsutawney, a terrible accident to him, proves to be his salvation. Change for Phil, although difficult, is possible. But he changes for the better only after his repertoire of cons is depleted. He must wrestle with his dilemma to the point of exhaustion. Only when he gives up does he discover a response that will solve his problem and get his life back on course.

Phil's journey begins as an infantile personality and ends with the potential for mature love. At the outset, he is not a candidate for a healthy relationship. His television personality is sufficient only for shallow affairs from which he can run when they get difficult. But because Rita is not interested in anything less than a whole relationship, he must look deeply into himself. What he sees through her eyes is that he is a user. To Phil, other people are not persons but merely a means for self-gratification.

Phil blames everybody else when things do not go the way he wants. Setbacks are never his fault. But this rationalization doesn't hold up as Groundhog Day repeats itself. People respond to Phil in a number of ways, but things still don't work out. Finally, he looks into the mirror and sees a person who wakes up every day stuck in the same place. He realizes that he alone must take responsibility for his problems because he is the one who is always around when things go bad.

This film can be viewed as a metaphor for therapy. Clients arrive with the problems they have not been able to solve through coping skills learned in the past. They are stuck. Moreover, many of these clients believe they are stuck because of others. They blame their parents, spouse, or boss for keeping them from being as happy as they think they should be. When these clients say they want change, they usually mean that somebody else should make the changes. They are frustrated because nobody cooperates with that fantasy.

Therapists encourage clients to take responsibility for their problems and stop the blame game. Clients improve by making basic changes in their behavior and in their attitudes toward others. For instance, a narcissistic client who complains that his wife is making an unreasonable demand by asking him to help out more around the house can begin to see that her demand is not only reasonable but also leads to a more satisfying relationship. His wife is simply asking that he start participating in the marriage. As long as clients blame other people, they are, like Phil Connors, stuck in insoluble problems. Clients get better when they look to themselves for solutions.

 **MARRIAGE**

The Bridges of Madison County
PG–13 • 130 min. • 1995

Quick Take

A fling that a lonely housewife has with a stranger passing through town becomes the love of her life and changes her forever.

Key Characters

Robert Kincaid. He's an unattached photographer with many loves but no commitments.

Francesca Johnson. She has been living on an Iowa farm for 20 years, married to a decent but emotionally distant man. Will she leave him and her two children for the stranger who offers romance?

Precautions

- Sexual situations.
- Brief nudity.
- Profanity.
- Therapists should be judicious in recommending the film to clients in troubled marriages, because the protagonist considers ending her own marriage.

Categories

Marriage, affairs, communication and conflict resolution, family-of-origin issues, grief and loss, death and dying, intimate relationships, parent–child relationships, women's issues.

Suggested Viewers

- Couples who have lost a sense of passion in their relationship.
- Grown children trying to understand their parents' life decisions.
- "Macho men" who need to learn about tenderness.

Main Lessons

---

1. Commitment is more than immediate gratification.
2. Communication is essential in keeping love alive.
3. Children learn from choices of their parents.
4. Partners must make decisions from a long-term rather than a short-term perspective.
5. An old love can never compare with an affair filled with romance and intensity. But it is risky to expect the new love to grow comfortable and self-sustaining with the passing of time.

Setting the Scene

After Francesca Johnson's death, her grown children discover that she left instructions to be cremated and her ashes strewn from a nearby bridge. They are horrified by the idea, but they find a letter to them explaining her unusual burial request.

Francesca's story begins the day she stayed at home while the rest of the family went to the state fair. As she is adjusting to welcomed time alone, a handsome, middle–aged man in a pickup truck stops by the house to ask directions. His name is Robert Kincaid, and he is on assignment from *National Geographic* to photograph covered bridges in Iowa. She rides with him to the bridge he is planning to shoot, and when he brings her back, she invites him in for a glass of ice tea. Supper follows, then more conversation, then a walk in the moonlight. By the time he leaves late that evening, they have fallen deeply in love.

Until that day, Francesca had been reasonably content, if not happy, with her traditional role as wife and mother despite isolation from an uncommunicative spouse. But Robert's unexpected arrival rekindles a sleeping sensuality, feelings she believed she had lost. Sitting alone after he has gone, she knows she must see him again. The next day she goes to town and buys the first dress she has bought for herself in years.

For the next three days, the two are not out of each other's sight. Francesca has yearned for the physical and emotional intimacy that Robert brings. And she makes him reconsider his decision to avoid committed relationships. When the time comes for him to leave, they know a choice must be made.

Scripting for Therapy

The outcome of the film reaffirms traditional values, albeit with an untraditional spin. Although Francesca has an affair with Robert, she decides that remaining with her family is the right course for her. She makes that decision not through loving Robert less or her husband more, but because marriage is permanent for her.

Clients in troubled relationships often consider similar dilemmas. They wonder if a more fulfilling relationship is waiting in the wings if they divorce. They may believe that their children are mature enough to handle a disruption, that romance has long been absent from their marriage, and that they need one last chance to find happiness. In effect, they reduce their decision to a checklist of positive and negatives: "11 reasons to stay; 17 to leave."

This film takes the focus away from such an arbitrary process and places it squarely on the meaning of commitment. Francesca has ample reasons to leave her husband, but she considers the effect that her leaving would have on her family. She believes that she cannot enjoy her love for Robert if it is overlaid by the guilt of having brought pain to her husband and children. And she respects the vows she had made to her husband, who, as she says, had done nothing to deserve her betrayal. In the end, those vows outweigh the absence of passion in her marriage.

To help clients think about their marriages while discussing this film, we suggest the following questions:

- Assuming you do leave your marriage, in what ways will your life be better in 10 years?
- If you have defined your present relationship as committed, what does commitment mean to you?
- How much does the degree of commitment you are willing to enter into depend on transient states (i.e., the health of your partner, your feelings for your partner)?
- What are the differences between a committed relationship and a romantic one?

- How does the argument that Francesca gave for remaining with her family agree or disagree with your thoughts about *your* relationship?

The Four Seasons
Rated PG • 108 min. • 1981

Quick Take

Couples learn about keeping love alive through changes in their group of friends.

Key Characters

Jack and Kate Burroughs.   He wants to control everybody and everything. She sees through him, but guards his ego.
Nick and Ann Callan.   They are the perfect couple, who fell out of love years before.
Danny and Claudia Zimmer.   He is anxious about everything. She tries to overlook his faults.
Ginny Newley.   She is the outsider who finds breaking into a tight group of friends a daunting task.

Precautions

- Brief nudity.
- Profanity.
- Sexual situations.
- A couple reacts to marital problems by choosing to divorce.

Categories

Marriage, affairs, aging, communication and conflict resolution, divorce, friends and support systems, grief and loss, intimate relationships, men's issues, stepparenting and blended families, women's issues.

Suggested Viewers

- Long-term partners who take each other for granted.
- Couples contemplating divorce.
- Clients dealing with friends or parents who divorce.

Main Lessons

1. Mature love takes work.
2. Entering new life stages requires reassessment and reordering of priorities to meet the changing needs.
3. Couples can grow together through commitment and flexibility.
4. Friendship involves compassionate honesty.
5. A friend's divorce can be a wake-up call for one's own marriage.

Setting the Scene

The Burroughs, Callans, and Zimmers are lifelong friends whose teasing sometimes gets out of hand. Ann Callan is a photographer who has spent the last year photographing three vegetables. Her husband Nick is a high-powered salesman. He has no respect for her, nor she for him. When he calls himself an estate planner "in the million-dollar roundtable," she sets the record straight: "Don't be silly, Nick. You're nothing but a life insurance salesman. That award got you a plastic statue and a trip to Puerto Rico."

Nick tells his best friend, Jack, that he has decided to get a divorce because he has been miserable for years. But Jack is furious that Nick would divorce and even angrier that Nick did not tell him sooner. Nick's decision stirs up feelings in his other friends too. They wonder why he cannot accept the ups and downs of married life as they do.

On the group's next vacation together, a bareboat sailing adventure, they listen through thin cabin walls to Nick and his new girlfriend, Ginny. They conclude that Nick is not acting his age, that he has lost his sense of direction, and that it is his fault that the group is drifting apart. Meanwhile, Jack and Danny cast lustful eyes on Ginny in her bikini. Eventually everybody realizes that what bothers them so much is that Nick has found what they have lost: the pizzazz.

Scripting for Therapy

This film addresses how long-term relationships stay vital. It facilitates such questions as: How do couples balance the need for personal growth against the demands of commitment? How can long-term relationships

209

be nourished? When good friends divorce, how does one continue to be a friend to both? Couples fall out of love (and friendships fail to mature) when the partners cease to grow; acceptance of the good times as well as the bad is necessary.

In the beginning, the group is too ritualized, too predictable, just like their long-term marriages. What appears as a spontaneous outpouring of feasting, song, and banter is a tightly scripted rite meant to protect them from the ravages of approaching old age. When Nick divorces Ann, their friends reevaluate their own marriages. What was acceptable before— Kate's complying with Jack's overcontrol, Claudia's quiet endurance of Danny's whining—becomes problematic. The group stops joking so much and starts arguing more. Nick's refusal to live in a loveless marriage forces the rest to examine what they are putting up with in their own marriages.

For clients, the threat of a divorce, or an affair, can serve much the same purpose. Couples endure years of minimal joy and unacknowledged resentment until one partner reaches a point of overload. If the couple has enough love left to look beyond the symptoms that emerge, they recognize the real problems that brought about the crisis. Once they verbalize what is wrong, they can agree to helpful changes. Clients should understand that recognizing significant marital differences does not inevitably lead to divorce; it can be an opportunity to make things better.

The film illustrates how burnout surfaces in relationships. When viewed from a stress model, the friends have all (with the exception of Nick) moved from the stage of alarm to the stage of adaptation. Before Nick's divorce, the group sees nothing wrong because they have grown accustomed to mediocrity. But Nick's love affair makes them recall what they no longer have together. When they hear the lovers cooing and cuddling, the friends are jealous. They realize that it has been years since they felt in their marriages the excitement that Nick and Ginny share. They want that back in their relationships too.

The film points out the value of cultivating good friends as an effective social support network. When couples isolate themselves, events may prove too formidable to be withstood. Friends are necessary, and the characters in this film recognize that. As Kate says to Jack at one point, "I don't want to grow old with just the two of us. I want to have friends around me." Good friendships, however, are built on honest confrontation and unconditional positive regard. The friendships in this film endure not because they are always running smoothly, but because these characters value each other and are willing to work things out.

MEN'S ISSUES AND WOMEN'S ISSUES

How to Make an American Quilt
Rated PG-13 • 116 min. • 1995

Quick Take

A young woman gets cold feet on the threshold of marriage. She spends a summer with relatives sorting things out.

Key Characters

Finn.   She's a college student with difficulties in committing to anybody or anything.

Grasse Quilting Bee.   As they quilt, they share their joys and sorrows.

Precautions

- Recreational drug use among senior citizens.
- Profanity.
- Premarital sex.
- Nudity.

Categories

Women's issues, affairs, aging, communication and conflict resolution, divorce, friends and support systems, grief and loss, intimate relationships,

---

Main Lessons

1. Forgiveness is an essential element in long-term relationships.
2. Emotional pain heals with time.
3. Having a support system of friends is necessary throughout one's life.
4. Affairs always damage relationships.
5. Older people can offer perspectives that peers cannot.

---

marriage, parent-child relationships, transition to adulthood, vocational and work-related issues.

Suggested Viewers

- Women dealing with commitment issues.
- Clients with destructive secrets in their family history.
- Clients who need to learn to forgive.

Setting the Scene

A Berkeley graduate student named Finn is having second thoughts about marrying her fiancee, Sam. He is a sweet man, but she finds him a little dull, not exactly the love of her life. He is, however, stable, and that is a quality she needs. She is working on her third dissertation, and this one is bogged down, too. Sam, on the other hand, is good at finishing things. Still, Finn wonders about romance. How can she agree to a lifetime commitment without feeling that special something?

To find the answer, she visits her maternal grandmother and great-aunt for a summer of soul-searching. It is a good place to go for advice. The women host a group called the Grasse Quilting Bee, made up of friends who gather to sew and reflect on their lives. This summer they intend to sew Finn's wedding quilt, made from squares of cloth that tell "where love resides." The bits and pieces of cloth symbolize wisdom obtained at a heavy price.

Indeed, the meaning that these women can find in the tattered remains of their relationships with men will go a long way in convincing Finn to marry. During the summer, Finn learns that marriage often means setting aside personal dreams, dealing with disappointments, and being willing to forgive. None of the women have entered middle age unscathed. But despite their tales of love's hard path, the group assumes that Finn too will soon be a married woman. Finn herself is not so sure.

Scripting for Therapy

Forgiveness is a major theme of the film. Each woman achieves a sense of peace to the extent that she forgives others for their transgressions— friends as well as husbands. Finn's aunt, Glady Joe, had discovered that her husband had a brief affair with her sister, and Glady Joe had built a wall of broken china. Through the years as she endured other disappointments, the wall grew taller. But after her husband's death, she suddenly tore it down. Why? She could not say. It just seemed she had resented him long enough.

Clients can discuss their own relationships in this light. We asked a couple to watch the film because their marriage was hampered by resentments. Several years before, they had divorced, then remarried. While they were apart, the woman had a brief but intense relationship with a high-school sweetheart. The husband had never forgiven her. After they watched the film, he said that he understood Glady Joe's need to build a wall. He had done much the same himself by refusing to let intimacy back into his marriage. He found it sad that Glady Joe had waited until her husband died before letting go of her resentments. It made him realize that his own marriage could not get back on track until he let go of his anger. As a result, he told his wife that although he could not forget the past, he was not going to let it ruin the love they had rediscovered.

Affairs are an undercurrent in the film. A woman named Em remains in a problematic marriage to an unfaithful husband, urged on by her parents who say it is her duty to stay with him no matter what. In the years that follow, he falls in love with a number of other women, and she finally decides to get a divorce. As she is walking through his studio on her way out, she sees for the first time a group of portraits he had painted each year. She was the one abiding subject of his art and, despite his infidelities, his one true love.

The question, of course, is whether this discovery really changes anything at all. Clients often ask this question about relationships in which a partner continues to behave inappropriately but swears fealty. Can hurtful behavior be pardoned because the heart of the transgressor is in the right place? Clients may find that they disagree with Em's decision to stay.

To some of these women, marriage has meant losing personal dreams. Sophia was a beautiful young woman who looked forward to a life of adventures. But her mother told her that she was not attractive enough to be on her own, so she decides to marry a geologist who promises to show her the world. They quickly have three children. Her geologist husband continues to pursue his vocation, but Sophia is confined to responsibilities of parenthood. Her dream is lost, and she becomes cynical and hard. Then, in a twist of fate, the husband who promised her the world leaves her as he found her except with children to rear. Clients might discuss options Sophia failed to exercise, choices she could have made that might have changed her situation for the better.

In their friendships with each other, the women in the film listen a lot and give limited advice. The men do not listen as well. The women ask for understanding, but the men misconstrue those requests as appeals for rescue. Male clients can learn from the film that intimacy requires an ability to empathize and that partners often are not asking for answers as much as expressing a need to be heard with compassion and without criticism.

Another issue of interest in this film is how young people benefit from the wisdom of older people. Young clients often try to solve their problems by taking advice exclusively from peers. But experience does count, and this film shows the value of seeking guidance from older persons. Adult mentors have not only faced similar problems but have also experienced the consequences of different courses of action. The film is helpful in encouraging an openness to the perspective that older generations bring.

The film also emphasizes the need for clients to find and maintain a support system of friends. Over an extended period of time, the women in this film have seen each other through a number of crises. They value their friendships. By contrast, many clients, married or not, view same-sex friendships as unimportant. This film shows that a support system offers nurture, understanding, and a different and helpful point of view.

Nothing in Common
Rated PG • 120 min. • 1986

Quick Take

A son reconciles with his father through caring for him after his divorce.

Key Characters

David Basner. He had given up on his father years before, but he cannot turn his back on the man when he is in need.

215

Max Basner. He had always boasted that he needed no one. When he becomes ill, he fears that no one will be around.

Precautions

- Sexual situations.
- Profanity.

Categories

Men's issues, aging, chronic illness and disabilities, communication and conflict resolution, death and dying, divorce, family-of-origin issues, friends and support systems, grief and loss, marriage, parent-child relationships, vocational and work-related issues.

Suggested Viewers

- Adult children of divorcing parents.
- Estranged family members.
- Couples with communication problems.
- Clients with family-of-origin issues.

Setting the Scene

David Basner is basically a nice guy, a high-octane achiever whose employees love him for taking them along on his rise to the top. His advertising agency is pursuing a lucrative contract with an airline, and Basner is the man they are counting on. Everything is rosy until he gets a call from his dad. It has been years since David had seen his father, and he still blames the man for not being around while David was growing up.

Main Lessons

1. Putting energy into repairing a breach with one's parents is worth the effort.
2. Forgiveness is essential in relationships.
3. You can love without condoning a person's lifestyle.
4. In strained relationships, somebody has to make the first move.
5. People who are unlovable need love nevertheless.

When his father says that David's mother wants a divorce, his first inclination is to hang up. But for some reason, he does not. Instead, he agrees to help them work things out.

Max Basner is a peddler who is fast with the jokes but hates life. He is bitter, isolated, and convinced that everybody is out to get him. He holes up in a dreary apartment staring at the floor and listening to Dixieland jazz. But after years of his verbal abuse, his wife blossoms when she finally walks out. David shuttles between his parents, encouraging his mother to spread her wings and trying to cheer up his depressed father. His mother will not go back, and he does not blame her.

In the coming weeks, David learns a lot about his parents. When his mother goes out for an evening and returns in tears because her date tried to kiss her, he demands an explanation from his father. "What did you do to her?" he asks. "Well since you ask," his father says, "I'll tell you. Your mother was frigid, so I went out and got what she couldn't give me." Ironically, the admission draws father and son closer. They are, after all, speaking honestly for the first time.

Suddenly Max is diagnosed with diabetes and is hospitalized. He wants to leave, but David forces him to follow his doctor's advice and undergo surgery. Max may lose both legs, and he is afraid but will not admit it. He wants his son to stay by his side, but he is too proud to ask. David stays and Max is shocked. "You're the last person I figured would come through for me."

Scripting for Therapy

Parental divorce is a crisis no matter what the child's age. David is in his 30s, but his parents' separation is as disruptive as if he were in his teens. He and his father have a strained relationship. Yet when his parents' dysfunctional marriage ends, it throws David's whole world into disarray. Through trying to help his father, David hopes to bring his life back to normal. He discovers that his parents' relationship, good or bad, is something he had always taken for granted. This film shows that even when children and their parents drift apart, a divorce still has far-reaching repercussions.

Clients often describe situations in which they would like to forgive relatives who have caused them harm, but other members of the family

217

will have no part of it. How does one reconcile with someone who is unapproachable? How does one forgive a person who doesn't ask for forgiveness? In this film, the father's infidelities and emotional absence have harmed his son as well as his wife, but Max is convinced he is the victim, not the aggressor. David knows that his father is not going to see things differently, not even as he nears his life's end. But David wants to forgive his father and enjoy the time they have left together, so he endures the put-downs and is quietly persistent in his offers of help. More important, David understands that the rage his father expresses is a substitute for the fear and loneliness he feels inside.

Relationships become more intense as people age, particularly when conflicts have not been resolved. Clients who believe that they have left behind their struggles when they move away from home are often surprised when a crisis opens the wounds. Before his father's telephone call, David rarely thought of his parents. He imagined that as he became more successful, they would quietly drift away; family conflicts would not be resolved so much as forgotten. That illusion was shattered when his parents separated. David was forced to confront the issues he had run away from in order to gain closure with his family.

This film also contains insights into the fears of severely ill medical patients. Clients sometimes ask why relatives choose the moment of critical illness to "show their true colors." They complain that the person who is ill should be grateful to helpers and cultivate a support system for the hard days ahead. But severe illness intensifies personality traits. In this film, Max knows he is very ill and he is terrified of death. He covers up his anxiety with bravado, but the fear is obvious in moments when he is alone. Max acts out because it is the response he knows best when under stress. David understands and gives his father the support he needs.

The Turning Point

Rated PG • 119 min. • 1977

Quick Take

Two old friends question choices they made about career and family.

Key Characters

Deedee Rodgers. She loves her family but wonders what she might have been.

Emma Jacklin. An aging ballet star at the end of her career, she has nowhere to go.

Precautions

- Premarital sex.
- Profanity.
- Long ballet sequences may be tedious for some clients.
- Unplanned pregnancy.

Categories

Women's issues, aging, communication and conflict resolution, friends and support systems, grief and loss, intimate relationships, marriage, parent-child relationships, transition to adulthood, vocational and work-related issues.

Suggested Viewers

- Clients making career and family decisions.
- Couples, regarding parenting questions.
- Persons who have become isolated from friends.
- Clients who are questioning their decisions of the past.

Main Lessons

1. What might have been is less important than what is.
2. Loving other people means granting them the freedom to search for their own answers.
3. Parents eventually have to let go of their older adolescents and encourage them to make their own choices.
4. Life involves choices. Not all roads can be taken.
5. Midlife reassessments are natural for men, women, and couples.

Setting the Scene

The American Ballet Company visits Oklahoma City. In the audience is Deedee Rodgers, who once was a promising ballerina before she quit to rear children. As she watches an electrifying performance by her best friend and former rival, Emma Jacklin, she ponders what might have happened if their lives had been reversed. Deedee remembers with lingering resentment that it was Emma who encouraged her not to have an abortion after learning she was pregnant; it was Emma who said that Deedee's husband, Wayne, would never forgive her if she did not have the baby. But in the years that followed, Deedee had questioned that advice, because once Deedee quit the company, Emma had gone on to stardom.

After the performance, the Rodgers host a reception at which the friends reminisce about old times. Deedee says she is happy to be a wife and mother, but she occasionally fantasizes about changing places. Emma is amazed by her envy. At the end of her career, with no family of her own, Emma finds many reasons to be jealous of Deedee.

One of Deedee's children, Emilia, is a beautiful young woman with a passion for ballet. She is a talented ballerina who already has professional experience. Emma volunteers to help Emilia join the ballet company for the summer. A few days later, Emilia and her mother leave for New York City. Although Deedee hopes to share in her daughter's excitement, she is treated like any other stage mother once rehearsals and classes begin. The mother-daughter ties weaken further as Emilia's friendship with her new mentor grows and as she is enticed by the glamour of an international troupe. Emilia falls in love with a Russian ballet star named Yuri, but quickly discovers that his affections are not exclusively her own. When he is unfaithful, she turns to Emma rather than to her mother. Deedee once again plays backup to her rival.

In the season's gala, Emilia dances brilliantly and is celebrated as a rising star—the mantle is passed from mentor to student. Just as Deedee must accept a diminished role in Emilia's life, so Emma must be content in her protégé's eclipse. In this heated emotional atmosphere, the strained feelings between the two old friends escalate. The tension comes to a head when Deedee delivers a biting insult and Emma douses her with champagne; the two follow up with a vicious fight. Once they are exhausted, the two women strike a truce. The unspoken resolution is that each woman made the life choice that was right for her.

Scripting for Therapy

Opportunities arise and people make choices. They imagine that if things do not work out as they plan, they can change directions. But life gets complicated. They have children, leave jobs, and move to places in which the old possibilities do not exist. With the approach of old age, people find it hard not to wonder what might have been, not to yearn for the road not taken.

Clients who question their choices will appreciate Deedee's dilemma. On the one hand, she loves her family. On the other, she longs to return to her first love of performing as a ballerina. Deedee discovers that although it is too late for her to reverse a decision made 20 years before, she *can* enjoy (but should not envy) the success of her daughter. Just as Emma must accept that she is no longer an ingenue, Deedee must accept the consequences of her decision to have a family.

Other relationships in this film are useful for clients. Deedee's husband, Wayne, shows how love entails risk. He recognizes the dangers in encouraging his wife to go with their daughter to New York. She could find someone else; she might leave him. Wayne knows that Deedee is in the midst of a midlife crisis and that her resolution of that crisis may destroy their marriage. He knows also, however, that if she does not resolve her questions, she will always be dissatisfied. When he encourages her to leave for the summer, she asks, "Are you trying to get rid of me?" He answers, "I'm trying to keep you." He demonstrates that no one preserves love by clutching it too tightly. Partners in the best relationships allow each other the freedom to ask hard questions and search for answers.

Another issue that the film introduces is the importance of mentors. The poet Robert Bly said that older men should mentor younger men, passing on what they have learned. This process celebrates the worth of the older man while initiating the younger one into the world of adults. In this film, Emma initiates Emilia into an artistic world of ballet as well as into adulthood. Emma manages her own grief over the loss of her physical abilities by training and promoting the career of a younger woman.

The relationship between Emilia and Yuri also merits comment. Although Emilia is artistically gifted, she is basically a young girl from Oklahoma who falls in love with an international star and is disillusioned. She must deal with her disappointment and decide how it will affect her choices. Will Yuri's rejection serve as a proof that she is not good enough to become a professional ballerina? Or will she take his betrayal for nothing more than it is and continue to pursue her goals? Her choice is to go on with her career and view Yuri realistically.

One client told us a story with a different ending. As a young woman, she had considered a career as an actor. She had talent and enjoyed early success, winning a place in a prominent acting school and appearing in an off-Broadway play. But she never believed that she was as good as her success indicated. One weekend she became ill with the flu. Lying in bed, she suddenly thought how absurd her fantasies were. Her illness was "proof" that she was in the wrong place. So as soon as she could travel, she took the next flight home and returned to college. But at age 40, she questioned if she had made the right choice. "I wish I'd just let the flu be the flu—instead of seeing it as an omen. I should have stayed around for another month." Clients should be encouraged to persist in their objectives and let setbacks merely be setbacks.

PARENT-CHILD RELATIONSHIPS

The Great Santini

Rated PG • 115 min. • 1979 (Also known as *Ace*)

Quick Take

A Marine pilot does not know how to show his family affection so he runs his home like a squadron.

Key Characters

Ben. He both hates his father and idolizes him. His problem is to assimilate the good traits and avoid the bad ones.

"Bull" Meechum. His legacy to his son is "Eat life, or it'll eat you."

Lillian. She is loyal to her husband and wants her children to be as strong as he is. But she teaches them that real strength comes from caring for others.

Precautions

- Domestic violence.
- Profanity.
- Adolescent drinking.
- Graphic depiction of a racially motivated murder.

Categories

Parent-child relationships, abuse (emotional, physical, sexual), adolescence, communication and conflict resolution, death and dying, family-of-origin issues, friends and support systems, grief and loss, marriage, prejudice, substance abuse, transition to adulthood.

Suggested Viewers

- Clients in abusive partnerships.
- Codependent clients.

Main Lessons

---

1. Parents must protect their children from physical and emotional abuse.
2. A spouse who is isolated needs a support system for reality testing.
3. Fierceness and compassion can exist in a healthy mix.
4. Assertiveness should be employed in breaking free from overbearing parents.
5. Real men are strong enough to cry.

- Partners of alcoholics.
- Clients with abusive childhoods.

Setting the Scene

The film begins at a farewell party for Marine fighter pilot Lt. Col. "Bull" Meechum, known fondly to his men as "The Great Santini." By the time the brawl breaks up, we know a lot about Bull. We know he is a guy whose troops would follow him to hell and back. We know he has been passed over for promotion because he is unpredictable and drinks too much. We also know that he is frustrated, represses his feelings, and has a thin ego. What we will learn is that he is devoted to his family and that they are devoted to him.

At home as well as at work, Bull is always in charge. His four children (he calls them the "Hogs") submit to white glove inspections and listen dutifully to his war stories. He expects his kids to be prettier, smarter, and above all, gutsier than other kids. For the Bull, winning is everything. Once, during a basketball game in which an opponent fouls his older son, Ben, Bull screams out: "You get that punk and put him on the deck. Get him or don't come home. It's an order."

Why his family loves him is anybody's guess, but they do—especially his wife Lillian. She knows he is a troublemaker and that he is too hard on her and the children. But she is a dyed-in-the-wool southern lady who watches over her man and walks softly around his rough edges. When she tells Ben to fetch his father late one night when Bull is drunk, she orders him to act fast: "You've got to bring your father back before the sun comes up and somebody finds him."

She explains to the children that their dad drives them so hard because he wants them to be winners. But they don't really believe that, nor does she. After a game of one-on-one basketball that Bull loses to his son, he takes out his anger by slamming the ball against Ben's head. The fact is, he hates to lose to anybody. The children are a prop for his ego. On the day that Ben was born, his father had burst into the hospital, knocked everybody out of the way, and shouted: "That's mine, the greatest little fighter pilot ever born!" He loves his family, but only as an extension of himself. Somehow they must deal with this complex and violent man.

Scripting for Therapy

The Great Santini is the proverbial military father who runs his home as if it were boot camp. Every year, he carries his family to a new Marine base and demands that they adjust quickly to their new surroundings. He stresses athletic and social victories over relationships and will not tolerate soft feelings. He hides behind alcohol and is physically abusive to his wife and children.

His wife, Lillian, is codependent and an enabler. She defends him by rationalizing his violent tendencies: "Harsh words never hurt anybody." But her son Ben sees through his mother's denial: "Harsh kicks do." Although she is a deeply sensitive woman, Lillian encourages her children to set aside their feelings and present a unified front in times of trouble. Even when she must deal with the death of a loved one, she emphasizes to her children that the family's suffering is to be carried out in private. They are not to let anybody see them cry because their behavior reflects on their father. Clients in abusive relationships can compare and contrast their experience to Lillian's. Therapists should note her rationalization of her husband's substance abuse and aggressiveness and should point out the damage to her and the children.

Clients who have grown up with a father like the Bull may paradoxically idealize their fathers. One of our clients, a man who drank too much and ran roughshod over his children, talked about growing up as "a military brat." He watched the film and identified with Ben, but differed in his view of his own father:

> It was tough having a dad who was a drill sergeant, just like in the movie. But it was also the best thing that ever happened to me. Other people felt sorry for themselves and complained that life wasn't fair. But I did what I had to do and I got ahead. I hated my dad all the time I was a kid, but now I love and respect him. He was never my best friend, but he equipped me to handle life.

We asked the client to discuss the costs his tough education had levied. After some hesitation, he admitted that he was uncomfortable with feelings, that he wished his children liked him more, and that his marriage was filled with conflict. In subsequent sessions, we worked with him to extract from his father an appreciation for "toughness" but to incorporate new skills that would lead to a warmer relationship with his wife and children. Ben is nowhere near as appreciative of his father as was our client. At night Ben prays that his father's plane will crash. Nevertheless, Ben is an amalgam of both parents. He dislikes his father but he has learned from Bull how to be a warrior. Ben knows that it is important to be tough, but not to be like his father. His problem is how to combine the fierceness of his father with the compassion of his mother.

Ben solves that problem by defying his father to help a friend in need. When his friend, a black man named Toomer, is threatened by local rednecks, Ben asks his father what he should do. "Stay out of it," the Bull commands, "and that is a direct order." But Ben gets involved anyway and is punished for his disobedience. Later, his mother says that defiance was when Ben became a man. By standing up to his father for a cause he considered right, Ben set himself free from his father's control. In the end, he combines courage with sensitivity, something his father never had learned how to do. Therapists can point out to clients who grew up in similar homes how Ben thrives despite his father's abusiveness. He refuses to let his father impose his own values; he appropriates what is useful but rejects what is destructive. He employs assertiveness in breaking free. Of course, for clients from severely abusive homes, finding positives in abusive parents may prove difficult or impossible. But therapists can help even these clients identify skills that allowed them to survive.

Parenthood

Rated PG • 124 min. • 1989

Quick Take

A group of siblings try to create better families than the one in which they grew up.

Key Characters

Gil Buckman.   He's a father torn between work and family.

Karen Buckman.   She's a mother raising an emotionally disturbed child.

Frank Buckman.   Gil's father dotes on his other son, Larry, who always lets him down.

Larry Buckman.   Gil's brother is a gambler down on his luck.

Helen.   Gil's sister is a single mother raising two teens.

Susan.   She's the other sibling, torn between an obsessive-compulsive husband and her daughter's needs.

Precautions

- Brief nudity and teenage sexuality.
- Profanity.
- Suggestion of adult sexuality.

Categories

Parent-child relationships, adolescence, communication and conflict resolution, divorce, emotional and affective disorders, family-of-origin issues, friends and support systems, grief and loss, intimate relationships, marriage, men's issues, stepparenting and blended families, transition to adulthood, understanding severe emotional illness, values and ethics, vocational and work-related issues, women's issues.

Suggested Viewers

- Anxious parents who question whether they are doing a good job raising their children.
- Clients dealing with resentments toward their parents.
- Single parents; blended families.
- Parents needing to set limits with their grown children.

Main Lessons

1. Family and work demands should be balanced.
2. Loving an emotionally disturbed child sometimes means asking for professional help.
3. Beyond managing their children, parents should also take time to enjoy them.
4. Parents must draw limits when grown children repeatedly call for rescue.
5. Parenthood is not a science; it is filled with surprises.

Setting the Scene

Gil Buckman must choose between the demands of a family and advancement at work. If he neglects work, his income and ability to take care of his family suffer. If he devotes himself to the job, his family gets the money but not necessarily Gil. He wants desperately to do the right thing. His own father, Frank, was self-absorbed throughout Gil's childhood. Now Frank is dealing with Gil's younger brother, Larry, who is even more narcissistic than his father. Larry returns home to ask for money when his latest get-rich-quick scheme falls apart. Gil has two other siblings, Helen and Susan. Helen is a divorced mother of two, trying to balance her own needs against the needs of her children. Susan is married to an obsessive-compulsive who treats their toddler as an educational experiment.

Strictly speaking, *Parenthood* has no plot other than these siblings' attempts to improve on their own childhood. But the scenarios present familiar family problems resolved largely through commonsense solutions. The film challenges the assumption that by mastering child management, parents can avoid the inconsistencies of family life. As Karen says to Gil at the film's end: "There are no guarantees. These are kids, not appliances; life is messy." Hence the message is an optimistic one to parents who feel overwhelmed by the stress of contemporary life.

Scripting for Therapy

Parenthood is filled with therapeutic insights. Clients will recognize themselves in one or more of the parents in this film but will find their problems treated with tasteful humor. The film features many of the stresses of contemporary families: too many "must do" activities, an ever present need to balance job and family responsibilities, and the challenges of single parenting. The characters referee sibling rivalries, contend with their children's emotional problems, and try to spread their energy among extended family, bosses at work, school authorities, spouses, and at the lowest rung of the ladder, their personal needs.

Nine-year-old Kevin Buckman is overanxious, breaks into tears unpredictably, appears socially stunted, and has a variety of school-related difficulties. When Karen and Gil meet with the school psychologist, who recommends that Kevin be transferred to a special education facility for children with emotional problems, Gil reacts the way many parents do. He belittles the expert, resolves to spend more time with his son, and tries to prove that Kevin is no different from any other child. Yet Gil finally recognizes that more than good intentions are needed to solve Kevin's serious problems. Parents with emotionally disturbed children can identify with Gil's pain.

The relationship between Gil, Larry, and their father shows sibling rivalry extending into adulthood. As the problematic child, Larry had always received the lion's share of his father's attention while Gil's stability and responsibility had been discounted. But Frank finally realizes the truth about his sons when Larry begs for financial help "just this one last time." Frank tells Larry he will give him money if Larry takes a steady job and joins Gamblers Anonymous. Larry readily agrees, but then brings up a new get-rich-quick scheme. How Frank handles the situation is a poignant and instructive lesson for clients who must contend with problematic grown children.

Frank's decision regarding Larry is, however, different from how Helen deals with her daughter, Julie. Helen knows from her own experience with a failed marriage that Julie is headed for trouble with a boyfriend who is long on romance but short on life skills. Helen's choice is whether to stand inflexibly on principle or to show a supportive and nonjudgmental commitment to her daughter. Her resolution reflects the wisdom of an adult able to see flaws in a child realistically, yet love without qualification.

Therapists might diagnose Helen's other child, 13-year-old Gary, as clinically depressed. He padlocks his room and is emotionally absent.

When he asks his birth father if he can live with him, Gary is cruelly rejected. He reacts by trashing his father's dental office. When Helen hears the news, she breaks into his room and discovers a cache of violent porno films. In desperation, she asks Julie's boyfriend, Tod, to talk with Gary because no other male role models are available. Tod learns that Gary has discovered masturbation and has assumed that he is losing his mind. Tod assures Gary that "we all, you know, did it," and Gary is vastly relieved. Tod's stock immediately goes up with Helen.

The other sibling in the family, Susan, must contend with her husband, Nathan, who has turned their home into an educational institution. He spends all his time training their daughter, Patti. He refuses to let her play with other children, fearing they will compromise her progress. Although a caricature, "Nathan" occasionally shows up at mental health clinics, usually accompanied by bright children who are socially delayed. Nathan offers a portrayal of a neurotically ambitious parent who manages to wake up before it is too late.

Perhaps this film can best be summed up as a love story about families. It shows that love is not contingent on how well children meet their parents' expectations but on an acknowledgment that children are gifts to be enjoyed. The family's matriarch offers a metaphor in which she likens parenthood to a roller coaster ride. Some people don't like the roller coaster, she says, preferring a safe and predictable ride on the merry-go-round. But she prefers the roller coaster "because you get more out of it. You go up, down, up, down, what a ride! It's amazing that you can feel so frightened, so scared, so sick, so excited, and so thrilled that you want to ride it again." What Grandma knows is that children always bring more than what was bargained for and therefore make life an adventure that is always fresh. This news is the reassurance that beleaguered parents in therapy sorely need.

Searching for Bobby Fischer
Rated PG • 107 min. • 1993

Quick Take

A brilliant young chess player and his parents weigh competitive success against a normal childhood.

Main Lessons

1. Children, geniuses or not, need support, not pushing.
2. Balance is important for children. They will have time in the future for specialization.
3. For young children, winning is *not* the only thing. Reducing peers to opponents socially delays a child.
4. Parents should not live vicariously through their children.
5. Parents should help children decide what is most important, then help them set limits.

Key Characters

Josh.   This seven-year-old has an extraordinary gift.

Fred.   He is awed by his son's prospects. For awhile, he forgets that his boy is still only a child.

Bonnie.   She stands up for her son's right to be a normal kid.

Bruce.   Seeing promises of greatness in his student, he pushes Josh to win at all costs.

Categories

Parent–child relationships, adolescence, communication and conflict resolution, friends and support systems, marriage, vocational and work-related issues.

Suggested Viewers

- Couples with conflicts about child rearing and family values.
- Children and teens who are pushed too hard to succeed; parents of such children.
- Educational discussion groups, regarding students and extracurricular activities.

Setting the Scene

Josh Waitzkin is a seven-year-old who stumbles upon a special gift while watching chain-smoking aficionados play speed chess in New York's Washington Square Park. When one of the players offers him a baseball for a chess piece Josh finds on the ground, he keeps the chess piece instead. Once he starts playing, everybody agrees that he has an unusual talent: "He's the next Bobby Fischer."

Josh's father is a sportswriter who knows the value of developing talent early, so he takes his son to a chess master rumored to be a great teacher. The teacher, Bruce Pandolfini, says he is not interested, but quickly changes his mind after watching Josh play. Bruce is soon instructing Josh in the strategy of competitive chess, especially in how to view the competition:

"Do you know what it means to have contempt for your opponent, Josh?"

"No."

"It means to hate them. You have to hate them, Josh. They hate you."

"But I *don't* hate them."

"Well then, you'd better start."

Josh enters tournaments in which he defeats all comers. The children are naive about competition, but their parents know what the stakes are all about. In one scene, a tournament director admonishes his audience to behave and reminds them that chess is only a game. Then the camera pans down to a group of intense parents sitting on the floor. Ignoring the official's good advice, they are teaching their children that chess is serious business and that there is no medal for second best.

Despite Josh's success, his schoolteacher notices that he is falling behind academically and socially. She asks his father not to take him to so many out-of-state tournaments. His father responds angrily: "Do you know how good he is? He's better at this than I've ever been at anything in my life. Better than anything *you'll* ever do." The next day Fred enrolls his son in a private school in which intense competition is viewed more sympathetically.

Scripting for Therapy

Searching for Bobby Fischer can be appreciated on many levels. The film is an informative and fascinating portrayal of the world of competitive chess and a study of one talented youngster. It is also a penetrating critique of the "winning-at-all-costs" philosophy as applied to children and adolescents. And it raises questions about how adults can help children put into perspective their many interests and how parents can help talented children nurture their gifts.

How *should* unique individuals with extraordinary gifts look upon the development of their talents? Is there an obligation to develop their gifts that necessitates sacrifice of a normal childhood? The film raises this question in its references to Bobby Fischer, who was arguably the greatest chess player of all time but whose life has been problematic. Is a genius's whole development less important than his or her art? How can parents of such children help them strike a balance? Parents don't want to hold their gifted children back, but they must help them look at the bigger picture and prioritize values.

Anybody who has been involved in children's sports, musical competitions, or other extracurricular activities knows that children are often pushed ahead by their parents, coaches, and teachers more quickly than they ought to be. Despite their successes, such children are frequently socially immature. Learning to interact with others requires developing a sense of fair play and compassion. But adults bent on winning encourage children to see peers as opponents. The film shows how adults harm children with this teaching.

For example, at the end of a baseball game that Josh's team has won, he watches the defeated team trudge off the field in shame. His expression says he knows what they feel and that he sympathizes. But the parents merely feign sympathy for the losers. They say the right words but they don't mean them. When Josh is playing competitive chess, his father demeans the opponents and his teacher stresses an even colder strategy: "You must have contempt." That attitude is not appropriate for seven-year-old children. It teaches them to categorize others into stereotypes and reduces their chances of good social adjustment.

STEPPARENTING AND BLENDED FAMILIES

Fly Away Home

Rated PG • 110 min. • 1996

Quick Take

A child learns about love and forgiveness as she cares for a family of orphaned geese.

Key Characters

Amy Alden.   A grieving child finds new hope in a gaggle of geese who depend on her for everything.

Thomas Alden.   He wants to help his child, but he does not know how.

Precautions

- Automobile accident in which an adolescent's mother dies.
- Mild profanity.

Categories

Stepparenting and blended families, adolescence, adoption and custody, communication and conflict resolution, death and dying, emotional

---

Main Lessons

1. It takes time for a child to deal with loss.
2. Children who are grieving often express their feelings through anger.
3. Stepparents must be patient. What matters most is mature love shown persistently through concrete acts.
4. The behavior of depressed children tells others to go away, but inside they are saying, "Please don't leave."
5. We learn to give and accept love by caring for others.

---

and affective disorders, family-of-origin issues, friends and support systems, grief and loss, inspiration, parent-child relationships.

Suggested Viewers

- Adolescents who are struggling with their parents' divorce.
- Parents needing positive role models in caring for difficult children.
- New stepparents who are finding the adjustments difficult.

Setting the Scene

Driving through a rainstorm in New Zealand, 13-year-old Amy Alden and her mother are involved in a terrible automobile accident. Her mother dies. Amy regains consciousness in a hospital with her father Thomas at her side. He tells her that he is taking her back to Canada, where she lived before her parents divorced. In one night, she has lost not only her mother but also her home.

Thomas is not comfortable in his role as a parent. He has little time or talent for taking care of a grieving adolescent. Working constantly at projects that pay little, he makes his living as an inventor and artist. To him, Amy is a complete mystery. Her moods are baffling, and he does not know how to help her deal with her mother's death. So he avoids her altogether, letting her sort out her feelings for herself. Thomas lives with his brother David and a lover named Susan. They both try to talk with Amy, to draw her out and cheer her. But she will have little to do with any of them, and she refuses their every attempt to reach out.

Amy skips school to wander in the countryside. One day she discovers a nest of eggs that has been abandoned. She hides them in a barn, wrapping the eggs in scarves and warming them with a light she takes from her father's workshop. One afternoon while she is watching them, the eggs hatch. And one by one, through imprinting, the goslings fix on her like Mother Goose.

The goslings follow Amy everywhere, but she soon discovers that a game warden plans to clip their wings. Without a mother to teach them to fly and migrate, the geese will become local pests. But Susan, Thomas, and David come up with a creative solution. Because the goslings are attached to Amy, perhaps they will let *her* teach them how to fly. Thomas's hobby is ultralight airplanes. The plan is a long shot, but the group figures that with Amy flying in the lead, the goslings might follow. So the family builds a craft that resembles a gigantic goose, and Amy gets a quick course in piloting. If the goslings cooperate, she can take them south to their winter home.

The plan has its rough moments (one gosling never learns and must be packed like a suitcase in the plane), but eventually Thomas, Amy, and the goslings take off. Thomas flies in his plane at her wing, and the geese follow behind in a V-formation. Although they have run-ins with hunters, dense fog, and a land developer, they ultimately reach their destination. They land to the applause of a crowd that has followed reports of their flight through the country. The geese are safe and sound, and so is Amy. In the course of carrying her charges to sanctuary, she finds a new family and learns to accept the love they have to share.

Scripting for Therapy

Amy responds to the death of her mother by withdrawing into depression and refusing to be comforted. Her grief is overwhelming. But she is also angry that she must live with a father she does not know, that she must enter a new school in a foreign country far from home, and that her father is involved in an intimate relationship. Her reaction is what children in blended families feel. Rage, suspicion, despondency, helplessness, and hopelessness make adjustment to a new family painful and arduous.

Susan and Thomas's frustrations are also familiar to stepparents who suddenly find a new and angry teenager in their home. They want to help the child get past the hurt, but nothing seems to work. Susan and Thomas know that Amy is in emotional pain, but her bitterness pushes them away. Susan tries to be a friend, but Amy will not allow it. Thomas doesn't know how to be a father to his unhappy child, so he retreats into his work. But neither adult gives up despite the setbacks. Parents in blended families must learn to persist in offering love to a displaced child despite minimal gains and frequent rebuffs.

Amy finally comes around when she begins nurturing her goslings. The story is a classic example of the healer who is healed through caring for others. The goslings have lost their mother, and so has Amy. They are alone, and she feels that way too. Both are dependent on strangers. So when she lavishes on them the love she needs herself, she begins to heal inside.

This film is beautiful. A distant father, doing the right thing, touches his child and she touches him. So few families can show love like this; they struggle to get it right. But the film shows that good intentions, persistence, and compassion are qualities that, with time, can put back the pieces of a broken life.

SUBSTANCE ABUSE

Clean and Sober

Rated R • 124 min. • 1988

Quick Take

A cocaine addict and alcoholic resists admitting his problem and getting help.

Key Characters

Darryl Poynter. A high-rolling real-estate salesman, he has worked a scam on everybody. Treatment professionals say he is an addict, but he won't accept their diagnosis.

Charlie. She is an alcoholic in a dysfunctional relationship. She has to choose between one person who facilitates her addiction and another who wants to rescue her.

Craig. This therapist gets beneath Darryl's skin.

Richard. He's an AA sponsor who models effective caregiving.

Precautions

- Much profanity.
- Nudity.

Main Lessons

1. The first step in dealing with drug or alcohol abuse is admitting that substances are ruining one's life.
2. Getting off drugs or alcohol is a struggle that never ends. The abuser is always one relapse away from calamity.
3. One cannot help people who won't accept it.
4. The effective caregiver determines who owns a problem.
5. Good relationships are based on honesty.

- Sexual situations.
- Abundant drug and alcohol use.

Categories

Substance abuse, chronic illness and disabilities, communication and conflict resolution, emotional and affective disorders, family-of-origin issues, friends and support systems, grief and loss, intimate relationships, parent-child relationships, understanding severe emotional illness, values and ethics, vocational and work-related issues.

Suggested Viewers

- Clients with substance abuse problems.
- Families of such clients.
- Couples, regarding dependency issues.

Setting the Scene

Darryl Poynter wakes up next to a woman he had met the night before. He reaches for the cocaine they had shared and offers her some, but then notices that she is not breathing and that her skin is cold. The police tell Darryl that she died from a heart attack, and they want to know who gave her the drugs. They tell him not to leave the city. He takes off as soon as they are gone, but doesn't know where to run. He had embezzled $92,000 from his company and had lost the money in the stock market. A radio ad he hears gives him an idea: hide in a drug and alcohol rehabilitation clinic, where he will be anonymous. The only catch is, he will have to pretend to be an addict.

Darryl does not have an attractive personality. He lies all the time. He calls his mother and asks for money—his first call to her since his last cry for help. He sees nothing wrong with cocaine or alcohol; he doesn't see how they are ruining his life. Once he checks into the rehabilitation clinic, he meets a therapist named Craig who is wise to all his tricks. Craig knows Darryl is calling buddies to ship cocaine packages to him and that he is trying to score with the female clients. Craig lets Darryl know that none of his deceptions will work.

In the hospital, Darryl meets a woman named Charlie, an alcoholic who lives with an abusive man. Once Darryl is discharged from the clinic, he asks Charlie out for a date. But Charlie is down on herself and thinks she has about the best she deserves. Darryl finally talks her into going out, but she has trouble with the demands of a healthier relationship. In the meantime, Darryl finds it difficult to stop lying and scheming. He goes to his boss to ask forgiveness but instead invents a series of lame excuses that the boss sees through. Some people hit rock bottom before they enter treatment. Darryl hits after he is out. Once that happens, his recovery begins.

Scripting for Therapy

This film is useful with substance abusers and their families because it focuses on an aspect of treatment usually given short shrift in similar movies: the long and difficult process of surrender. Many films deal with substance abuse, but this one is unique in illustrating the ploys that addicts use to avoid admitting their problem.

One of our clients, a professional woman in her 20s, had seen this film while she was still using cocaine; she was even high at the movie theater. Nevertheless, the film helped motivate her to get treatment. What struck her was how Darryl believed he was fooling everybody, but nobody was taken in. Like Darryl, she too had been making up excuses. She thought she had been doing her job well, but her boss's assessment was critical. Most important, she too thought she could handle the drug: "I saw Darryl kidding himself, and I realized that I was doing the same thing." A few weeks after viewing the film, she called a hospital and admitted herself for treatment.

Besides showing users the transparency of their excuses, the film also illustrates the impossibility of helping a person who does not want help. Once Darryl invests himself in treatment, he does not return to drugs. But Charlie, dependent on a man who is an active user, does not do as well. Darryl believes that he can, by sheer force of will, convince her to leave. When he fails, his AA sponsor, Richard, points out the arrogance of such an intention.

For clients who are in codependent relationships, Richard is the role model of a mature helper. He offers specific information and advice and he is supportive as long as Darryl plays by the rules, but he draws boundaries to keep himself from falling into traps. He has a clear understanding of who owns a problem, and he does not blame himself for Darryl's relapses.

The therapist, Craig, also is an effective role model. He confronts Darryl's lies without taking them personally. He is realistic and respectful of his clients who are trying to give up drugs. He looks for ripe opportunities to let his clients assume personal responsibility, but he checks out their stories. When one woman in the group appears to be *too* happy, Craig confronts her and asks if she is using again. No matter how close he becomes to his clients, his relationship with them is always based on evidence. If they are trying hard he is supportive. When they stop trying, he asks them to leave.

Charlie's relationship with her live-in illustrates how abused persons continue to stay with an abuser. She knows the relationship is bad for her, but she feels sorry for him when he is sober and finds meaning in taking care of him. She fails to see that she is too vulnerable to be a caregiver. And because her self-esteem is so fragile, she believes that she deserves the punishment he delivers. She is afraid to leave him even when others encourage her and offer to protect her from him. Clients who stay in abusive relationships sometimes offer similar reasons for not leaving. But the film shows the consequences of staying in a destructive relationship.

When a Man Loves a Woman
Rated R • 126 min. • 1994

Quick Take

An alcoholic woman and her husband renegotiate their relationship after her treatment in a rehabilitation clinic.

Key Characters

Alice.   She is a witty and attractive young woman before alcohol turns her life into a nightmare.

Michael.   He solves her problems and speaks for her. But eventually he sees that one of her biggest problems is him.

Main Lessons

1. Loved ones contribute to an alcoholic's problems through co-dependent behavior.
2. Partners should give support but let others learn to solve problems for themselves.
3. A healthy relationship requires good communication.
4. When a partner has a substance abuse problem, recognize the signs early. It saves time and heartache.
5. Love means setting reasonable limits.

Precautions

- Mild sexual situations.
- Profanity.
- A drunken episode in which the protagonist strikes a child.

Categories

Substance abuse, communication and conflict resolution, friends and support systems, intimate relationships, marriage, understanding severe emotional illness.

Suggested Viewers

- Clients who are abusing alcohol or drugs but are in denial.
- Clients in recovery, and their families.
- Couples with communication and power issues.

Setting the Scene

No one escapes harm as Alice Green, a junior high school counselor, descends from the preppy fun of social drinking to outright self-destruction. She tells lies that cover up her abuse of alcohol ("I had to meet my friend at the bar. She's going through a lot in her marriage and needed to talk.") She hides liquor in the chest of drawers and wraps empty bottles in newspapers before throwing them into the garbage. Her husband, Michael, is an airline pilot who is accustomed to taking charge, but he cannot stop Alice from drinking. Michael's problem is that he likes

Alice when she is drinking: She is fun, romantic, and lets him do what he does best, take care of things. Still, he sees that her drinking is getting out of hand. There are nights when she passes out and mornings that begin with apologies. So when Alice slaps her daughter and crashes through a shower door, Michael is finally ready for her to get help. Once at the treatment center, however, he cannot let go. As he wraps his jacket around her and prepares to say goodbye, he argues with the center's director about the house rules. Michael cannot say what he really feels: "If I'd tried harder, I could have taken care of this myself."

The real battles start after Alice leaves the treatment center where she has learned about alcohol and herself. She has learned to identify with other alcoholics, even when they differ in social status. She, like they, share a dependency on people as well as chemicals; they use the same cons in trying to get what they want. Michael, however, cannot understand the changes in his wife. He wants to put her hospitalization behind them and pretend that nothing has happened. He wants Alice to be the same fun-loving, casual, undemanding person she was before—only sober. She knows that is impossible; she *is* different than before, and her treatment will go on for as long as she lives. What puts their marriage in jeopardy is that she now finds it easier to talk to other alcoholics than to her husband.

Scripting for Therapy

For problem drinkers and their loved ones, there is no joy in the day-to-day grind as alcohol ravages the alcoholic and destroys a family's cohesion. Alcoholism is truly a social virus. It damages everybody in contact with the host. Through this realistic portrayal of what families experience in coping with substance abuse problems before, during, and after clinical treatment, this film helps clients get an outside perspective on themselves and their behavior.

One couple to whom we assigned the film, both recovering alcoholics, reported that the film was difficult for them to watch because it paralleled so many aspects of their history. Nevertheless, they appreciated the film's insight into the way alcoholics mask their drinking. They also agreed that, like the couple in the film, the thorniest difficulty they encountered once they were sober was in renegotiating their marriage contract without alcohol. They liked the ending of the film, which doesn't answer the question about whether Alice and Michael's marriage will survive. "That's like real life," they said. "The movie ends where we are now."

The film contains a number of insights about alcoholics and their codependent partners that clients in recovery will recognize:

- Michael criticizes his wife as she gets more out of control, but he is far more engaged when she is mildly intoxicated, which subtly encourages her to drink. Other people do not cause alcoholism, but they can facilitate it.

- Michael confuses power with love. He is most comfortable in his role as an airline captain responsible for the safety of his passengers and crew, and he tries to assume that role in his marriage. For him, love means taking care of people and making decisions for them—thus robbing them of learning how to take care of themselves.

- The couple's communication is fundamentally flawed through Michael's unwillingness to take Alice seriously. He says what he thinks is needed without paying attention to what she is really communicating. He hears most conversations as questions to be answered rather than as a sharing of concerns between equals. She finally tells him how he is failing her: "You always tell me how to do things, but you never listen to me."

- Michael does not want to make fundamental changes in the relationship. He believes that the only problem in their marriage was Alice's drinking. By the end of the film, he has started to understand that he is an integral part of the problem.

What recovering couples know is that when they are drinking, the relationship, in a bizarre sense, works. When they get sober, it may very well not. The problem is how to manage the relationship successfully without alcohol as a buffer. One of our clients, the husband of a woman who became sober through Alcoholics Anonymous, echoed Michael's criticism that treatment itself had ruined his marriage. He agreed that his wife was better because she attended AA meetings frequently. But he resented her being gone so much and criticized her for valuing their relationship less. "You were always there for me before," he said to her. "Why can't you be there now that you're not drinking?"

Although we use this film primarily with substance abuse clients, we also assign it to couples who play rescue games and to those with stereotypic male versus female communication patterns. Michael encourages Alice to get help, but when that help threatens his own self-image as her protector, he encourages her not to go overboard. The close of the film shows an interchange between them that should be required viewing for premarital counseling. She doubts she can work things out with him because he tries to take care of her. He listens but he does not really understand. He gives answers that prevent her from learning to solve her own problems.

By contrast, the couple's housekeeper, Amy, is a good example of a person who knows how to set limits and let others solve their own problems. When the children balk at staying with their grandparents while Michael is away on a trip, Amy doesn't let them manipulate her into giving up her weekend: "Surely you're not saying that your life is more important than mine." Amy defines who owns a problem, sets reasonable limits, and forces Michael to make hard decisions. She won't solve his problems; he must solve them for himself. We have had clients react to her by saying that she was unsympathetic, cold, and self-centered. But Amy demonstrates that love often is clothed in rough garments. The film shows the consequences of dependency and illustrates that mature relationships must include individual autonomy for both partners.

VALUES AND ETHICS

Short Cuts
Rated R • 189 min. • 1993

Quick Take
Stories of life and death and ethical decisions in the fast-paced world of southern California.

Key Characters
A host of characters trying to deal with a fragmented world.

Precautions
- Nudity.
- Deprecating treatment of women.
- Very strong profanity (phone sex).
- Explicit sexual situations.
- Violence (rape).
- A young boy dies in a gripping emotional scene. The film is not suitable for parents who have recently lost a child.

Main Lessons
1. Bad things happen without easily identified causes.
2. If we knew all the circumstances that led to a tragedy, blame might be irrelevant.
3. Emotional survival depends on connecting with other people.
4. Solving personal problems means looking at one's whole life, not just a piece of it.
5. We often do not know the value of what we have until after we lose it.

Categories

Values and ethics, abuse (emotional, physical, sexual), affairs, communication and conflict resolution, death and dying, divorce, family-of-origin issues, friends and support systems, grief and loss, intimate relationships, marriage, parent-child relationships, substance abuse.

Suggested Viewers

- Groups, regarding victim empathy, ethics.
- Clients recovering from loss or burdened with unreasonable guilt.
- Couples with issues such as affairs, abuse, communication.

Setting the Scene

This film is based on nine short stories and a poem by Raymond Carver. Summing up the various episodes is not feasible. The film's theme is that modern-day life has become irrational and that nothing is simple.

In one story, for instance, an eight-year-old boy named Casey is hit by an automobile. The driver stops to see if he is all right. When he tells her he is, she offers to take him home, but his parents have warned him not to get into cars with strangers. So he walks home, lies down on a couch, and then slips into a coma. Casey's mother carries him to a hospital, where a physician assures the parents that their son will recover. But the doctor has little patience with their questions; he is anxious about his wife, whom he suspects of having an affair. Some time later, Casey regains consciousness for a moment, and then he dies.

Who is to blame—the child, the doctor, the driver, his parents? The child was late for school and ran into the street without looking. His parents had not worried about him because he was always so careful. The doctor, although distracted, could do nothing to save him. The driver could not avoid hitting him because he had stepped out in front of her car. For every potential answer, the story shows how some odd event influenced the outcome. The conclusion is that nobody really caused the accident.

In *Short Cuts,* the city of Los Angeles festers with such inexplicable events. All vignettes are complex, making conclusions difficult. A mother, grieving for her lost love, misses the warning signs from her depressed daughter who later commits suicide. An older man, long estranged from his son, comes back but then does not know what to say. A middle-aged woman hates her husband's alcoholism but stays with him because he is kind to her when he is sober. In every relationship, the past is filled with promises made and broken, and the future is a gamble. Yet these characters make choices as best they can.

A Carver poem titled "Lemonade"—cited by Director Robert Altman as an inspiration for *Short Cuts*—epitomizes the movie. While going back to his truck for a thermos of lemonade, a boy on a fishing trip falls into a river and drowns. Months later, his father can think of nothing else and is consumed by regrets. He blames himself for sending his son to the truck for the lemonade, but he also blames the grocery store for the attractive display that made him buy lemons instead of oranges. He blames the people who shipped the lemons from the valley, the pickers who picked them, the truckers who brought them, even the first lemon cultivated on the earth. He cannot stop the obsession because he cannot pinpoint what killed his son. If just one thing had been different, he reasons, his son would still be alive. Nobody intended the tragedy, but everything came together to make it happen. What hurts the most, the poem goes on to say, is not just that things happen for no one reason. What hurts is that once tragedies happen, we are haunted from then on by the memories of how wonderful life had been before.

Scripting for Therapy

In this film, the characters *don't* notice those things that matter most until they lose them. Couples ignore each other until one has an affair. A father plans to contact the son he abandoned but he does not. A child dies on the way to school. Even when these characters finally notice what *is* important, the film suggests that life has a way of slipping back into familiar patterns and they stop noticing once again.

One of our clients, in describing his reaction to the film, talked about his son's hospitalization for a life-threatening condition, a medical emergency that fortunately ended well. Before his son became ill, the father had been worrying about a number of business problems and had spent little time with the boy. Of course, those worries became irrelevant when he learned his child might die. For several days he thought of nothing else and made promises about how things would be if the child recovered. The child did get better, but within six months, the man's life was just like it had been before. In hindsight, he wondered how he found it so easy to break promises he had made when his child was ill.

These characters do not communicate well with each other, but when they do, their conversations are healing. In the episode cited earlier, Casey's parents receive taunting phone calls after his death, which they finally trace to a baker who had been making Casey's birthday cake. Because no one had come for the cake, the baker assumed he had been cheated and made the calls. When the parents confront him, he is angry, then ashamed, then empathetic. The conversation that follows is an exercise in redemption. The episode teaches that healing comes about through a connection to others who share one's grief. The scene is an affirmative response to clients who ask, "Will talking really help?"

Therapy is often criticized for concentrating on individual personality while ignoring social and environmental factors that also impact a person. Marital problems are artificially treated in isolation from the society in which partners live. Therapy with children ignores school policies that can undo treatment gains. And job complaints center on what clients can do personally, with little reference to employers who limit their true options. This film is useful to clients because it views the problems of these characters in a wider social context. These characters are influenced by their families, of course, but other significant or casual relationships play at least as important a part. Likewise, therapists can encourage clients to solve their problems by considering the totality of the environments in which they live.

VOCATIONAL AND WORK-RELATED ISSUES

Apollo 13
Rated PG • 135 min. • 1995

Quick Take

True-life adventure of the crew of NASA's Apollo 13 on a mission to the moon that depends on teamwork and effective response. The ultimate job stress.

Key Characters

Jim Lovell, Fred Haise, Jack Swigert. The crew confronts a potential disaster and must pull together to get back home.
Ken Mattingly and Gene Kranz. They demonstrate the power of a good support system.

Precautions

- Profanity.
- Harrowing depiction of a crisis in space that may frighten some young children.

Main Lessons

1. In teamwork, working for the greater good takes precedence over personal agendas.
2. Never say "can't!" Creative responses to problems bring about unpredictable solutions.
3. A leader's attitude and style set the mood for the team.
4. Be willing to take responsibility for actions and decisions.
5. Families are teams too.

Categories

Vocational and work-related issues, communication and conflict resolution, friends and support systems, inspiration, values and ethics.

Suggested Viewers

- Organizations, in discussing problems that prevent successful teamwork.
- Parents, in learning how to delegate authority, support each other, focus on solutions.
- Families who need to learn to function as a team.

Setting the Scene

Only hours before Apollo 13 is scheduled for launch, Commander Jim Lovell's boss summons him to a meeting with the flight surgeon. The doctor reports to Jim that Ken Mattingly, the crew's pilot, has been exposed to measles. His presence on the crew jeopardizes the entire mission because he will likely become ill while in space. Jim has two choices: Take a different pilot, or let an entire backup crew make the trip. The crew meets behind closed doors. They discuss the options, but the decision has already been made. Jim says that another pilot, Jack Swigert, is going to the moon. A disappointed Ken Mattingly tries to shift the blame to the flight surgeon, but Jim owns up to the responsibility "It was my call," he says.

The next morning's liftoff is followed by a series of disasters. First an oxygen tank explodes, making a moon landing impossible. Then other technical problems turn the spaceship into a life raft and shift NASA's priority to getting the three men back alive. No one wastes time with blame; the scientists in Houston team with the astronauts to get the wounded ship home.

One of their problems is that a device that clears carbon dioxide out of the cabin, a scrubber, suddenly does not work. The staff in Houston gathers a garbage bag full of items that are available in the Apollo 13 cabin and goes to work making a replacement. An hour or so later, the staff has a model of a new scrubber that the astronauts can assemble on board.

It is Mission Control Director Gene Kranz's job to orchestrate this brilliant ground crew. He must see the big picture, encourage his staff, and make demands when necessary. It is also his job to change negative attitudes to positive ones. When a bureaucrat says that the accident is likely to be the greatest disaster NASA has ever faced, he corrects him: "With all due respect, sir, I believe this may be our finest hour."

Scripting for Therapy

Apollo 13 is a marvelous adventure, an old-fashioned hero saga that is inspirational in its triumph over adversity. We think the film teaches seven rules of effective teamwork in organizations. These rules apply to smoothly functioning families as well as to effective business teams.

1. Success is meeting a team's objectives, not satisfying personal ambition. Someone once said that when we are in our 20s, we are more interested in putting our names on the map than in anything else. Corporate observers might amend that group to include overambitious executives of almost any age who view the needs of an organization as second to their own. In today's interdependent organizations, self-absorbed mavericks are out. Individuals must act for the good of the team and its goals.

2. Solve problems, don't attack personalities. The one criticism that the astronauts had of this movie was that, in truth, no conflict arose between Fred Haise and Jack Swigert when the oxygen tank blew. Even with the fictionalized conflict, however, no one attempts to fix blame. The attentions of the crew are firmly riveted on finding solutions. In Houston, Gene Kranz says, "Let's work the problem, people." Turning on each other would merely be a waste of valuable time.

3. Own up to responsibility. When Jim Lovell decides to scrub Ken Mattingly from the mission, he tells Ken outright and doesn't hide behind the flight surgeon or his boss. Ken doesn't like what he hears, but because it's a statement of fact, he can accept it. Effective teams depend on individuals owning responsibility.

4. Admit real limits. The scientist responsible for providing a start-up routine to reactivate the spacecraft's computer demonstrates how team players must deal with the real world. When someone asks him to compromise, he answers: "You're telling me what you need. I'm telling you what you have." Minimizing problems unrealistically gives a team false hopes.

5. *Extraordinary problems require creative solutions.* The problem of the damaged vessel cannot be solved by conventional methods. When his staff tells Gene Kranz that the material available to serve as a jury-rigged scrubber is incompatible with where it must be placed, he says: "Then invent a way to put a square peg in a round hole."

Social psychologists have demonstrated that groups are more willing to assume risks than individuals are because responsibility is shared. When problems have no obvious solutions, all options contain some risk. Thus teams bring a measure of creativity to problem solving that surpasses that of individuals.

6. *Don't try to predict how things will turn out.* Results can't be seen until the preliminary steps are taken. Outcomes are far more complex than simple cause and effect, and no one should try to predict the future.

Jim Lovell, in a television interview, describes a harrowing experience as a fighter pilot that taught him patience. He was searching on a dark night for a carrier on which he was to land. His instrumentation had failed him, and he had little hope of visually spotting the ship. He turned a small map light on and every light in the cockpit suddenly went dead. As his eyes adjusted to the dark, he looked out and saw a trail of phosphorus plankton in the wake of the ship. Had the cockpit lights not failed, he would not have seen the plankton and would have been lost. He concluded: "You never know what events are going to transpire to get you home."

7. *Optimism is a basic prerequisite.* Gene Kranz refuses to believe that the astronauts might be lost. When the NASA director introduces a note of pessimism into the room, Gene quickly disagrees. He is not naive, but he realizes that people work more intensely when they think their efforts are going to result in success.

Consultants who teach teamwork to traditional organizations say that failure to make a transition to teams is often caused by using sticks rather than carrots. Organizations that stress the worst make it difficult for employees to focus on what is possible. But Gene Kranz knows optimism opens up doors that pessimism closes. By convincing his team that success is inevitable, he creates an energy level adequate to the task.

The Doctor
Rated PG–13 • 128 min. • 1991

Quick Take

A surgeon learns to appreciate his patients' feelings after undergoing treatment for cancer. His experience makes him a better man and a more compassionate physician.

Key Characters

Jack McKee.   He had always thought of doctors and patients as "us" and "them." When he becomes ill, he discovers what "they" had always felt.
Anne McKee.   She wants to understand her husband, but she cannot. When he asks for more than a marriage of convenience, she is not sure if the relationship can hold up.
June.   A dying patient, she teaches Jack how to live.

Precautions

- Profanity.
- Sexually oriented jokes.

Categories

Vocational and work-related issues, chronic illness and disabilities, communication and conflict resolution, death and dying, friends and support systems, grief and loss, intimate relationships, marriage, values and ethics.

Suggested Viewers

- Clients who need to develop empathy.
- Clients who are angry with the medical community.

Main Lessons

---

1. Empathy is a life lesson often learned through difficult experience.
2. To handle the inevitable struggles that will occur, a couple should develop communication skills before crises arrive.
3. Critically ill patients sometimes push family away and bond with other patients. This process is normal and does not mean they love their family less.
4. Solid family relationships require time and attention.
5. Health care professionals should separate the business of medicine from the task of relieving suffering.

- Health care professionals.
- Couples, regarding communication.

Setting the Scene

Jack McKee is a technically superb heart surgeon who develops a nagging cough. The family doctor says the cough is nothing, but a week later Jack sees blood on his white shirt and consults a specialist, who detects a mass in his throat. She orders a biopsy, and the diagnosis is cancer of the larynx. She suggests radiation but gives no guarantees. Overnight, the prosperous and esteemed physician Dr. McKee steps into the medical world as an ordinary patient.

Before the illness, Jack was at the top of the feeding chain. Cocky, certain of himself, he held to high-tech, low-compassion medicine. His motto: "Get in, fix it, get out." He warned surgery residents against becoming enmeshed: "There is a danger in feeling too strongly about your patients, in becoming too involved. Surgery is about judgment, and the judge needs to be detached." Jack poked fun at his patients behind their backs. He put a patient's call on his speakerphone so his wife could listen in and gave silly advice to pertinent concerns. And in a postsurgery interview, he demeaned a woman's anxieties regarding her husband's reactions to a chest scar: "Tell him you look like a Playboy centerfold, and you have the staple marks to prove it."

255

But Jack finds out about life on the other side. The specialist who diagnoses his cancer is a no-nonsense doctor who ignores Jack's discomfort during her competent but rough examination and dismisses his fears. Other hospital personnel are polite but indifferent. Given a stack of documents to complete, Jack is incensed: "I've been an attending surgeon on the staff of this hospital for eleven years" A clerk replies: "Then you should know all about filling out forms."

Jack meets a patient named June, who is dying from a brain tumor. Her doctors had misdiagnosed the problem when it might still have been treatable, and she balances a sense of outrage against an uneasy acceptance of her fate. Jack finds comfort in talking with her, comfort he cannot find with his wife, Anne, who wants to help but doesn't know how. Gradually June teaches Jack to get the most from every day by concentrating on the things that count.

The doctors tell Jack that his tumor is not responding to radiation and that he must undergo surgery. If it is successful, a full recovery is possible. If not, he could lose his ability to speak. Jack realizes that a qualified but cold physician, similar to the doctor he once was, holds his future in her hands. So he replaces her with a colleague who believes that empathy is the key ingredient in healing. When Jack returns to his practice, he has become a healer as well as a physician.

Scripting for Therapy

Although many health professionals are empathic, too many are not. When our six-year-old son was hospitalized several years ago, we encountered a specialist who described the risks of a scheduled surgical procedure (the most significant risk being death) in front of our obviously frightened child. We asked the specialist to step outside before continuing to talk—a request we thought was reasonable but to which he took offense. "What I have to say shouldn't bother the boy," he argued. "Statistically speaking, there is only nominal risk of impairment."

The events of this film are not surprising to anyone who has been a patient in the health care system. We know that patients wait long past appointment times and that when doctors arrive, they say only, "Sorry I'm late. It's been one of those days." We are no longer shocked that doctors cover up each other's mistakes in malpractice litigation nor that they lack bedside manners. Nevertheless, this film has been assigned to clients who have had bad experiences with doctors and hospitals, and they return feeling better because others understand what they went through. For such clients, assigning this film opens up discussions that lead to better perspective about their experiences.

The film is useful also to clients dealing with issues other than medical concerns. Jack learns to take his patients' feelings more seriously, but he also learns to take more time for his family. Parents who are too busy to spend time with their children should note Jack's family life. In one scene, Anne chides her husband for agreeing to address a PTA meeting and then forgetting to show up—for the second straight year. Jack is a doctor, but he could just as easily be a corporate CEO or any fast-track professional. The point is that Jack learns there is more to life than his career and that successful families require time and attention.

A parallel issue is the way Jack and Anne have settled into a marriage of convenience in which few emotionally honest conversations take place. She is irritated by his superficiality, but she has learned to take him as he is—at a cost to their relationship. She does not require much from him and does not believe that he requires much from her either. So she is unprepared for his "neediness" when he fears that he might lose his voice. "I don't know what you want from me, Jack," she says. "How do you want me to be?" Married clients who suddenly must deal with traumatic events find that speaking with emotional honesty is hard to do if they've avoided it in the past. Clients in relationships can use this film as an incentive to learn better ways to communicate effectively.

Finally, the film addresses a phenomenon that occurs in patients who are critically ill. Such patients often prefer to be with others who are ill and may even avoid their loved ones. This preference is not unusual, but family members are threatened by what they take to be rejection. In this film, Jack forms a close relationship to another patient. His wife does not understand and fears that the friendship may be more than platonic. Her concerns are reasonable, but misplaced. This theme is helpful in discussing a client's feelings about changed relationships with a seriously ill family member.

Ruby in Paradise

Not Rated • 115 min. • 1993

Quick Take

A young woman finds her calling in a Florida souvenir shop.

Key Characters

Ruby.   She is looking for a vocation, not just a job, and she wants to be independent.
Mildred.   She is the first strong woman Ruby has ever met.
Ricky and Mike.   These boyfriends want to take care of Ruby.

Precautions

- Nudity.
- Profanity.
- Explicit sex.

Categories

Vocational and work-related issues, friends and support systems, intimate relationships, transition to adulthood, values and ethics, women's issues.

Suggested Viewers

- Women seeking to leave an abusive relationship.
- Women wanting to be more self-assured and independent.

Main Lessons

1. When abuse is severe, the first step is to get out. Be scared, be unsure, but do it anyway!
2. Breaking free from culturally determined roles is hard but necessary in pursuing life's meaning.
3. Having a supportive mentor can help in taking risky steps.
4. Vocations are unique, measured according to each person's desires.
5. Mistakes are common. What counts is the recovery.

- Couples in which abuse is an issue.
- Individuals looking for their true vocation.

Setting the Scene

Ruby Lee Gissing has escaped from what was probably an abusive relationship, and she is hoping for better days ahead. She considers herself fortunate to "get out of Manning, Tennessee, without getting pregnant or beat up." According to Ruby, her deceased mother hoped for a better life to come "all the while getting kicked around in this one." Ruby does not want the same thing to happen to her.

Just drifting, Ruby lands a job in a Panama City, Florida, souvenir shop. The owner of the store is a tough-minded woman named Mildred Chambers, the only woman Ruby has ever met who is in charge of her own life. Mildred has built her business without help from any man, an ideal role model for a young woman like Ruby who was raised to think of men as tickets to security. But Ruby is seduced by Mildred's selfish and manipulative son, Ricky. After a half-hearted attempt at resistance, she gives in and spends a night in his bed. Later she writes in her journal: "Like Ricky said, we might as well get it over with."

Shortly thereafter, Ruby's knight-in-shining-armor wanna-be appears on the scene. Mike McCaslin, a stuck-in-the-60s young cynic, abandons his plans to save the planet and decides to save Ruby instead. His solution to Ruby's problem is simple: "Leave him and move in with me. I'll take care of you." She is not so sure that Mike is a step up. In her mind, Mike's rejection of this world is not much better than her mother's faith in the sweet bye and bye. But Ruby's nerves are wearing thin, and she is becoming discouraged. So although she doubts Mike's long-range potential she decides on a short-term basis to trade Ricky for Mike.

In retaliation, Ricky lies to his mother about Ruby. She loses her job and is quickly driven into poverty. On the verge of taking a job as a stripper, she almost lets Mike rescue her. But living next door to Ruby is a young girl named Debrah Ann, a high school graduate who is playing house with two men at the same time. Her eyes sparkle when she describes the advantages of her liberated relationship: "I've learned so much in the past two weeks." Ruby agrees that Debrah Ann has learned a lot— how to make coffee, cook supper, and be around whenever these men want her. Debrah Ann is the polar opposite of what Ruby wants to be and is proof positive that "in sacrificing for love, it's usually the woman who does all the sacrificing."

Eschewing both Ricky's harassment and Mike's overprotection, Ruby goes to work in a commercial laundry. The work is back breaking, and she is still just one step away from the welfare rolls. But Ruby takes comfort in everything she is *not:* not a slave, not a prostitute, not somebody's alter ego. The job is a trade-off she can handle.

Eventually Mildred figures out that Ricky has deceived her and asks Ruby to come back and manage the gift shop. The film ends with Ruby busily marking sale items while tourists descend on the town. Ruby is now an independent woman in charge of her store and of herself.

Scripting for Therapy

A major value of this film is the mature view it takes about life goals. Clients need to set reasonable objectives—to be happy with their work and satisfied with peaceful homes. Ruby's notion of paradise is modest and attainable. She finds a job that utilizes her people skills and offers room for advancement. And she can do her work without being dependent on a man.

The film dramatizes the way we sometimes slip into poor life choices despite our best intentions. Ruby enters into a relationship with Ricky even after her best friend tells her to avoid him. The affair seems the easiest course at the time, and Ruby is not accustomed to saying no to men. But she learns from her mistake and breaks off the relationship despite the cost in his retaliation. Clients can recall times when they, too, found it easier to go along even though their best instincts warned them to pull away. Therapists can emphasize that we all occasionally make bad decisions but that damage control means reversing course and accepting the consequences.

Unlike the relationship between Ruby and Ricky, Ruby's mentor relationship with Mildred is mutually beneficial and honest. Clients might find Mildred somewhat cold, but if Mildred were to rescue Ruby without asking anything in return, Ruby would become as dependent on Mildred as she had been on men. Mildred offers herself as a willing mentor, not just from altruistic motives, but also because Ruby is bright, effective, and an asset to the business. Their relationship is straightforward in that both women have something to gain. By contrast, clients report that their mentor relationships sometimes fail because the people involved have not articulated what they want from the relationship.

Finally, some clients will see this film as an example of how women have characteristically been the victims of men, and that interpretation is certainly viable. With such clients, therapists might ask not only how the men in the story encourage Ruby to be a victim but also how Ruby manages to escape from their not-so-subtle traps. The film shows a strong woman who stands on her own.

PART **III**

Therapists' Film Reference

✎ Quick Picks: Category Index to Films

Films listed in this index include all the films from the anthology as well as other films that can have therapeutic benefits. Films from the anthology have page numbers included for clinicians' easy reference.

ABUSE (EMOTIONAL, PHYSICAL, SEXUAL)

Dolores Claiborne (1995). Rated R. A woman tries to protect her daughter from an abusive father. Useful for clients with histories of abuse who are angry not only with the perpetrator but also with the parent who was unable to stop the abuse. (page 82)

Matilda (1996). Rated PG. A young girl grows up in an abusive home, but makes her dreams come true through her own initiative as well as through attention from a teacher who cares. Raises issues of parental neglect and emotional mistreatment. Shows how a nurturing adult can help. A good film for clients with abusive backgrounds. (page 85)

The Prince of Tides (1991). Rated R. A man who is burdened with a dark past tries to make sense of his dysfunctional family. Suitable for sexual abuse victims or relatives of a victim, particularly those who were told by parents to guard a family's terrible secret. (page 89)

Radio Flyer (1992). Rated PG-13. Two brothers use their wits against a violent stepfather. Illustrates the fantasies abused children use in surviving a destructive home. The plot may strain credulity for some clients with histories of abuse, but others will make a connection.

This Boy's Life (1993). Rated R. A true-life story of how a boy struggles with a sadistic stepfather while his mother denies the truth. Features emotional and physical abuse. Particularly useful in showing parents how adolescents who feel powerless identify with peer groups involved in delinquent behavior. (page 92)

What's Love Got to Do With It? (1993). Rated R. Tina Turner's fight to escape from a cruel and violent husband. Suitable for abused clients who deny they are in destructive relationships and who need encouragement to get away.

ADOLESCENCE

The Breakfast Club (1985). Rated R. This film is about the bonding of five truant adolescents who are sentenced to "makeup days" at school. Normalizes teen behavior for parents and emphasizes the value of individual differences among family members.

Ferris Bueller's Day Off (1986). Rated PG-13. An adolescent helps a friend overcome his fears by showing him how to enjoy each day to its fullest. The film shows adolescent clients and their parents the need to encourage thoughtful risk taking and the value of supporting one's friends. Also helps parents see that mild acting out is not aggression but a normal expression of the adolescent's desire for adult independence.

Hoop Dreams (1993). Rated PG-13. Six years in the lives of two high school basketball players. The film is about family cohesion, the pros and cons of organized competition, and the power of individual initiative. Inspiring film that will encourage adolescents to give their best and will cause adults to think about kids and competition. (page 99)

My Bodyguard (1980). Rated PG. Terrific film about one bright boy who co-opts the toughest kid in school to watch over him. This film helps adolescents talk about peer pressure, avoidance of conflict, and their developmental concerns.

Powder (1996). Rated PG-13. A story about a boy who must contend with the prejudice of others because he is an albino. The film shows how harmful prejudice is for adolescents. Helpful in encouraging young clients who are teased by peers to verbalize their emotional pain.

Sixteen Candles (1984). Rated PG. Coming-of-age film in which a young girl's 16th birthday is forgotten by her family in the flurry of excitement over an older sister's wedding. Helpful to adolescent clients in discussing ambivalent feelings common to younger adolescents. Probably more appropriate for younger rather than older adolescents.

Stand and Deliver (1988). Rated PG. A tough-minded teacher refuses to accept his school's patronizing attitude toward underachieving students. He expects his kids to learn; he teaches to a high level, and his students succeed. Very useful for professionals and parents in illustrating how expectations often match performances. Also helpful as an example of how clearly defined consequences facilitate behavior change.

Stand by Me (1986). Rated R. Four boys learn about their strengths and weaknesses on an overnight search for the body of a boy who is missing. A beautiful story of adolescent friendship, self-discovery, and conquering fears and anxieties. Suitable for adolescent clients and their parents.

White Squall (1996). Rated R. A boat crewed by troubled adolescents sets sail on a voyage that will bring out the best in behavior as well as the worst. Although the parental style of the captain is sometimes questionable, he makes a team of his ragged crew. Helpful for adolescents who need to learn about teamwork, respect for authority, and overcoming fears.

ADOPTION AND CUSTODY

The Good Mother (1988). Rated R. A custody suit alleges sexual molestation in the home of a custodial parent. This film serves as a focus of discussion regarding sexual repression, single parents' intimacy concerns, and sexual abuse. The film is also helpful in encouraging divorcing parents not to involve their children in their conflicts. (page 103)

Losing Isaiah (1995). Rated R. A social worker and her family adopt a crack-addicted baby. The birth mother undergoes rehabilitation and wants her child back. Appropriate for divorcing couples in stressing the need for compromises that will serve the best interests of their children. (page 106)

AFFAIRS

Alice (1990). Rated PG-13. She has suspicions that her husband is having an affair, but he denies it. When she discovers the truth, she realizes his unfaithfulness is only one symptom of what's wrong in her life. Therapists can use this film with couples in discussing the meanings of affairs in a problematic relationship.

Something to Talk About (1996). Rated R. After a wife sees her husband with another woman, she moves back home with her parents. Her mother says it is her job as a wife to forgive and forget. But behind Mom's advice is a family secret that soon comes to light. A good film for clients whose families blame them for leaving an unfaithful spouse and for couples in discussing what commitment means in a relationship.

AGING

Cocoon (1985). Rated PG-13. Heart-warming fantasy about senior citizens discovering a fountain of youth. Encourages older people to get back into the swim of things and dissolves stereotypes that younger people may have about old age.

Strangers in Good Company (1991). Not rated. A group of older women share memories, hope, and fears when their tour bus breaks down. Helpful in discussing the challenges of aging and in fostering empathy among younger people. (page 110)

The Trip to Bountiful (1985). Rated PG. An aging woman seeks to return to her roots and is thwarted by her son and daughter-in-law, who want her to let go of the past. A useful film for older clients and their families in stressing the need to share memories, visit places that have meaning, and talk together about the things that matter. (page 113)

Wrestling Ernest Hemingway (1994). Rated PG-13. This film is a sensitive character study of two older men who meet and become friends late in life. They understand and accept with quiet dignity the imminence of death. A useful film in discussing aging with older clients and their children. Also, a good film for men of all ages in discussing the value of same-sex friendships.

CHRONIC ILLNESS AND DISABILITIES

An Early Frost (1985). Not rated. Attorney tells his prejudiced family that he is gay and dying of AIDS. A film that shows the anguish of dealing with a terrible disease and the prejudice that surrounds it. For clients and their families with either or both of these concerns and for others in encouraging empathy.

Lorenzo's Oil (1992). Rated PG-13. An emotionally riveting true story of a couple's race to save their severely ill son. They refuse to accept the authorities' advice that his cause is hopeless, and through persistence and active love, they find a way. An inspiring film that is suitable for clients who have lost hope. (page 117)

Mask (1985). Rated PG-13. True story of a boy afflicted with craniodiaphyseal dysplasia (elephantitis). Wonderful role modeling by a mother who emphasizes her son's strengths and encourages him to get on with his life. This is a good film for disabled clients as well as clients who need to learn to empathize.

Passion Fish (1992). Rated R. An automobile accident leaves a soap opera actress paralyzed. She becomes defiant and cynical, but a reality-oriented nurse spurs her out of self-pity and back into life. An effective film for chronically ill or disabled clients who must regain their will to live.

Philadelphia (1994). Rated PG–13. A young Philadelphia attorney sues his law firm when he is fired for being gay and having AIDS. This film shows the plight of persons who are the objects of prejudice as well as terminally ill. It is a useful assignment for families with gay and lesbian children and for clients who are homophobic. (page 120)

The Waterdance (1992). Rated R. An autobiographical account of the ordeals of a writer after a hiking accident leaves him paralyzed. Realistic portrayal of the physical readjustments that disabled persons must make. A helpful film for clients who need to develop empathy, who are dealing with loss, or who face any unwanted life change. (page 123)

COMMUNICATION AND CONFLICT RESOLUTION

The Accidental Tourist (1988). Rated PG. A couple separates after the death of their son. The man meets another woman and must confront his repressed feelings. For clients who avoid sharing their feelings with those they love and for couples who avoid confrontation. (page 127)

Forget Paris (1996). Rated PG–13. A film about an on-again, off-again relationship. Suitable for clients who love someone but get bogged down in daily upsets.

He Said, She Said (1991). Rated PG–13. A humorous look at a couple that disagrees about everything; a collection of stereotypic male-female communication faux pas. This nonthreatening film allows couples to examine their communication problems and conflicts over power.

Terms of Endearment (1983). Rated PG. A mother lives vicariously through her daughter and is anxious about everything she does. This film is helpful for clients who live in families without boundaries, for clients dealing with grief, and for couples with a history of extramarital affairs. (page 131)

Who's Afraid of Virginia Woolf? (1966). Not rated. A film about verbal abuse and physical violence in which alcohol makes a bad problem worse. Not recommended for couples with severe marital difficulties. Best for viable relationships in showing how verbal abuse escalates.

DEATH AND DYING

Corrina, Corrina (1994). Rated PG. Light-hearted comedy centering on a withdrawn eight-year-old whose mother has died. Valuable in teaching adult clients how to talk with children about the death of a loved one.

My Life (1993). Rated PG-13. A successful but narcissistic young executive is dying from cancer and tries to come to terms with his past. Useful for clients who are workaholics, for clients with family-of-origin issues, and for groups discussing values clarification. (page 135)

Shadowlands (1993). Rated PG. A marriage late in life and a wife's terminal illness teach a repressed intellectual how to love. A beautiful film that models mature love for couples in therapy. Also illustrates how to help children deal with the death of a loved one. (page 138)

A Woman's Tale (1992). Rated PG-13. A deeply moving account of the last few days in the life of a 78-year-old woman dying from cancer. The tender relationship with a young nurse personifies effective caregiving. Excellent film for younger clients in developing empathy for the aged.

DIVORCE

Bye, Bye Love (1995). Rated PG-13. A film about three divorced dads who juggle their kids' needs and their own. Suitable for divorced clients in discussing problems that arise between ex-spouses, the noncustodial parent's fear of being excluded from a child's life, and concerns about beginning new relationships. (page 143)

First Wives Club (1996). Rated PG. When a friend commits suicide after her husband files for divorce, three ex-wives decide to get even. This film shows the damage that divorce does to self-esteem, the economic disparities between divorced men and women, and traps that ensnare women who are trying to build postdivorce lives. Useful for divorced men and women in exploring ways to minimize the damage of a failed marriage.

Kramer vs. Kramer (1979). Rated PG. A troubled marriage fails and the father is left to take care of his son. This film helps divorcing clients keep the needs of a child uppermost and shows all parents how time spent with a child deepens the parent-child bond. (page 146)

Mrs. Doubtfire (1993). Rated PG-13. A divorced man disguises himself as a woman to get a job as his children's nanny. The film is useful for divorced clients in discussing how each parent can have a viable relationship with the children.

Starting Over (1979). Rated R. A film about a man who reenters the dating world after his wife asks for a divorce. Helpful in talking with divorced men about problems in dating and about ambivalent feelings toward an ex-spouse.

An Unmarried Woman (1978). Rated R. A companion piece to the film *Starting Over*, but from a woman's perspective and more realistic. For divorced clients in discussing the difficulties of adjustment to single life.

The War of the Roses (1989). Rated R. A bitter divorce from which literally no one walks away. Shows how selfishness and blind ambition can ruin a marriage. For clients whose marriages are still salvageable. (page 150)

EMOTIONAL AND AFFECTIVE DISORDERS

Best Little Girl in the World (1981). Not rated. Excellent made-for-television drama about an adolescent suffering from anorexia. Useful in showing the family dynamics of eating disorders.

Dead Poets Society (1989). Rated PG. A teacher encourages his student to pursue a passion for acting against his father's orders. When things go wrong, the adolescent commits suicide and the father holds the teacher responsible for his son's death. The film illustrates successful as well as unsuccessful strategies in working with adolescents and their families. It cautions that adolescents are particularly vulnerable to suicide attempts because they think of suicide in magical and unrealistic terms. (page 154)

Down Came a Blackbird (1995). Rated R. After being tortured for his political opinions, a journalist enters a clinic for Holocaust survivors. Shows post-traumatic stress disorder (PTSD) and an effective treatment. Useful for clients diagnosed with PTSD as well as for their families.

Eating (1990). Not rated. At a 40th birthday party, four women share thoughts about life and food. Eating is their best friend and their worst enemy. Their obsession with being thin leads to a lifelong struggle with food. A useful film for clients with eating disorders.

Fearless (1993). Rated R. After a man survives a plane crash, he can't come to grips with his brush with death. Finally he heals himself by helping another survivor of the accident put her life back in order. Useful for clients with survivor's guilt, for those clients with post-traumatic stress disorder, and for clients experiencing difficulties in adjusting to significant life changes.

Fried Green Tomatoes (1991). Rated PG-13. A tale of four southern women, close friendships, male chauvinism, racism, and an eating disorder. Shows the interactions between a troubled marriage and ambivalence toward weight loss. Also shows the value in transgenerational friendships.

The Hospital (1971). Rated PG. A satirical look at medicine that illustrates the difference between normal mood swings and severe depression. Useful in showing clients and their families how untreated depression can lead to suicide.

Multiplicity (1996). Rated PG-13. When a man finds a way to clone himself, he thinks his problems are all solved. In the end, however, he discovers that his solution created an even bigger problem. A helpful film for clients who complain of being stressed–out, underappreciated, and unable to set effective priorities.

The Slender Thread (1965). Not rated. True-life story about a crisis center volunteer who tries to save a potential suicide victim. Useful for professionals as well as lay persons in understanding the depths of clinical depression and in seeing how toxic relationships contribute to a sense of helplessness and hopelessness.

What's Eating Gilbert Grape? (1994). Rated PG-13. A film about a family with a mentally retarded child and a mother with a severe eating disorder. Shows clients in troubled families that they can recognize each others' problems but still be loving and supportive. (page 157)

FAMILY-OF-ORIGIN ISSUES

Hannah and Her Sisters (1986). Rated PG. A film in which family enmeshments are made worse through alcoholism. Helpful in discussing the need for setting boundaries and limits with loved ones.

Home for the Holidays (1996). Rated PG. When this family gathers to celebrate, all its dysfunctions show up too. Illustrates how triangulation, cutoffs, and enmeshment damage family relations.

The Joy Luck Club (1993). Rated R. Three generations of Chinese Americans tell stories of abuse, prejudice, and marital discord. A film that shows how a family's character strengths overcome tragedy and misfortune. Inspirational as a model of healing, it is also an instructive study of mother–daughter relationships.

Like Water for Chocolate (1993). Rated R. In Spanish with English subtitles. A narcissistic mother tries to keep her daughter from growing up. Shows how clients in destructive family relationships should set boundaries and act forcibly to individualize from parents who will not let them go. (page 161)

On Golden Pond (1981). Rated PG. A film about the troubled relationship of a woman and her father. Shows clients the necessity of honest communication with aging parents and a positive resolution with loved ones.

Stuart Saves His Family (1995). Rated PG-13. Allegedly a spoof on the self-help industry, this film shows a dysfunctional family confronting a father's alcoholism, a son's drug problem, and a daughter's poor choices in marital partners. Gives hope to clients from troubled families.

FRIENDS AND SUPPORT SYSTEMS

Bang the Drum Slowly (1973). Rated PG. A beautiful film about the friendship of two men, one of whom is dying from Hodgkin's disease. Illustrates the value of sticking up for a friend and how support systems enhance quality of life for a severely ill person. Suitable for clients in caretaking roles and for other clients in discussing qualities of a healing relationship.

The Big Chill (1983). Rated R. A group of college friends gather for the funeral of a former classmate who committed suicide. This film helps 35- to 55-year-old clients whose youthful ambitions did not work out, who have regrets and second guesses about the past.

Circle of Friends (1995). Rated PG-13. Three young Irish women explore friendship, first loves, and sexuality. A useful film for young clients and their parents in understanding problems that accompany transition to adulthood. (page 165)

City Slickers (1991). Rated PG-13. Three friends in the midst of midlife crises find meaning on a cattle drive. This film is about male bonding, job and marriage burnout, and fear of commitment. It is useful for 30- to 40-year-old male clients and for all clients who are questioning the purpose of their lives. (page 168)

Peter's Friends (1992). Rated R. The British version of *The Big Chill* but with a shocking and ironic ending. Shows how good friends stay together through thick and thin. Suitable for clients dealing with regrets about the past, grief over significant loses, and indecision about the future.

Steel Magnolias (1989). Rated PG. A diabetic woman marries and gives birth to a child against her doctor's advice. This useful film shows clients the importance of a support system of same-sex friends. It also illustrates the feelings that family members experience following the death of a loved one and how others can help ease the pain. (page 172)

GRIEF AND LOSS

The Lion King (1994). Rated G. This animated children's film can be used with adults and adolescents in encouraging them to overcome their fears, take assertive action, and fulfill their responsibilities.

Mr. Holland's Opus (1996). Rated PG. A composer's temporary teaching job turns into a lifetime commitment to his students. This film addresses the concerns of middle-aged clients who regret having given up youthful dreams and who question the value of their sacrifices.

Ordinary People (1980). Rated R. The death of a son in a boating accident throws a family out of balance. The son who survives becomes the scapegoat for their grief. A film that illustrates how feelings are hidden behind insincere speech and avoidance of engagement. Useful for couples with communication difficulties and for individuals with family-of-origin issues. (page 176)

A River Runs through It (1992). Rated PG. A family tries to understand its prodigal son's death. A moving film that illustrates the therapeutic dictum that no one can help a person who will not accept help. Teaches that we can love other persons even when we do not completely understand them. (page 179)

Truly, Madly, Deeply (1991). Rated PG. A tender comedy that is about holding on to the memory of a deceased loved one and turning one's back on life. For grieving clients who need to go on as well as for clients who have suffered significant loss.

INSPIRATION

Being There (1979). Rated PG. A mentally retarded gardener, whose knowledge of the world comes from television, is taken for a genius. This film shows how projection plays a part in our assessments of others and how answers to life's important questions are often quite simple.

Chariots of Fire (1981). Rated PG. Runners competing in the 1924 Olympics face challenges to their principles as well as to their athletic abilities. An uplifting musical score and rich cinematography make this film ideal for evoking a spirit of hope in clients who face challenges of their own.

Field of Dreams (1989). Rated PG. Emotionally inspiring story of a man who listens to his heart and is willing to risk censure by his detractors. Encourages clients to pay attention to their intuition, take thoughtful risks, and allow old interpersonal wounds to heal. (page 183)

Forrest Gump (1994). Rated PG. This film is about being true to oneself, persevering through adversity, and helping others. It is well suited for clients who are depressed, feel inadequate, suffer from disabilities, or are having difficulty getting over the loss of a loved one.

Gandhi (1982). Rated PG. A moving account of Mahatma Gandhi's use of passive resistance in winning independence. Ideally suited for clients who perceive themselves as victimized and without power.

It's a Wonderful Life (1946). Not rated. Heartwarming story about a man who gives up his dreams of travel and adventure in order to help his family and friends. For discouraged clients who feel trapped by life's circumstances and who grieve for opportunities that have passed them by. (page 186)

Jonathan Livingston Seagull (1973). Rated G. This film is a beautiful and peaceful story that teaches the power of love, encourages a spirit of adventure, and supports a person who marches to a different drummer. It is also useful for clients who are wrestling with spiritual concerns.

Places in the Heart (1984). Rated PG. A young widow struggles to raise her son and survive an economic depression aided by a blind veteran and a drifter. To save their farm, they must fight the Ku Klux Klan, prejudice against women, and the hot Texas sun. Particularly inspiring for clients who feel overwhelmed by responsibilities and change.

Rudy (1993). Rated PG. A pint-sized athlete sets out to play college football against the advice of his family and friends. An uplifting story for adolescents or young adults with goals but no support from loved ones. (page 190)

The Shawshank Redemption (1994). Rated R. This film shows how one man responds when he is accused of a crime he did not commit. It illustrates the importance of letting go of resentments, taking effective action to meet daily challenges, and avoiding becoming victimized. A very helpful film for clients who feel oppressed but do not exercise personal power. (page 193)

Star Wars (1977). Rated PG. A film about being true to one's purpose, being loyal to one's friends, and coming to terms with the negative parts of oneself. A useful film assignment for adolescents and other clients who prefer action films.

INTIMATE RELATIONSHIPS

About Last Night (1986). Rated R. Fear of commitment, interference of friends, problems not shared: these doom a budding love affair. Clients in an early stage of a relationship can use this film as an object lesson in how to approach these common issues. Suitable for young marrieds as well as singles. (page 197)

Groundhog Day (1993). Rated PG. A bittersweet comedy about a man's learning to care for others. Useful for self-involved clients who manipulate others and whose relationships are superficial and one-sided. (page 201)

Nine Months (1996). Rated PG-13. When a child psychologist's girlfriend tells him she is pregnant, his life changes overnight. Now he must deal with his fear of commitment, a bare tolerance for children, and the prospects of far less attention from his girlfriend. This film is an excellent focus of discussion for young couples who are weighing the pros and cons of starting a family. It is also a good film for male clients who have been told by former lovers that they need to grow up.

An Officer and a Gentleman (1982). Rated R. This film is about one man's transition from narcissism to genuine care for others. It teaches that you cannot love another until you stop adoring yourself. It is useful for couples in which selfishness limits intimacy. If applied to parenting, it is also an intriguing model of tough love.

Out of Africa (1985). Rated PG. She wants him to settle down. He tells her she wouldn't love him if he did. A story of a woman's resignation

278

to the limits of a free-spirited man's intimacy. Suitable for clients who are confused about the requirements of commitment for a long-term relationship.

Il Postino (The Postman) (1996). Rated PG. In Italian with English subtitles. A tender story of an improbable friendship between an illiterate postman and a famous poet. The postman feels love for a woman but cannot speak; the poet teaches him to put his feelings into words. Therapists can use this film with insightful clients as a metaphor for developing better communication in relationships.

Singles (1992). Rated PG-13. Young adults in Seattle try to balance careers and intimate relationships. The film is useful for singles or young marrieds in discussing long-term commitments, autonomy versus inclusiveness, and identity issues.

When Harry Met Sally (1989). Rated PG. Romantic comedy that follows a man and a woman on their road to a successful relationship. A film for young adults about friendship, communication, forgiveness and, of course, falling in love.

MARRIAGE

The Bridges of Madison County (1995). Rated PG-13. This film is about a woman who sacrifices the love of her life to stay with her children and with a kind but emotionally inaccessible husband. It is about passion, caring, commitment, tenderness, and long-range thinking. For couples who want to improve a viable relationship that has become apathetic. (page 205)

Enchanted April (1992). Rated PG. On a holiday in Italy, four women find ways to rejuvenate their spirits and rebuild their relationships with the men in their lives. This film addresses the problem of burnout in marriage and is useful for couples who yearn for more pizzazz.

The Four Seasons (1981). Rated PG. Three couples learn what counts in a marriage when two friends get a divorce. Useful for older couples who take each other for granted, don't say what they mean, and don't always know how they feel. (page 208)

Husbands and Wives (1992). Rated R. A couple considered by others to have a perfect marriage shock their friends by announcing that they are getting a divorce. This film is about trust, commitment, and mature love. It provides an honest look at the problems that beset many marriages and is suitable for clients in marital therapy.

Mr. and Mrs. Bridge (1991). Rated PG-13. A polite but emotionally fragile couple has lived together, more or less successfully, for many years. He shows no real feelings; she accepts the limit that he imposes on intimacy. This film is a sobering description of how a need for respectability drains a relationship of its élan vital and is a useful object lesson for couples in emotionally repressed marriages.

Scenes from a Marriage (1974). Rated PG. Dubbed in English. This lengthy film (168 minutes) follows a relationship from its reasonably happy days until 10 years after a divorce. It is a painful autopsy, instructive in showing how small but unresolved problems escalate into fatal flaws. This film is recommended for discussion groups as well as for insightful couples.

MEN'S ISSUES

Da (1988). Rated PG. A man goes home to Ireland after his father dies and works things out with his father's ghost. A useful film for male clients who have unfinished business with their fathers, alive or deceased.

I Never Sang for My Father (1970). Rated PG. "Death ends a life. But it does not end a relationship." This film is about regrets, flawed communications, and feelings that are too proud. It is useful for male clients who have trouble speaking honestly with their older parents or with partners.

Nothing in Common (1986). Rated PG. An estranged son becomes reconciled to his father by caring for him after he becomes seriously ill. This film illustrates difficulties some men have in talking about subjects that matter with their loved ones. It is highly suitable for adult male clients in conflicted relationships with their fathers. (page 215)

Tootsie (1982). Rated PG. When an unemployed actor cross-dresses to land a role in a soap opera, he becomes a better man through considering things from a woman's point of view. Teaches male clients to appreciate values such as emotional honesty, compassion, and generosity.

PARENT-CHILD RELATIONSHIPS

A Bronx Tale (1993). Rated R. A young boy compares his father's honesty and middle-class values against a flashy gangster who wants to be his mentor. This film illustrates that children learn from a variety of experiences, not always ones their parents would have preferred. This film is useful for parents of older children and adolescents.

The Great Santini (1979). Rated PG. A Marine pilot doesn't know how to show his family affection, so he runs his home like a boot camp. The film illustrates the problems that develop in children when discipline becomes abuse. Also a useful film about substance abuse. (page 223)

Parenthood (1989). Rated PG. This wonderful comedy is about the struggles of parents in trying to give their children a better childhood than their own. It is filled with examples of parenting strategies that work well, as well as examples of those that don't. Recommended for all parents. (page 227)

Searching for Bobby Fischer (1993). Rated PG. A young chess genius and his parents measure competitive success against a normal childhood. Introduces issues related to the hurried child syndrome and is an effective focus for discussion about children and competition. (page 230)

PREJUDICE

Do the Right Thing (1989). Rated R. This film is about racial tensions between blacks and whites in Brooklyn. The issues it raises are common, however, to all metropolitan areas in which racial disputes spill over into violence. It is useful in discussions with clients for whom prejudice interferes with job performance or those struggling with adaptation to a changing neighborhood.

STEPPARENTING AND BLENDED FAMILIES

Fly Away Home (1996). Rated PG. A child learns about love and forgiveness as she cares for a family of orphaned geese. This film illustrates how grieving children often act out in anger against adult caretakers and shows how to help them express their feelings constructively. (page 234)

Unstrung Heroes (1995). Rated PG. His mother's cancer forces a young boy to live with two eccentric uncles. The film is appropriate for clients who have recently become stepparents or guardians in illustrating the emotional needs of a suffering child.

SUBSTANCE ABUSE

Clean and Sober (1988). Rated R. A cocaine addict and alcoholic resists admitting his problem and seeking help. This film is a realistic account of treatment for substance abuse and is suitable for clients who deny their addiction. (page 238)

The Days of Wine and Roses (1962). Not rated. Problems of a couple that spiral into serious abuse of alcohol. He wants help and she does not. Illustrates the concept of enabling. For clients with loved ones who abuse alcohol or other drugs.

Leaving Las Vegas (1996). Rated R. Starkly realistic portrait of an alcoholic's self-destruction and his dysfunctional relationship with a call girl who has serious problems of her own. A shocking film for problem drinkers and their families in showing how some addicts reach a point of no return.

When a Man Loves a Woman (1994). Rated R. An alcoholic woman and her husband renegotiate their relationship after her treatment. This film is highly useful in showing how spouses enable a loved one's addiction. Also useful in showing stereotypic communication problems between men and women. (page 241)

TRANSITION TO ADULTHOOD

Breaking Away (1979). Rated PG. Excellent film about four high school friends who are contemplating their futures. Illustrates to adolescents and young adults how loyalties change as objectives are revised. Also useful to families who are having trouble letting older children grow up. (page 96)

The Graduate (1967). Rated PG. A film about the ambivalence of young people in joining an adult world. Useful for young adults in verbalizing fears, hopes, dreams, and disappointments.

Little Women (1994). Rated PG. A tender story of four sisters who care for their family yet feel the tugs of love and marriage. An appropriate film for young clients entering adulthood and for their parents.

Say Anything (1989). Rated PG-13. A film about discovering the truth about one's parents, yearning for a better life, and trusting one's own instincts. A good film for clients in late adolescence or early adulthood who are weighing their options.

UNDERSTANDING SEVERE EMOTIONAL ILLNESS

Bill (1981) and *Bill: On His Own* (1983). Not rated. Sensitive treatments about a mentally retarded man who pursues an independent life after years in an institution. Two helpful films for understanding the challenges that retarded persons face.

Birdy (1984). Rated R. An evocative film that illustrates the problems of schizophrenia. Appropriate for discussion groups about mental diseases.

Rain Man (1988). Rated R. The father of a self-centered man dies and leaves a fortune to an autistic brother. The man begins a ploy to get the money for himself, but comes to appreciate his brother and grows up in the process. A useful film for clients who need to develop empathy for family members who are mentally ill.

VALUES AND ETHICS

Before and After (1996). Rated PG-13. A couple's teenage son is accused of the murder of his girlfriend, and the couple disagrees on how they should respond. A film about trust, family communication, and redemption. It is appropriate for families in discussing how family loyalties relate to community responsibility.

Quiz Show (1994). Rated PG-13. This is a film about dishonesty, greed, and the difference between appearance and truth. The film is useful for clients who are struggling with ethical dilemmas.

Short Cuts (1993). Rated R. Insightful scenarios that depict characters who operate without clear moral guidelines. The film provides a vehicle for discussion in helping clients to identify ethical standards that work for them. (page 246)

Whose Life Is It Anyway? (1981). Rated R. This film focuses on a sculptor who has been paralyzed and no longer wishes to live. It asks under what circumstances individuals can make life-and-death decisions for themselves. A useful film for group discussion of medical ethics, it also is an effective portrayal of the depths of major depression.

VOCATIONAL AND WORK-RELATED ISSUES

Apollo 13 (1995). Rated PG. True-life adventure of the crew of NASA's Apollo 13 on a mission to the moon that depends on teamwork. This film illustrates creative problem solving, leadership attributes, and personal responsibility. It is useful as a focus of discussion of teamwork in organizations and in families. (page 250)

The Doctor (1991). Rated PG-13. A surgeon learns to appreciate his patients' feelings after undergoing treatment for cancer. His experience makes him a better man and a more compassionate physician. This film helps professionals establish empathy with clients or patients. Also useful in showing couples how to communicate more effectively with each other. (page 254)

Ruby in Paradise (1993). Not rated. This film is about searching for one's vocation, having the courage to admit mistakes, and achieving independence. It is highly useful in encouraging clients to set realistic goals and to persist in obtaining them. (page 258)

Top Gun (1986). Rated PG. A young pilot must learn to be part of a team rather than a maverick. This film teaches that individual ambitions must be subservient to group goals. It is a good film for organizations that stress teamwork.

Working Girl (1988). Rated R. A film about a young woman who gets ahead by using her brains and her initiative. Helps clients who want to advance in their professions but who also value honesty and fair play.

WOMEN'S ISSUES

How to Make an American Quilt (1995). Rated PG-13. A young woman on the threshold of marriage questions her decision. She spends a summer with relatives to sort things out. A film appropriate for clients in discussing commitment, differences between infatuation and mature love, and how to forgive loved ones. (page 212)

A League of Their Own (1992). Rated PG. Wonderful comedy about the women who played professional baseball during World War II. Touches on stereotypes that are still in effect, showing women who must be more exceptional than their male counterparts to have a chance at the big leagues.

Thelma and Louise (1991). Rated R. The first feminist buddy-movie, these two women turn chauvinism on its head. (The ending, a mutual suicide, is unfortunate.) A cathartic film assignment for both women and men.

The Turning Point (1977). Rated PG. Two friends question career decisions made years before. The film is useful for clients who have second thoughts about their life decisions and who need to see the value in choices they made. Also shows how trust is an essential ingredient in successful marriages. (page 218)

Title Index to Films

Films listed in this index include all of the films from the anthology as well as other films that can have therapeutic benefits. Films from the anthology have page numbers included for clinicians' easy reference. Bold-face indicates primary classification.

About Last Night, Rated R. Categories: **Intimate relations,** communication and conflict resolution, friends and support systems, men's issues, transition to adulthood, women's issues. (page 197)

The Accidental Tourist, Rated PG. Categories: **Communication and conflict resolution,** affairs, death and dying, divorce, family-of-origin issues, friends and support systems, grief and loss, intimate relationships, marriage, parent–child relationships, stepparenting and blended families. (page 127)

Alice, Rated PG-13. Categories: **Affairs,** communication and conflict resolution, divorce, grief and loss, marriage, women's issues.

Apollo 13, Rated PG. Categories: **Vocational and work-related issues,** communication and conflict resolution, friends and support systems, inspiration, values and ethics. (page 250)

Bang the Drum Slowly, Rated PG. Categories: **Friends and support systems,** aging, death and dying, inspiration, men's issues, chronic illness and disabilities, vocational and work-related issues.

Before and After, Rated PG-13. Categories: **Values and ethics,** adolescence, communication and conflict resolution, family-of-origin issues, friends and support systems, grief and loss, marriage, parent-child relationships.

Being There, Rated PG. Categories: **Inspiration,** emotional and affective disorders, chronic illness and disabilities, understanding severe emotional illness, values and ethics.

Best Little Girl in the World, Not rated. Categories: **Emotional and affective disorders,** adolescence, communication and conflict resolution, family-of-origin issues, friends and support systems, parent-child relationships, chronic illness and disabilities.

The Big Chill, Rated R. Categories: **Friends and support systems,** affairs, communication and conflict resolution, death and dying, grief and loss, intimate relationships, marriage, men's issues, substance abuse, women's issues.

Bill and *Bill: On His Own,* Not rated. Categories: **Understanding severe emotional illness,** emotional and affective disorders, family-of-origin issues, friends and support systems, inspiration, chronic illness and disabilities.

Birdy, Rated R. Categories: **Understanding severe emotional illness,** adolescence, emotional and affective disorders, family-of-origin issues, friends and support systems, parent-child relationships, chronic illness and disabilities, transition to adulthood.

The Breakfast Club, Rated R. Categories: **Adolescence,** communication and conflict resolution, friends and support systems, parent-child relationships, prejudice, stepparenting and blended families, transition to adulthood.

Breaking Away, Rated PG. Categories: **Transition to adulthood,** adolescence, communication and conflict resolution, family-of-origin issues, friends and support systems, intimate relationships. (page 96)

The Bridges of Madison County, Rated PG-13. Categories: **Marriage,** affairs, communication and conflict resolution, family-of-origin issues, grief and loss, death and dying, intimate relationships, parent–child relationships, women's issues. (page 205)

A Bronx Tale, Rated R. Categories: **Parent–child relationships,** adolescence, family-of-origin issues, friends and support systems, men's issues, transition to adulthood, values and ethics.

Bye, Bye Love, Rated PG-13. Categories: **Divorce,** adoption and custody, affairs, communication and conflict resolution, friends and support systems, grief and loss, intimate relationships, marriage, men's issues, parent–child relationships, stepparenting and blended families, women's issues. (page 143)

Chariots of Fire, Rated PG. Categories: **Inspiration,** communication and conflict resolution, friends and support systems, prejudice, transition to adulthood, values and ethics.

Circle of Friends, Rated PG-13. Categories: **Friends and support systems,** adolescence, affairs, communication and conflict resolution, family-of-origin issues, grief and loss, intimate relationships, marriage, parent–child relationships, transition to adulthood, values and ethics, women's issues. (page 165)

City Slickers. Rated PG-13. Categories: **Friends and support systems,** affairs, aging, communication and conflict resolution, divorce, family-of-origin issues, grief and loss, intimate relationships, marriage, men's issues, parent–child relationships, transition to adulthood, values and ethics, vocational and work-related issues. (page 168)

Clean and Sober, Rated R. Categories: **Substance abuse,** chronic illness and disabilities, communication and conflict resolution, emotional and affective disorders, family-of-origin issues, friends and support systems, grief and loss, intimate relationships, parent–child relationships, understanding severe emotional illness, values and ethics, vocational and work-related issues. (page 238)

Cocoon, Rated PG-13. Categories: **Aging,** chronic illness and disabilities, death and dying, friends and support systems, grief and loss, marriage.

Corrina, Corrina, Rated PG. Categories: **Death and dying,** friends and support systems, grief and loss, intimate relationships, parent–child relationships, prejudice, stepparenting and blended families.

Da, Rated PG. Categories: **Men's issues,** aging, communication and conflict resolution, death and dying, family-of-origin issues, grief and loss, parent-child relationships.

The Days of Wine and Roses, Not rated. Categories: **Substance abuse,** chronic illness and disabilities, communication and conflict resolution, emotional and affective disorders, friends and support systems, grief and loss, intimate relationships, marriage, understanding severe emotional illness.

Dead Poets Society, Rated PG. Categories: **Emotional and affective disorders,** adolescence, communication and conflict resolution, death and dying, family-of-origin issues, friends and support systems, grief and loss, inspiration, men's issues, parent-child relationships, transition to adulthood, values and ethics, vocational and work-related issues. (page 154)

Do the Right Thing, Rated R. Categories: **Prejudice,** communication and conflict resolution, friends and support systems, stepparenting and blended families, values and ethics.

The Doctor, Rated PG-13. Categories: **Vocational and work-related issues,** chronic illness and disabilities, communication and conflict resolution, death and dying, friends and support systems, grief and loss, intimate relationships, marriage, values and ethics. (page 254)

Dolores Claiborne, Rated R. Categories: **Abuse (emotional, physical, sexual),** adolescence, affairs, communication and conflict resolution, emotional and affective disorders, family-of-origin issues, friends and support systems, grief and loss, marriage, parent-child relationships, substance abuse, understanding severe emotional illness, women's issues. (page 82)

Down Came a Blackbird, Rated R. Categories: **Emotional and affective disorders,** abuse (emotional, physical, sexual), friends and support systems, grief and loss, understanding severe emotional illness.

An Early Frost, Not rated. Categories: **Chronic illness and disabilities,** communication and conflict resolution, death and dying, family-of-origin issues, friends and support systems, grief and loss, parent-child relationships, prejudice.

289

Eating, Not rated. Categories: **Emotional and affective disorders,** adolescence, aging, chronic illness and disabilities, communication and conflict resolution, family-of-origin issues, friends and support systems, grief and loss, marriage, understanding severe emotional illness, values and ethics, women's issues.

Enchanted April, Rated PG. Categories: **Marriage,** aging, communication and conflict resolution, friends and support systems, grief and loss, intimate relationships, women's issues.

Fearless, Rated R. Categories: **Emotional and affective disorders,** chronic illness and disabilities, death and dying, friends and support systems, grief and loss, understanding severe emotional illness.

Ferris Bueller's Day Off, Rated PG-13. Categories: **Adolescence,** communication and conflict resolution, family-of-origin issues, friends and support systems, parent-child relationships, transition to adulthood.

Field of Dreams, Rated PG. Categories: **Inspiration,** communication and conflict resolution, family-of-origin issues, friends and support systems, grief and loss, intimate relationships, marriage, men's issues, parent-child relationships, transition to adulthood, values and ethics, vocational and work-related issues. (page 183)

First Wives Club, Rated PG. Categories: **Divorce,** affairs, communication and conflict resolution, death and dying, emotional and affective disorders, friends and support systems, grief and loss, intimate relationships, marriage, substance abuse, values and ethics, women's issues.

Fly Away Home, Rated PG. Categories: **Stepparenting and blended families,** adolescence, adoption and custody, communication and conflict resolution, death and dying, emotional and affective disorders, family-of-origin issues, friends and support systems, grief and loss, inspiration, parent-child relationships. (page 234)

Forget Paris, Rated PG-13. Categories: **Communication and conflict resolution,** friends and support systems, intimate relationships, marriage.

Forrest Gump, Rated PG. Categories: **Inspiration,** chronic illness and disabilities, death and dying, family-of-origin issues, friends and support systems, grief and loss, parent-child relationships.

The Four Seasons, Rated PG. Categories: **Marriage,** affairs, aging, communication and conflict resolution, divorce, friends and support systems, grief and loss, intimate relationships, men's issues, stepparenting and blended families, women's issues. (page 208)

Fried Green Tomatoes, Rated PG-13. Categories: **Emotional and affective disorders,** aging, communication and conflict resolution, death and dying, friends and support systems, grief and loss, marriage, women's issues.

Gandhi, Rated PG. Categories: **Inspiration,** communication and conflict resolution, prejudice, values and ethics, vocational and work-related issues.

The Good Mother, Rated R. Categories: **Adoption and custody,** abuse (emotional, physical, sexual), affairs, communication and conflict resolution, divorce, family-of-origin issues, friends and support systems, grief and loss, intimate relationships, marriage, parent-child relationships, prejudice, stepparenting and blended families, values and ethics, women's issues. (page 103)

The Graduate, Rated PG. Categories: **Transition to adulthood,** adolescence, communication and conflict resolution, parent-child relationships, values and ethics.

The Great Santini, Rated PG. Categories: **Parent-child relationships,** abuse (emotional, physical, sexual), adolescence, communication and conflict resolution, death and dying, family-of-origin issues, friends and support systems, grief and loss, marriage, prejudice, substance abuse, transition to adulthood. (page 223)

Groundhog Day, Rated PG. Categories: **Intimate relationships,** communication and conflict resolution, men's issues, transition to adulthood, values and ethics, vocational and work-related issues. (page 201)

Hannah and Her Sisters, Rated PG. Categories: **Family-of-origin issues,** affairs, communication and conflict resolution, divorce, emotional and affective disorders, friends and support systems, intimate relationships, marriage, men's issues, parent-child relationships, substance abuse, women's issues.

He Said, She Said, Rated PG-13. Categories: **Communication and conflict resolution,** intimate relationships, vocational and work-related issues.

Home for the Holidays, Rated PG. Categories: **Family-of-origin issues,** communication and conflict resolution, parent-child relationships.

Hoop Dreams, Rated PG-13. Categories: **Adolescence,** friends and support systems, parent-child relationships, substance abuse, transition to adulthood, values and ethics, vocational and work-related issues. (page 99)

The Hospital, Rated PG. Categories: **Emotional and affective disorders,** aging, chronic illness and disabilities, death and dying, grief and loss, understanding severe emotional illness, values and ethics, vocational and work-related issues.

How to Make an American Quilt, Rated PG-13. Categories: **Women's issues,** affairs, aging, communication and conflict resolution, divorce, friends and support systems, grief and loss, intimate relationships, marriage, parent-child relationships, transition to adulthood, vocational and work-related issues. (page 212)

Husbands and Wives, Rated R. Categories: **Marriage,** affairs, aging, communication and conflict resolution, divorce, friends and support systems, grief and loss, intimate relationships, values and ethics.

I Never Sang for My Father, Rated PG. Categories: **Men's issues,** aging, chronic illness and disabilities, communication and conflict resolution, death and dying, family-of-origin issues, grief and loss, parent-child relationships.

It's a Wonderful Life, Not rated. Categories: **Inspiration,** friends and support systems, grief and loss, marriage, parent-child relationships, transition to adulthood, values and ethics, vocational and work-related issues. (page 186)

Jonathan Livingston Seagull, Rated G. Categories: **Inspiration,** adolescence, aging, communication and conflict resolution, death and dying, family-of-origin issues, friends and support systems, grief and loss, parent-child relationships, prejudice, transition to adulthood, values and ethics, vocational and work-related issues.

The Joy Luck Club, Rated R. Categories: **Family-of-origin issues,** aging, death and dying, friends and support systems, grief and loss, intimate relationships, marriage, parent-child relationships, prejudice, transition to adulthood, women's issues.

Kramer vs. Kramer, Rated PG. Categories: **Divorce,** adoption and custody, communication and conflict resolution, grief and loss, marriage, parent-child relationships, values and ethics, vocational and work-related issues. (page 146)

A League of Their Own, Rated PG. Categories: **Women's issues,** grief and loss, inspiration, prejudice, transition to adulthood, vocational and work-related issues.

Leaving Las Vegas, Rated R. Categories: **Substance abuse,** abuse (emotional, physical, sexual), chronic illness and disabilities, death and dying, emotional and affective disorders, friends and support systems, grief and loss, understanding severe emotional illness.

Like Water for Chocolate, Rated R. Categories: **Family-of-origin issues,** adolescence, communication and conflict resolution, emotional and affective disorders, friends and support systems, grief and loss, intimate relationships, marriage, parent-child relationships, transition to adulthood, understanding severe emotional illness, values and ethics, women's issues. (page 161)

The Lion King, Rated G. Categories: **Grief and loss,** adolescence, death and dying, friends and support systems, parent-child relationships, transition to adulthood.

Little Women, Rated PG. Categories: **Transition to adulthood,** adolescence, chronic illness and disabilities, family-of-origin issues, friends and support systems, grief and loss, intimate relationships, parent-child relationships, vocational and work-related issues, women's issues.

Lorenzo's Oil, Rated PG–13. Categories: **Chronic illness and disabilities,** death and dying, friends and support systems, grief and loss, inspiration, marriage, parent-child relationships. (page 117)

Losing Isaiah, Rated R. Categories: **Adoption and custody,** communication and conflict resolution, friends and support systems, grief and loss, marriage, parent-child relationships, stepparenting and blended families, substance abuse, values and ethics. (page 106)

Mask, Rated PG–13. Categories: **Chronic illness and disabilities,** adolescence, communication and conflict resolution, friends and support systems, grief and loss, inspiration, parent-child relationship, prejudice, values and ethics.

Matilda, Rated PG. Categories: **Abuse (emotional, physical, sexual),** adoption and custody, family-of-origin issues, friends and support systems, grief and loss, parent-child relationships, stepparenting and blended families. (page 85)

Mr. and Mrs. Bridge, Rated PG–13. Categories: **Marriage,** aging, communication and conflict resolution, divorce, grief and loss.

Mr. Holland's Opus, Rated PG. Categories: **Grief and loss,** aging, friends and support systems, marriage, men's issues, vocational and work-related issues.

Mrs. Doubtfire, Rated PG–13. Categories: **Divorce,** communication and conflict resolution, grief and loss, marriage, men's issues, parent-child relationships, stepparenting and blended families, vocational and work-related issues.

Multiplicity, Rated PG–13. Categories: **Emotional and affective disorders,** communication and conflict resolution, intimate relationships, marriage, men's issues, vocational and work-related issues.

My Bodyguard, Rated PG. Categories: **Adolescence,** communication and conflict resolution, friends and support systems, parent-child relationships.

My Life, Rated PG–13. Categories: **Death and dying,** aging, chronic illness and disabilities, communication and conflict resolution, family-of-origin issues, friends and support systems, grief and loss, marriage, parent-child relationships. (page 135)

Nine Months, Rated PG-13. Categories: **Intimate relationships,** communication and conflict resolution, grief and loss, marriage, men's issues, transition to adulthood, women's issues.

Nothing in Common, Rated PG. Categories: **Men's issues,** aging, chronic illness and disabilities, communication and conflict resolution, death and dying, divorce, family-of-origin issues, friends and support systems, grief and loss, marriage, parent-child relationships, vocational and work-related issues. (page 215)

An Officer and a Gentleman, Rated R. Categories: **Intimate relations,** affairs, communication and conflict resolution, emotional and affective disorders, men's issues, parent-child relationships, stepparenting and blended families, substance abuse, transition to adulthood.

On Golden Pond, Rated PG. Categories: **Family-of-origin issues,** aging, communication and conflict resolution, grief and loss, marriage, parent-child relationships.

Ordinary People, Rated R. Categories: **Grief and loss,** adolescence, communication and conflict resolution, death and dying, divorce, emotional and affective disorders, family-of-origin issues, friends and support systems, marriage, parent-child relationships, prejudice, understanding severe emotional illness, vocational and work-related issues. (page 176)

Out of Africa, Rated PG. Categories: **Intimate relationships,** communication and conflict resolution, death and dying, grief and loss, intimate relationships, marriage.

Parenthood, Rated PG. Categories: **Parent-child relationships,** adolescence, communication and conflict resolution, divorce, emotional and affective disorders, family-of-origin issues, friends and support systems, grief and loss, intimate relationships, marriage, men's issues, stepparenting and blended families, transition to adulthood, understanding severe emotional illness, values and ethics, vocational and work-related issues, women's issues. (page 227)

Passion Fish, Rated R. Categories: **Chronic illness and disabilities,** communication and conflict resolution, friends and support systems, grief and loss, marriage, women's issues.

Peter's Friends, Rated R. Categories: **Friends and support systems,** chronic illness and disabilities, communication and conflict resolution, death and dying, divorce, grief and loss, intimate relationships, marriage, substance abuse.

Philadelphia, Rated PG-13. Categories: **Chronic illness and disabilities,** communication and conflict resolution, death and dying, family-of-origin issues, friends and support systems, grief and loss, intimate relationships, marriage, parent-child relationships, prejudice, values and ethics, vocational and work-related issues. (page 120)

Places in the Heart, Rated PG. Categories: **Inspiration,** chronic illness and disabilities, death and dying, friends and support systems, grief and loss, parent-child relationships, prejudice, women's issues.

Il Postino (The Postman), Rated PG. Categories: **Intimate relationships,** chronic illness and disabilities, death and dying, friends and support systems, grief and loss, inspiration.

Powder, Rated PG-13. Categories: **Adolescence,** friends and support systems, grief and loss, prejudice.

The Prince of Tides, Rated R. Categories: **Abuse (emotional, physical, sexual),** affairs, emotional and affective disorders, family-of-origin issues, grief and loss, marriage, parent-child relationships, substance abuse, understanding severe emotional illness, values and ethics, vocational and work-related issues. (page 89)

Quiz Show, Rated PG-13. Categories: **Values and ethics,** communication and conflict resolution, marriage, vocational and work-related issues.

Radio Flyer, Rated PG-13. Categories: **Abuse (emotional, physical, sexual),** adolescence, family-of-origin issues, friends and support systems, grief and loss, marriage, parent-child relationships, stepparenting and blended families, substance abuse.

Rain Man, Rated R. Categories: **Understanding severe emotional illness,** chronic illness and disabilities, communication and conflict resolution, emotional and affective disorders, friends and support systems, values and ethics.

A River Runs through It, Rated PG. Categories: **Grief and loss,** death and dying, family-of-origin issues, friends and support systems, inspiration, parent-child relationships, substance abuse, transition to adulthood. (page 179)

Ruby in Paradise, Not rated. Categories: **Vocational and work-related issues,** friends and support systems, intimate relationships, transition to adulthood, values and ethics, women's issues. (page 258)

Rudy, Rated PG. Categories: **Inspiration,** friends and support systems, parent-child relationships, transition to adulthood, values and ethics, vocational and work-related issues. (page 190)

Say Anything, Rated PG-13. Categories: **Transition to adulthood,** adolescence, communication and conflict resolution, family-of-origin issues, friends and support systems, grief and loss, intimate relationships, parent-child relationships, values and ethics.

Scenes from a Marriage, Rated PG. Categories: **Marriage,** affairs, communication and conflict resolution, divorce, grief and loss.

Searching for Bobby Fischer, Rated PG. Categories: **Parent-child relationships,** adolescence, communication and conflict resolution, friends and support systems, marriage, vocational and work-related issues. (page 230)

Shadowlands, Rated PG. Categories: **Death and dying,** chronic illness and disabilities, communication and conflict resolution, friends and support systems, grief and loss, inspiration, marriage, parent-child relationships, stepparenting and blended families. (page 138)

The Shawshank Redemption, Rated R. Categories: **Inspiration,** communication and conflict resolution, friends and support systems, grief and loss. (page 193)

Short Cuts, Rated R. Categories: **Values and ethics,** abuse (emotional, physical, sexual), affairs, communication and conflict resolution, death and dying, divorce, family-of-origin issues, friends and support systems, grief and loss, intimate relationships, marriage, parent-child relationships, substance abuse. (page 246)

Singles, Rated PG-13. Categories: **Intimate relationships,** communication and conflict resolution, friends and support systems, transition to adulthood, values and ethics.

Sixteen Candles, Rated PG. Categories: **Adolescence,** communication and conflict resolution, family-of-origin issues, friends and support systems, grief and loss, parent-child relationships.

The Slender Thread, Not Rated. Categories: **Emotional and affective disorders,** friends and support systems, grief and loss, understanding severe emotional illness.

Something to Talk About, Rated R. Categories: **Affairs,** communication and conflict resolution, divorce, family-of-origin issues, grief and loss, marriage, parent-child relationships.

Stand and Deliver, Rated PG. Categories: **Adolescence,** communication and conflict resolution, friends and support systems, inspiration, parent-child relationships, prejudice, stepparenting and blended families, transition to adulthood, values and ethics, vocational and work-related issues.

Stand by Me, Rated R. Categories: **Adolescence,** death and dying, friends and support systems, parent-child relationships.

Starting Over, Rated R. Categories: **Divorce,** affairs, communication and conflict resolution, friends and support systems, grief and loss, intimate relationships, marriage.

Star Wars, Rated PG. Categories: **Inspiration,** adolescence, communication and conflict resolution, family-of-origin issues, friends and support systems, grief and loss, parent-child relationships, prejudice, transition to adulthood, values and ethics.

Steel Magnolias, Rated PG. Categories: **Friends and support systems,** aging, chronic illness and disabilities, communication and conflict resolution, death and dying, grief and loss, marriage, parent-child relationships, transition to adulthood, women's issues. (page 172)

Strangers in Good Company, Not rated. Categories: **Aging,** chronic illness and disabilities, death and dying, family-of-origin issues, friends and support systems, grief and loss, women's issues. (page 110)

Stuart Saves His Family, Rated PG-13. Categories: **Family-of-origin issues,** communication and conflict resolution, emotional and affective disorders, friends and support systems, grief and loss, marriage, parent-child relationships, substance abuse, values and ethics.

Terms of Endearment, Rated PG. Categories: **Communication and conflict resolution,** affairs, chronic illness and disabilities, death and dying, emotional and affective disorders, family-of-origin issues, friends and support systems, grief and loss, marriage, parent-child relationships, substance abuse, women's issues. (page 131)

Thelma and Louise, Rated R. Categories: **Women's issues,** abuse (emotional, physical, sexual), friends and support systems, marriage, substance abuse.

This Boy's Life, Rated R. Categories: **Abuse (emotional, physical, sexual),** adolescence, communication and conflict resolution, emotional and affective disorders, family-of-origin issues, friends and support systems, grief and loss, marriage, parent-child relationships stepparenting and blended families, substance abuse. (page 92)

Tootsie, Rated PG. Categories: **Men's issues,** communication and conflict resolution, friends and support systems, intimate relationships.

Top Gun, Rated PG. Categories: **Vocational and work-related issues,** adolescence, communication and conflict resolution, death and dying, friends and support systems, grief and loss, intimate relations, men's issues, transition to adulthood.

The Trip to Bountiful, Rated PG. Categories: **Aging,** communication and conflict resolution, family-of-origin issues, friends and support systems, grief and loss, parent-child relationships, values and ethics. (page 113)

Truly, Madly, Deeply, Rated PG. Categories: **Grief and loss,** death and dying, intimate relationships, marriage.

The Turning Point, Rated PG. Categories: **Women's issues,** aging, communication and conflict resolution, friends and support systems, grief and loss, intimate relationships, marriage, parent-child relationships, transition to adulthood, vocational and work-related issues. (page 218)

An Unmarried Woman, Rated R. Categories: **Divorce,** affairs, communication and conflict resolution, friends and support systems, grief and loss, intimate relationships, marriage.

Unstrung Heroes, Rated PG. Categories: **Stepparenting and blended families,** adolescence, death and dying, friends and support systems, grief and loss, parent-child relationships.

The War of the Roses, Rated R. Categories: **Divorce,** abuse (emotional, physical, sexual), communication and conflict resolution, grief and loss, marriage, values and ethics. (page 150)

The Waterdance, Rated R. Categories: **Chronic illness and disabilities,** communication and conflict resolution, friends and support systems, grief and loss, intimate relationships, men's issues, prejudice, values and ethics. (page 123)

What's Eating Gilbert Grape? Rated PG-13. Categories: **Emotional and affective disorders,** chronic illness and disabilities, family-of-origin issues, friends and support systems, intimate relationships, parent-child relationships, transition to adulthood, understanding severe emotional illness. (page 157)

What's Love Got to Do with It? Rated R. Categories: **Abuse (emotional, physical, sexual),** affairs, communication and conflict resolution, friends and support systems, marriage, substance abuse, women's issues.

When a Man Loves a Woman, Rated R. Categories: **Substance abuse,** communication and conflict resolution, friends and support systems, intimate relationships, marriage, understanding severe emotional illness. (page 241)

When Harry Met Sally, Rated PG. Categories: **Intimate relationships,** communication and conflict resolution, divorce, friends and support systems.

White Squall, Rated R. Categories: **Adolescence,** communication and conflict resolution, emotional and affective disorders, friends and support systems, parent-child relationships, transition to adulthood.

Who's Afraid of Virginia Woolf? Not rated. Categories: **Communication and conflict resolution,** abuse (emotional, physical, sexual), emotional and affective disorders, grief and loss, marriage, substance abuse, understanding severe emotional illness.

Whose Life Is It Anyway? Rated R. Categories: **Values and ethics,** chronic illness and disabilities, death and dying, emotional and affective disorders, friends and support systems, grief and loss, intimate relationships.

A Woman's Tale, Rated PG-13. Categories: **Death and dying,** aging, chronic illness and disabilities, communication and conflict resolution, family-of-origin issues, friends and support systems, grief and loss, parent-child relationships, values and ethics, women's issues.

Working Girl, Rated R. Categories: **Vocational and work-related issues,** communication and conflict resolution, friends and support systems, intimate relationships, prejudice, transition to adulthood, values and ethics, women's issues.

Wrestling Ernest Hemingway, Rated PG-13. Categories: **Aging,** communication and conflict resolution, death and dying, friends and support systems, grief and loss, men's issues.

References

American Psychiatric Association. (1994). *Diagnostical and statistical manual of mental disorders (4th ed.)*. Washington, DC: Author.

Anderson, D. (1992). Using feature films as tools for analysis in a psychology and law course. *Teaching of Psychology, 19*(3), 155–158.

Anderson, H., and Goolishian, H. (1988). Human systems as linguistic systems. *Family Process, 27,* 371–395.

Aumont, J., Bergala, A., Marie, M., and Vernet, M. (1992). *Aesthetics of film*. Austin: University of Texas Press.

Bandler, R., and Grinder, J. (1982). *Reframing*. Moab, UT: Real People Press.

Bandura, A. (1969). *Principles of behavior modification*. New York: Holt, Rinehart and Winston.

Beitman, B. D. (1987). *The structure of individual psychotherapy*. New York: Guilford Press.

Berg-Cross, L., Jennings, P., and Baruch, R. (1990). Cinematherapy: Theory and application. *Psychotherapy in Private Practice, 8*(1), 135–157.

Brown, E. F. (1975). *Bibliotherapy and it's widening applications*. Metuchen, NJ: Scarecrow Press.

Budman, S. H., and Gurman, A. S. (1988). *Theory and practice of bibliotherapy*. New York: Guilford Press.

Christie, M., and McGrath, M. (1989). Man who catch fly with chopstick accomplish anything: Film in therapy: The sequel. *Australian and New Zealand Journal of Family Therapy, 10*(3), 145–150.

Connors, M., and Furtaw, J. (Eds.). (1995). *VideoHound's golden movie retriever: 1995*. Detroit:Visible Ink Press.

Dermer, S. B., and Hutchings, J. B. (1997). *Utilizing movies in family therapy: Applications for individuals, couples, and families*. Manuscript in preparation.

Ebert, R. (1996). *Roger Ebert's movie home companion 1996 edition*. Kansas City: Andrews and McMeel.

Eisenberg, L. (1986). Does bad news about suicide beget bad news? *New England Journal of Medicine, 315*(11), 690–694.

Friedman, S. (Ed.). (1993). *The new language of change*. New York: Guilford Press.

Gergen, K. (1991). *The saturated self.* New York: Basic Books.

Greenberg, H. R. (1993). *Screen memories: Hollywood cinema on the psychoanalytic couch*. New York: Columbia University Press.

Harry, B. (1983). Movies and behavior among hospitalized, mentally disordered offenders. *Bulletin of the American Academy of Psychiatry and the Law, 11*(4), 359–364.

Haley, J. (1973). *Uncommon therapy*. New York:W. W. Norton.

Hill, G. (1992). *Illuminating shadows: The mythic power of film*. Boston: Shambala.

Horenstein, M. A., Rigby, B., Flory, M., and Gershwin, V. (1994). *Reel life/real life*. Burlington,VT: Fourth Write Press.

Kael, P. (1991). *Movie love*. New York: Penguin.

Lewis, C. S. (1961). *A grief observed*. New York: Bantam Books.

Menninger, W. C. (1937). Bibliotherapy. *Bulletin of the Menninger Clinic, 1*(8), 263–274.

Newby, R. F., Fischer, M., and Reinke, B. (1992). Just a spoonful of sugar helps the therapy go down. *Psychotherapy in Private Practice, 11*(4), 41–49.

Pearce, S. S. (1996). *Flash of insight*. Needham Heights, MA: Allyn and Bacon.

Pardeck, J. T. (1993). *Using bibliotherapy in clinical practice*. Westport, CT, and London: Greenwood Press.

Rubin, R. J. (1978). *Using bibliotherapy: A guide to theory and practice*. Phoenix, AZ: Oryx Press.

Sample, H. (1940). *Pitfalls for readers of fiction*. Chicago: National Council of Teachers.

Solomon, G. (1995). *The motion picture prescription.* Santa Rosa, CA: Aslan Publishing.

Starker, S. (1988). Psychologists and self-help books: Attitudes and prescriptive practices of clinicians. *American Journal of Psychotherapy, 42,* 448–455.

Staudacher, C. (1987). *Beyond grief.* Oakland, CA: New Harbinger Publications.

White, M., and Epstein, D. (1990). *Narrative means to therapeutic ends.* New York: W. W. Norton.

Zimbardo P. G. (1977). *Shyness: What it is, what to do about it.* Reading, MA: Addison-Wesley.

About the Authors

JOHN W. HESLEY, PhD is a psychologist with a consulting and psychotherapy practice in the Dallas–Ft. Worth area. In addition to scientific papers, he has written numerous articles for popular magazines, newspapers and trade publications. **JAN G. HESLEY, MSSW,** is an advanced clinical practitioner who specializes in marriage and family therapy. She has taught at the university level and has consulted with agencies, churches, and public and private schools. The Hesleys' Web site is www.hesley.com. Their e-mail address is movietalk@hesley.com.